Biological and Cultural Bases of Human Inference

T0347492

BIOLOGICAL AND CULTURAL BASES OF HUMAN INFERENCE

Edited by

Riccardo Viale
*University of Milano–Bicocca
and Rosselli Foundation, Torino*

Daniel Andler
*Université Paris–Sorbonne (Paris IV)
and Ecole normale supérieure, Paris*

Lawrence Hirschfeld
New School for Social Research, New York

Psychology Press
Taylor & Francis Group

LONDON AND NEW YORK

First published 2006 by Lawrence Erlbaum Associates, Inc.

Published 2014 by Psychology Press
27 Church Road, Hove, East Sussex, BN3 2FA

and by Psychology Press
711 Third Avenue, New York, NY 10017

First issued in paperback 2014

Psychology Press is an imprint of the Taylor & Francis Group, an informa business

Cover design by Kathryn Houghtaling Lacey

Library of Congress Cataloging-in-Publication Data

Biological and cultural bases of human inference / edited by R. Viale,
    D. Andler, L. Hirschfeld.
        p.   cm.
    Includes bibliographical references and index.

        1. Inference—Congresses.   2. Cognitive science—Congresses.   3. Social
    sciences—Congresses.   I. Viale, Riccardo.   II. Andler, D. (Daniel)
    III. Hirschfeld, Lawrence A.

BC199.I47B56   2006
160—dc22   2005052185
                                                                        CIP

ISBN 978-0-8058-5395-7 (hbk)
ISBN 978-1-1380-0417-7 (pbk)

Contents

Preface

The present volume is the outcome of a conference held in Paris, June 7–9, 2001. It was the sixth and last in a series of workshops sponsored by the European Science Foundation (ESF) on the general topic of *Human Reasoning and Decision Making*. The ESF Scientific Network, which oversaw the series, was coordinated by the Rosselli Foundation and co-chaired by Riccardo Viale, LaSCoMES (Laboratory of Cognitive, Methodological, Sociological, and Economic Sciences) of the Rosselli Foundation, Torino, and Jean-Paul Caverni, Université de Provence. The first of these workshops was held in Torino and focused on *Cognitive Theory of Social Action* (June 11–13, 1998). Milan hosted the second workshop on *Probabilistic Reasoning and Decision Making* (February 19–20, 1999). The third was devoted to *Explaining Social Norms: Rationality and Cognition* (Paris, October 14–16, 1999). The fourth, held in Amsterdam, was concerned with *Risk and Decision Making* (December 9–11, 1999). Alexandria and Torino jointly sponsored the fifth on *Cognitive Economics* (November 15–18, 2000).

The general aim of the Network was to encourage the development, in Europe, of the interface between social science and cognitive science. Specifically, there was a growing awareness that theories of action and decision making central to the mainstream of economics and social science need to be informed by recent research in the psychology of reasoning and, more broadly, by the advances in cognitive developmental psychology, formal models, comparative studies in anthropology, linguistic investigations, and conceptual and critical analysis conducted by empirically minded philosophers.

As its title indicates, the last conference focused on the distinctive perspective afforded by anthropology and social psychology. Since its inception, cognitive science's relationship with the social sciences has been a one-way affair: Cognitive science has been moving into the social sciences, questioning both explicit and tacit assumptions and proposing alternatives. This is not surprising: Cognitive science was the newcomer. Its project of substituting a scientifically based model for a schematic, commonsensical reconstruction of the economic agent has historically been an important motivating force in the conception of cognitive science. It has been and still is a productive orientation within the general project of bringing the two domains in closer contact.

The first workshops quite appropriately gave pride of place to descriptive psychological models of individual reasoning and decision making, and to the ways in which theories of social processes need to change to accommodate these models. By contrast, the present volume's overall import explores the opposite direction of influence. Several of the volume's chapters provide reflections by social scientists or philosophers on the social dimensions of thought. Others take a critical stance, often inspired by evolutionary considerations, toward some central assumptions of cognitive science. It would seem that the moment is ripe for the pendulum to swing back toward "population thinking" without letting go of what we have learned and are constantly learning about the individual mind's capacities and the importance of insisting on causal accounts that necessarily implicate the capacities of individual cognitive systems.

There are both strategic and substantial reasons for this turn toward population-level approaches. First, the social sciences have accumulated over the last century, and with a notable acceleration in the last 50 years, an enormous body of facts, concepts, methods, and know-how. As every reasonable cognitive scientist should acknowledge, it is neither feasible nor desirable to attempt a total reconstruction (or reduction) of this work, however distant or problematic it may appear from her own perspective. The time has now come to actually connect these two traditions in a constructive and cumulative way, rather than stick to the binary choice between correcting mistaken models or keeping at large. In other words, cognitive science must piggy-back on carefully selected programs within mainstream social science if it wants to make significant progress in understanding social processes.

Second, in the course of its own internal development, cognitive science has of late encountered manifold reasons for adverting to collective phenomena. On the negative side, it has become increasingly clear that the individual mind is not a self-contained universal thinking system akin to a powerful inference engine coupled to a vast database. Instead, the mind's primary raison d'être is to provide the organism with a number of competencies essential for surviving and thriving in the environment in which it evolved. The architecture of the mind reflects this, and, to a large extent, it operates as a collection of functional, domain-specific agencies. From this perspective, the mind is seen as intrinsically, from its inception, a social organ, not simply as an organ that, among other things, can be recruited in social processes. This distinction parallels Ernst Mayr's famous distinction between distal and proximal causes: Sociality figures among the distal causes of the human mind, whereas certain specific properties of the human mind proximally account for the contemporary mind's ability to engage in social processes.

This is where the positive reasons for the social turn in cognitive science come into play. We now have at our disposal a powerful set of hypotheses and methodologies for investigating the social dimension of the mind, accounting for human society as "an interaction of minds," in Perner's and Kühberger's phrase. To put it in a slightly different light, and to paraphrase once more Warren McCulloch's famous title ("What Is a Number, That a Man May Know It, and a Man, That He May Know a Number?"), there is a shared sense that we are now in a position to begin to answer the question, "What is culture, such that it is supported by minds, and what are minds, such that they support culture?"

When we were planning the workshop from which the present volume emerged, the research program just sketched was far from figuring on the agenda of cognitive science. It does now. In fact, there is something of an epidemic of publications and projects under the twin labels of *social cognition* and *cognitive approaches of social phenomena*. The workshop, we like to think, contributed to this movement of ideas, building on some pioneering intellectual and organizational work by some of the senior participants in the workshop. This initial impetus has by now set in motion a rather large current of research occupying a distinctive position within the broader movement at the interface of the cognitive and social sciences. We feel privileged to have benefited from and, to a small measure, contributed to this current.

The workshop was organized by the newly established Département d'études cognitives, directed by Daniel Andler at Ecole normale supérieure, with considerable logistic help from the Rosselli Foundation, whose contribution is gratefully acknowledged. We thank Dr. Marta Spranzi for her critical role as chair of the local organizing committee, which was comprised of two preternaturally efficient and enthusiastic graduate students, Edouard Machery, now a professor at the University of Pittsburgh, and Emmanuel de Vienne. The funding was provided by the ESF, the Institute for Social Research and the International Culture and Cognition Consortium of the University of Michigan, and the Rosselli Foundation. Additional contributions came from the Université Paris–Sorbonne

(Paris IV), the GDR "Développement Cognitif et Diversité Culturelle," a CNRS unit headed by Dan Sperber, by Ecole normale supérieure, and by the journal *Mind and Society*. The preparation of the volume is almost entirely the work of Riccardo Viale, for whose disproportionate contribution his two co-editors are deeply and embarrassingly grateful. We would also like to thank Laura Gilardi for her secretarial work, Daniela Corsaro for her editorial processing, and Gabriella Passerini for the preparation of author and subject indexes.

—Daniel Andler
Lawrence Hirschfeld
Riccardo Viale

Editors and Contributors

Daniel Andler, Department of Philosophy, University of Paris–Sorbonne (Paris IV) and Department of Cognitive Studies, Ecole normale supérieure, Paris, France. E-mail: daniel.andler@ens.fr

Scott Atran, Centre National de la Recherche Scientifique, Institut Jean Nicod, Paris, France and Institute for Social Research, The University of Michigan, Ann Arbor, USA. E-mail: satran@umich.edu

Maria Bagassi, Faculty and Department of Psychology, University of Milano–Bicocca, Milano, Italy. E-mail: maria.bagassi@unimib.it

Lawrence A. Hirschfeld, Department of Psychology, New School for Social Research, New York, NY, USA. E-mail: hirschfl@newschool.edu

Anton Kühberger, Department of Psychology, University of Salzburg, Salzburg, Austria. E-mail: anton.kuehberger@sbg.ac.at

Laura Macchi, Faculty and Department of Psychology, University of Milano–Bicocca, Milano, Italy. E-mail: laura.macchi@unimib.it

Takahiko Masuda, Department of Psychology, University of Alberta, Canada. E-mail: tmasuda@ualberta.ca

Douglas L. Medin, Department of Psychology, Northwestern University, Evanston, IL, USA. E-mail: medin@northwestern.edu

Shaun Nichols, Department of Philosophy, University of Utah, Salt Lake City, UT, USA. E-mail: snichols@philosophy.utah.edu

Richard E. Nisbett, Institute for Social Research, 3229 East Hall, University of Michigan, Ann Arbor, MI, USA. E-mail: nisbett@umich.edu

Ara Norenzayan, Department of Psychology, University of British Columbia, Vancouver, Canada. E-mail: ara@psych.ubc.ca

Daniel Osherson, Psychology Department, Princeton University, Princeton, NJ, USA. E-mail: osherson@princeton.edu

Josef Perner, Department of Psychology, University of Salzburg, Salzburg, Austria. E-mail: josef.perner@sbg.ac.at

Norbert Ross, Department of Anthropology, Vanderbilt University, Nashville, TN, USA. E-mail: norbert.o.ross@vanderbilt.edu

Dan Sperber, Institut Jean Nicod (CNRS, EHESS, ENS), Paris, France. E-mail: dan@sperber.com

Stephen Stich, Department of Philosophy & Center for Cognitive Science, Rutgers University, New Brunswick, NJ, USA. E-mail: stich@ruccs.rutgers.edu

Riccardo Viale, Department of Sociology and Social Research, University of Milano–Bicocca, Milano, Italy and Rosselli Foundation, Torino, Italy. E-mail: riccardo.viale@fondazionerosselli.it

Jonathan M. Weinberg, Department of Philosophy, Indiana University, Bloomington, IN, USA. E-mail: jmweinbe@indiana.edu

Introduction: Local or Universal Principles of Reasoning?

Riccardo Viale
Rosselli Foundation

INNATE PRINCIPLES OF REASONING

In the past, philosophers used to put infants and children on the opposite side from science in the spectrum of cognitive rationality. Their supposed cognitive immaturity did not allow them to approach the ideal image of rational beings. Two psychologists, Gopnik and Meltzoff (1997), declared, at the end of the introduction to their book: "Ultimately, our reason for watching and talking to children is the same as Socrates'. The most central questions in cognitive science are questions that only they can answer" (p. 9).

One of the questions that children seem to answer in their book is about the analogy of the child as a little scientist. The central idea of the book is that "the processes of cognitive development in children are similar to, indeed perhaps even identical with, the processes of cognitive development in scientists" (Gopnik & Meltzoff, 1997, p. 3).

Infants are endowed with an innate set of principles that allows them to begin to interact with the world. Among these principles, one of the most important allows a causal attribution to relations between physical events. At around the age of 6 months, the infant is able to apply the principles of *cohesion*—a moving object maintains its connectedness and boundaries—*continuity*—a moving object traces exactly one connected path over space and time—and *contact*—objects move together if and only if they touch (Spelke, Phillips, & Woodward, 1995). A child has an

1

intuition of what characterizes a living being from an artifact or an object. Between the ages of 2 and 5, the child assumes that external states of affairs may cause mental states and that there is a causal chain from perception to beliefs to intentions and to actions (see Sperber, Premack, & Premack, 1995). According to Viale (1999), these results on causal cognition in infants seem to justify the anti-Humean thesis of causal inferences based on synthetic a priori principles.

What are the features of these principles? Data from developmental studies and a certain universality of causal perception in cross-cultural studies seem to support the hypothesis that we are endowed with early developed cognitive structures corresponding to maturational properties of the mind-brain. They orient the subject's attention toward certain types of clues, but they also constitute definite presumptions about the existence of various ontological categories, as well as what can be expected from objects belonging to those different categories. Moreover, they provide subjects with "modes of construal" (Keil, 1995)—different ways of recognizing similarities in the environment and making inferences from them. Moreover and more surprisingly, contrary to the Piagetian theory, according to which the notion of causality is domain-general and gradually modified by experience,

> different conceptual domains are structured by different principles which 1) carry information about the types of stimuli that are likely to correspond to particular ontological categories, 2) convey expectations about non-obvious properties of objects in different domains, 3) constrain the manner in which spontaneous inductive inferences are made about objects from different domains. (Boyer, 1995, p. 623)

The previous Piagetian notion of formally defined stages, characterized by principles that apply across conceptual domains, has been replaced by a series of domain-specific developmental schedules, constrained by corresponding domain-specific principles. These principles constitute a core of probably innate "intuitive theories," which are implicit and constrain the later development of the explicit representations of the various domains. As Gelman (1990) highlighted, "different sets of principles guide the generation of different plans of action as well as the assimilation and structuring of experiences" (p. 80). They establish the boundaries for each domain, which single out stimuli that are relevant to the conceptual development of the domain.

The three main intuitive theories individuated by cognitive science are the theory of physical objects, the theory of biology, and the theory of psychology. These theories allow infants to individuate some theory-specific causal mechanisms to explain interactions among the entities in a domain. A child has an intuition of what characterizes a living being from an artifact or object. Between the ages of 2 and 5, the child assumes that external states of affairs may cause mental states and that there is a causal chain from perception to beliefs to intentions to actions.

The intuitive theory of physical causality is the least controversial and very rich in empirical data. Intuitive physical principles orient the child's understanding of the physical environment from infancy. Principles specifying that solid objects are cohesive, continuous, and not susceptible to action at a distance seem to emerge before 4 months (Baillargeon & Hanko-Summers, 1990; Leslie, 1988; Spelke, 1990). At around 6 months, the infant is able to apply the principle of support (i.e., that objects fall if they are not supported; Spelke, 1990). The specific patterns of movements allow him to make ontological distinctions between self-generated and non-self-generated movement (Massey & Gelman, 1988). This distinction gives an initial skeleton to the differentiation between animate and inanimate kinds of objects, which has important consequences for causal reasoning in the biological and psychological domains.

Research on causal cognition has shown that there are perceptions of causality that are not affected by previous experiences, whether of the same specific kind of relations or of an analogous kind. Besides, there is a great amount of empirical data showing that there is, in many cases, a strong cognitive tendency to infer a priori the effect of observing a cause without any dependence on previous experienced regularity. These empirical data seem to meet Hume's challenge (i.e., to show examples of perception and of a priori inference of a nonexperienced causal relation; Viale, 1999).

Starting from these data, Gopnik and Meltzoff (1997) introduced "The Little Scientist Thesis":

> There is strong empirical evidence that starting from their innate endowed principles, children propose abstract entities, coherently organised with causal relations among them. They make ontological commitments and hold counterfactuals. These entities serve to provide characteristic explanations, predictions and interpretations. Children initially ignore certain kinds of counter-evidence, then account for such evidence with auxiliary hypotheses, then use the new theoretical idea in limited contexts, and only finally reorganise their knowledge so that the new theoretical entities play a central role. When the new theory is under construction, they engage in extensive experiments relevant to the theory and collect empirical generalisations.

The innate theories function as a start-up of the conceptual development—but while innate, they would be defeasible. They are later modified and revised by new evidence: "Innate theories are like the Neurath boat that pushes off from the pier. The boat you start out in may have considerable effect on the boat you end up with, even if no trace of the original remains" (Gopnik & Meltzoff, 1997, p. 51).

Children resemble scientists in their method of theory change. One theory can substitute another when it fits the empirical evidence better and allows one to make better predictions. Counterevidence to a theory is ignored unless it manifests itself persistently. The methodological criteria of theory change in little scientists are not the guarantee of truth and representational success. Many false hypotheses are generated using these criteria. Nonetheless they seem to be a guarantee of conceptual learning from errors to generate theories that fit the world better.

ARE CHILDREN RATIONAL?

Norms and criteria of theory change and conceptual development in children give a positive representation of the rational attitude of humans. On the contrary, there is a dark side of the coin. Little scientists seem not to satisfy elementary canons of correct reasoning. For example, one candidate principle of inductive reasoning concerns the diversity of evidence in support of a general hypothesis. It is widely claimed that greater diversity entails greater support (e.g., Franklin & Howson, 1984; Hempel, 1966). Why did Newton's theory end up commanding so much assent? One reason is that in the presence of various background assumptions, the theory accurately predicts heterogeneous phenomena, such as the trajectories of balls thrown into the air, the behavior of gyroscopes, and the orbit of celestial bodies. At the end of the 17th century, these phenomena appeared very diverse, which forced respect for the theory despite reservations about the reliance on occult, nonmechanical entities like gravity.

The diversity principle has been the object of psychological investigation. Osherson, Smith, Wilkie, López, and Shafir (1990) discovered that it is one of the phenomena present in category-based induction tasks.

A general inductive argument is one in which the category in the conclusion properly includes the categories in the premises. For example, the conclusion category MAMMAL in Argument 1 includes the premise category HIPPO and HAMSTER:

(1) *Hippos have ulnar arteries.*
Hamsters have ulnar arteries.

———————————————————————

All mammals have ulnar arteries.

An argument is strong if belief in the premises causes people to believe the conclusion.

American adults seem to support a general or specific conclusion more when the premises are more different than when they are more similar. On the contrary, studies by López, Gelman, Gutheil, and Smith (1992) and Gutheil and Gelman (1997) among 6- and 9-year-olds show an opposite attitude. For example, 6-year-olds prefer Argument 2:

(2) *Cows have ulnar arteries.*
 Buffalos have ulnar arteries.
_____
 All animals have ulnar arteries.

to the alternative Argument 3:

(3) *Cows have ulnar arteries.*
 Cats have ulnar arteries.
_____
 All animals have ulnar arteries.

Moreover, both 6- and 9-year-olds prefer more homogeneous premises to more diverse premises in arguments with specific conclusions like Argument 4:

(4) _____
 Kangaroos have ulnar arteries

Children seem not to apply a fundamental norm of inductive reasoning. Therefore, the little scientist hypothesis might be weakened.

The diversity principle is a genuine feature of rational inquiry, hence part of the meaning of the "little scientist" hypothesis. Viale and Osherson (chap. 1, this volume) argue against the use of the diversity principle as a normative standard of inductive reasoning. The diversity variable is not related in such a simple fashion to argument strength, even at the prescriptive level. This is because so-called *blank* predicates (i.e., predicates that are indefinite in their application to given categories, but clear enough to communicate the kind of property in question) often retain enough meaning to open the door to legitimate reasoning that violates the diversity principle. An example is provided by the predicate *often carry the parasite Floxum*. It counts as blank because the parasite *Floxum* is unfamiliar, so nothing can be divined about which mammals are more or less likely to suffer from it. Now consider Arguments 5 and 6:

(5) *Housecats often carry the parasite Floxum.*
    Fieldmice often carry the parasite Floxum.

    All mammals often carry the parasite Floxum.

(6) *Housecats often carry the parasite Floxum.*
    Tigers often carry the parasite Floxum.

    All mammals often carry the parasite Floxum.

It seems undeniable that housecats resemble tigers more than they resemble fieldmice. Yet it appears perfectly defensible to judge Argument 6 to be stronger than Argument 5 on the grounds that housecats might catch Floxum from fieldmice (their prey), whereas they have little contact with tigers. In this case, reasonable judgments about strength run counter to the advice offered by the diversity principle. Hence, the latter is discredited as a basis for evaluating inductive intuition. Of course the example does not show that diversity always gives the wrong advice, only that it sometimes does. But this is enough to undermine its claim to normative status.

If we accept the Bayesian probability theory as a normative account of scientific inference, as most contemporary philosophy of science is doing (Howson & Urbach, 1993), we may propose that it is the probability of premises prior to accepting the conclusion that governs its strength (Horwich, 1982). Under these conditions, argument strength stands in a simple relation to premise probability.

Premise Probability Principle (PPP)

Suppose that Arguments A,B/C and A,B'/C are given where C logically implies A,B and B'. Then the strength of the first argument is greater than the strength of the second if and only if $P(A \& B) < P(A \& B')$.

The less probable the premises, the stronger the argument. Diversity of premises is often (but not systematically) associated with low premise probability. For example, it seems less likely that cows and cats have ulnar arteries than that cows and buffalos do. Based on this assumption, PPP accounts for the greater strength of Argument 3 compared with Argument 2. Likewise, given their unrelated habitats, housecats and tigers seem less likely to carry common parasites than do housecats and mice. For anyone sharing the latter judgment, PPP rules Argument 6 to be stronger than Argument 5.

From the proof of PPP, it can be seen that the principle applies to arguments with any predicate, blank or not. Its normative status is thereby enhanced because inductive reasoning almost invariably involves meaning-ful predicates. Observe also that PPP is a consequence of no more than the axioms of probability along with our definition of argument strength.

The experiments on PPP, summarized in Viale and Osherson (chap. 1, this volume), come from Lo, Sides, Rozelle, and Osherson (2002). All experiments were designed to collect judgments about argument strength versus premise probability in two-premise general arguments with blank predicates. The crucial items were arguments evaluated at separate times for strength and premise probability.

In Experiment 1, American preschoolers showed reliable (albeit imperfect) conformity to PPP. Indeed, they showed more conformity to PPP than to the diversity principle. In Experiment 3, it was seen that Taiwanese children showed as much conformity to PPP as their American counterparts.

The PPP has better credentials because it follows from the axioms of probability and a plausible definition of argument strength. The experiments reveal tenuous but detectable conformity to PPP on the part of young children in different cultures. If these findings are supported and extended by further experimentation, they provide one clear sense in which young children's inductive methodology can be interpreted as properly scientific.

Furthermore, these studies show how, prior to environmental conditioning resulting from different latitudes and longitudes, there is cognitive uniformity that appears to be based on a common genetic endowment of the same principles of reasoning.

REASONING BIASES OR EXPERIMENTAL ERRORS?

If the studies on biases and errors during developmental age do not generate great concern about the image of human rationality, on the contrary, the enormous amount of empirical evidence collected over the past 40 years on suboptimal ways of human reasoning and decision making has provoked great bewilderment. "How can we go to the Moon with so many constant errors of judgement?" was the question asked by a colleague to Nisbett and Ross after having read the proofs of the first eight chapters of their book *Human Inference: Strategies and Shortcomings of Social Judgement* (1980). The image of man that is portrayed in the book is of a person unable to use formal criteria of reasoning and decision making like those that scientists use in their activity. Man chooses samples that are biased by systematic tendencies; he is not able to assess the covariation between events; he is biased in the causal attribution; he makes predictions ignoring base rate and regression toward the mean; he tends to confirm the theory instead of falsifying it.

Nevertheless, man goes to the Moon—that is, he is quite able to adapt to his social and natural environments. He is able to understand, predict, and control many aspects of his life and environment. He is able to plan his career, make diagnoses from his symptoms, and discuss rationally many problems.

There are two important aspects of human irrationality that can find a moderate interpretation. The first concerns suboptimality in assessing covariation among events, which is a crucial ability for generating hypotheses. Outside the laboratory, in real life, there are many circumstances that allow good performance in covariation:

1. Because sometimes the stimuli are well perceived, evident, close, and motivationally relevant.
2. Because when covariation is very strong, a single prototypical case can offer a reliable representation of the general relation.
3. Because most of our theories are founded on covariations made by experts (scientists, advisers, consultants) in particular fields.

The second and most important concern about human rationality is the "perseverance bias." People tend to persevere in their beliefs even when faced with data that falsify them. This phenomenon seems to undermine the dynamic image of theory change of the little scientists thesis. Actually, the dynamics of theory change of the child compared with the adult is much stronger. In fact, the *little scientist* metaphor finds its justification in the greater analogy between child and scientist than child and adult. Adults, for many acceptable and unacceptable reasons, are more conservative in maintaining their theories of the world. They prefer stability of their system of thought and find it difficult to integrate, in the quick flow of contemporary life, empirical counterevidence into new alternative theories. Nevertheless:

a) The maintenance of a theory in front of anomalies, until we are sure that it is systematic, seems a sound methodological rule also in the scientific community.
b) The adult seems more close to the model of the technologist rather than the scientist. He needs to apply theories in everyday problem-solving. He has no time to worry about the truth of the theory. What is important is that it functions in solving practical problems. He fears more a casual error in applying the theory in a given pragmatic context than a systematic error that would need the generation of an alternative theory. Nevertheless, as in technology, the solution works if the embodied theory is

valid. Therefore, sooner or later, even the adult is obliged to change ill-functioning theories. (Viale, 2001, p. 225)

However, not all people accept a picture of man as being naturally inclined to systematic errors and bias. Following the tradition of studies on probabilistic judgment, the mainstream, represented by Kahneman, Slovic, and Tversky (1982), sees in natural heuristics the "strategies of simplification that reduce the complexity of judgement tasks, to make them tractable for the kind of mind that people happen to have" (p. XII). Availability heuristic and representativeness heuristics are an example of these inferential tools used by the human mind and based on the limits of memory. Their activation appears to be responsible for probability judgments that do not comply with the canons of Bayesian theory. These results have been criticized by Gigerenzer (1991, 1994) and Cosmides and Tooby (1996), who, following evolutionist psychology, regard probabilistic reasoning as based on observed frequencies, sequences of events, and limited samples. Contrary to the frequentist approach, the Bayesian method adopted by Kahneman et al. uses probability expressed in percentages that are a highly processed cultural product and consequently do not seem to be a natural representation to study probabilistic reasoning. As a result, many errors and biases identified in the experiments undertaken in the past few years appear not to be an expression of irrationality in human cognition, but rather the effect of an unnatural method of studying probabilistic reasoning. This offers contrast between two opinions on the natural dimension of probabilistic reasoning: The first focuses on the limitations of the mind and the use of heuristics, whereas the second stresses the categorization of events through sequences and frequencies. According to Macchi and Bagassi (chap. 9, this volume), this characterization is inadequate. In fact, both approaches fail to take account of an important explanatory element for the formation of errors and biases: the pragmatic effect of context-dependent variables activated by the formulation of a problem. As the studies described in the chapter show, the difficulties and suboptimal features of many tests on probabilistic reasoning are related more to the structure of the text than to the heuristic factors or the statistical format in which the probabilities are expressed. This consideration is true irrespective of the use of cultural percentages or natural frequencies.

CULTURAL DIFFERENCES IN THE STYLES OF REASONING

When we analyze the cognitive rationality stemming from the cognitive tests on everyday reasoning, one important question concerns the cultural variability of the styles of reasoning. Are cognitive abilities universal or context-dependent? Can we discover common patterns of thinking among different cultures or does each sociocultural environment shape its system of thought?

An answer to this question comes from Nisbett and Masuda (chap. 2, this volume); Nisbett, Peng, Choi, and Norenzayan (2001); and Nisbett (2003) on the differences between Asian and American thinking. They rely on an impressive number of cognitive tests that try to compare the way of reasoning of North Americans, mainly university students, and East Asians (Korean, Chinese, and Japanese), mainly university students. The East Asians and Americans respond in qualitatively different ways to the same stimulus situation in many different tests.

For example, American participants showed large primacy effects in judgments about covariation, whereas Chinese participants showed none. Control illusion increased the degree of covariation seen and the reported accuracy of Americans, but tended to have the opposite effects on Chinese. Koreans were greatly influenced in their causal attribution by the sort of situational information that has no effect for Americans. Koreans showed great hindsight bias effects under conditions where Americans showed none. Finally, Americans responded to contradiction by polarizing their beliefs, whereas Chinese responded by moderating their beliefs. I can summarize the results as follows.

The *American* versus *East Asian style of thinking* (Nisbett et al., 2001):

1. *Explanation*: East Asians tend to explain events, both social and physical, more with respect to the field, whereas Americans tend to explain events more with respect to a target object and its properties.

2. *Prediction* and *postdiction*: East Asians tend to make predictions with reference to a wider variety of factors than Americans do. Consequently, they are less surprised by any given outcome, and they are more prone to "hindsight bias" or the tendency to regard events as having been inevitable in retrospect.

3. *Attention*: Because East Asians locate causality in the field instead of the object, they tend to be more accurate at "covariation detection"—that is, the perception of relationship within the field.

4. *Control*: Americans are more subject to the "illusion of control"— that is, a greater expectation of success when the individual is involved in interaction with the object—even when that interaction could not logically have an effect on the outcome.

5. *Relationships and similarities* versus *rules and categories*: East Asians tend to group objects and events on the basis of their relationships to one another (e.g., "A is a part of B"). Americans would be expected to group them more on the basis of category membership (e.g., "A and B are both Xs"). Americans are inclined to learn rule-based categories more readily

than East Asians and rely on categories more for purposes of inductive and deductive inference.

6. *Logic* versus *experiential knowledge*: East Asians are more influenced by prior beliefs in judging the soundness of a formal argument. Americans are more able to set aside prior beliefs in favor of reasoning based on logical rules.

7. *Dialectics* versus *the law of noncontradiction*: East Asians are inclined to seek compromise solutions to problems ("middle way") and reconcile contradictory propositions. Americans tend to seek solutions to problems in which a given principle drives out all but one competing solution, to prefer arguments based on logic, and to reject one or both of two propositions that could be construed as contradicting one another.

These differences are reflected in the different kinds of errors and biases that affect East Asians and Americans. We cannot say that one culture is normatively better than another. East Asians are better at causal covariation and less prone to illusion of control. Americans are better at deductive reasoning in category-based induction and less prone to hindsight bias. Obviously, better does not mean that they satisfy, absolutely, the normative canons of rational reasoning. It is well known that the tradition of investigation into deductive and probabilistic errors and biases started in American colleges.

Therefore, we can say that we are faced with two different mixes of rational and irrational reasoning. But the crucial thesis of Nisbett et al. (2001) and Nisbett and Masuda (chap. 2, this volume) is that the different ways of reasoning are not a contingent and superficial feature, but are rooted in two completely different systems of thinking—that is, in different metaphysical and epistemological principles that shape the American and East Asian cognition differently. These two different systems of thinking originated causally from two different sociocultural environments: the old Greek trading society and classical philosophy, on the one hand, and the old Chinese agricultural society and Confucian philosophy, on the other hand.

Different socioeconomic variables gave birth to different styles of thought that we can summarize under the headings of *holistic* and *analytic* thought. Nowadays, these different styles of thought continue to be effective in differentiating the reasoning processes of contemporary Americans and East Asians.

Norenzayan (chap. 3, this volume) also confirms the results of Nisbett and Masuda (chap. 2, this volume), Nisbett (2003), and Nisbett et al. (2001). The cultural differences between Western and Asiatic populations are examined in a variety of cognitive tasks that involve formal and intuitive reasoning.

Formal reasoning is rule-based, emphasizes logical inference, represents concepts by necessary and sufficient features, and overlooks sense experience when it conflicts with rules of logic. Intuitive reasoning is experience-based, resists decontextualizing or separating form from content, relies on sense experience and concrete instances, and overlooks rules and logic when they are at odds with intuition. The reasoning of Euro-American, Asian American, and East Asian university students was compared under conditions where a cognitive conflict was activated between formal and intuitive strategies of thinking. The central hypothesis was that Euro-Americans would be more willing to set aside intuition and follow rules than East Asians. (Norenzayan, chap. 3, this volume)

The chapter contains the results of four experiments. In the first experiment, participants are asked to apply complex rules to classify imaginary animals correctly. Then, to test the inductive category learning, a conflict is stimulated between the complex rule and the memory of animals seen previously. The second experiment explores judgments of similarity and drawing classification. These judgments use either a solution based on rules or a family-resemblance-based solution. The last two experiments attempt to examine the conceptual processes. In the third experiment, participants are asked how convincing deductive reasoning is when logic comes into conflict with the typicality of the conclusion. In the fourth experiment, Norenzayan examines deductive reasoning when the logical structure opposes the credibility of the conclusion.

The results confirm the starting hypothesis that Euro-American students have a much stronger tendency to ignore intuition and follow the rules of reasoning when the latter conflict with the former.

THE APPARENT DIVERSITY OF TRIBAL
AND CIVILIZED STYLES OF REASONING

The first consideration about this anti-universal conception of cognition comes from the supporters of the universal endowment of cognitive abilities. If the innate theories of physics, biology, and mind are true, then these theories form a common universal cognitive basis for the thought of every human in the world. Other investigators are even more radical. There are even common essential beliefs about the nature of the social world (Hirschfeld, 1996; see also chap. 5, this volume), and even religious conceptions, such as spirits and superhuman agents, are remarkably similar from one culture to another (Boyer, 1993).

In my opinion, this position may be consistent with the anti-universal thesis of Nisbett et al. The little scientist hypothesis can explain why. We know that conceptual and theory change in the developmental age does not start from nothing, but from an innate endowment of theory about causality, the physical world, and so on. The change toward new theories is triggered by empirical evidence and informative inputs that come from the environment. These evidential and informative inputs obviously are variable in relation to the particular developmental contexts. Therefore, they drive the generation of different theories on how to interpret and understand the world. They are the metaphysical and epistemological theories representing the implicit premises of our reasoning and thinking. In conclusion, it is likely that such different sociocultural contexts as the East Asian and American ones are able to lead, in the developmental age, to the generation of different metaphysical and epistemological theories that have a different effect on ways of reasoning.

Norenzayan (chap. 3, this volume) agrees with the previous consideration. The human mind is equipped with basic cognitive primitives and possesses cognitive processes that carry out many tasks, such as exemplar-based categorization, deductive reasoning, causal attribution, and so on. However, this basic endowment does not rule out differentiated development in response to cultural and environmental stimuli. These differences are manifested in various ways. First, different cultural practices can make a given cognitive process, which is universally available in principle, accessible in a differentiated way. Asians appear to have a greater propensity than Westerners for exemplar-based categorization and a lesser propensity to decontextualize deductive arguments and more to explain behavior by referring to the situational context. Second, through discoveries and inventions, societies often introduce artificial and complex new ways of thinking that differentiate one culture from another. One needs only think of the statistic and probabilistic revolution in the 17th century and its impact on Western rationality and decision-making models—or the development and influence of the ancient Taoist notion of yin and yang in the contemporary Chinese way of reasoning in relation to modal concepts like change, moderation, and relativism.

The second consideration about the thesis proposed by Nisbett et al. relates to the implicit support of a kind of cognitive relativism. This is the natural consequence of the socioeconomic determinism present in their thesis. In fact, according to them, social organization and economic structure are the major determinants of the causal chain metaphysics–epistemology–cognition. Different socioeconomic configurations generate fixed, irreversible, different causal chains. The world seems shaped with different and incommensurable causal chains related to the different socioeconomic structures.

One of the results that Nisbett et al. bring to support their thesis seems to go in the opposite direction. It deals with the difference principle mentioned in a previous paragraph. According to them: "Koreans make less use of categories for purposes of inductive inference than do Americans and therefore are not able to follow the difference principle in an argument with a specific conclusion" (Nisbett et al., 2001).

Faced with Arguments 7 and 8, Koreans prefer Argument 7 because they are less able than Americans to generate the inclusive category MAMMALS from the category in the conclusion RABBIT, and therefore to estimate that LIONS and TIGERS have a lesser coverage of the category MAMMAL than LIONS and GIRAFFES (Choi, Nisbett, & Smith, 1997).

(7) *Lions have ulnar arteries.*
   Tigers have ulnar arteries.
   _____
   Rabbits have ulnar arteries.

(8) *Lions have ulnar arteries.*
   Giraffes have ulnar arteries.
   _____
   Rabbits have ulnar arteries.

On the contrary, if the category MAMMAL is made salient by changing the conclusion to:

(9) _____
   Mammals have ulnar arteries.

the principle of difference is satisfied.

Data that seem more severe about the ability to use categories come from a study that has been carried out in Vietnam at the University of Ho Chi Min City (Viale & Osherson, 2000). The sample seems to show that even using arguments with a general conclusion, and not only with a specific conclusion, the East Asian students are unable to apply the difference principle. Does this mean that there are fixed wired-in limitations in the cognitive processing of categories in some people (e.g., East Asians), but not in others (e.g., Americans)? I don't think so.

The answer comes from the studies carried out among traditional Itza' Mayans from the Peten region of Guatemala (López, Atran, Coley, Medin, & Smith, 1997; see Atran, Medin, & Ross, chap. 4, this volume) to identify the universal cultural features of folk-biological inductions on mammal categories. They discovered that, as in the previous case of Vietnam, Itza' did not follow the diversity principle with general and specific conclusions. These data were very different from those found in many American colleges, where the diversity principle was always followed. They tried to explain, through a number of follow-up studies, what the reasons were for this difference. The conclusion was not one of radical cognitive differences, but rather an ecology-based reasoning stemming from the particular pragmatic context where they were living.

> Itzaj participants had extensive knowledge of the habits, characteristics, and ecological proclivities of Peten mammals; this ecological knowledge appears to have blocked diversity-based reasoning by rendering the premises implausible on the basis of what the Itzaj know to be true. Cultural knowledge available to the Itzaj may have rendered the diversity strategy irrelevant. (López et al., 1997, p. 288)

In fact, they tried to control the hypothesis of ecology-based reasoning in two following studies. One was made on Itza', using arguments stemming from real-world scenarios and not from natural taxonomy. The tests were about saving money, inspecting farmland, and buying corn. It showed that they were able to follow the diversity principle when reasoning about everyday life and pragmatic problem solving. One of the tests was the following:

> Imagine you want to buy several bags of corn from a given person. Before buying them, this person will show you only two cobs of corn to check whether all the corn is good. Do you prefer him to show you two cobs from one and the same bag (non-diversification response), or do you prefer him to show you one cob from one bag and another cob from another bag (diversification response)? (López et al., 1997, p. 284)

The majority of Itza' chose the diversification response because, according to their theory based on real-life experience, they had good reasons to widen the sample.

The other study was made on American tree experts. They discovered that the less expert the individuals were (e.g., maintenance personnel), the more subject they were to ecology-based reasoning and the less they followed the diversity principle. On the contrary, expert taxonomists were able to extrapolate the inclusive categories more easily and to follow the diversity principle. Scientific knowledge enables the taxonomists to generate more salient categories at a rank higher than genus and family. When an individual, as in the case of the maintenance personnel, has knowledge based on concrete examples of trees at the genus level, he is not able to reason using categories at a higher rank and, consequently, cannot follow the diversity principle. On the contrary, the taxonomist can generate more generalized theories about the same object of everyday experience (e.g., the trees), therefore he is able to categorize at a more abstract level. These more abstract theories enable him to generate and use inclusive categories, and therefore to satisfy the diversity principle.

LAY FOLKS' REASONING

These tests appear capable of demonstrating that cognitive styles from other cultures (e.g., like those used by the Indios, which seem so different, in terms of performance, from Western ones) in fact present similar cognitive skills. The data presented earlier are reported by Atran, Medin, and Ross (chap. 4, this volume), who tackle various topics linked to folk biology. The first set of experiments was carried out with Yukatek Maya and urban American children and showed how the former, but not the latter, were able to reason on the members of the biological world without using analogies with humans. American children, in contrast, show an anthropocentric bias that can be explained by their different experience and interaction with animals and plants compared with the Indios children, who have lived in the rain forest since birth. Therefore, it would seem that "humans are not the prototype that organizes the domain of animals."

The second set of experiments was carried out with 4- and 5-year-old children belonging to the Maya Indios tribe and on Brazilian and American children living in cities. Both appear to use "concepts of innate species potential, or underlying essence, as an inferential framework for projecting known and unknown biological properties to organisms in the face of uncertainty." Together with the first set of experiments, these studies confirm the hypothesis that folk biology does not come from folk psychology. Children from different cultures relied on the concept of underlying essence, not on the properties of human beings, to reason on the properties of animals and plants.

The third set of experiments was carried out with adult Maya Indians and Americans living in the Midwest. Both sample populations showed a common tendency to prefer the generic-species level—the level of robin and oak—as the taxonomic rank to reason and make inductive inferences. This result appears to be counterintuitive among American adults owing to their scant knowledge and culture of individual animal and plant species. One would have expected that, for reasons of experience and similarity reasoning, the preferred level would be that of life forms—the level of tree and bird. Instead, also among the Americans, the level of generic species is preferred to make inductions on the distribution of biological properties and for "predicting patterns in the face of uncertainty." This result is a further confirmation of the presence of concept of underlying essences, the "generic-species level as a partitioning of the ontological domains of plant and animal into mutually exclusive essences."

The fourth set of experiments was carried out with adult Mayas, American college students, and various groups of biological experts (landscapers, park workers, birdwatchers, professional taxonomists). It showed that all groups tend to categorize generic species spontaneously into taxonomies with higher and lower levels. "People from diverse societies build topologically-similar biological taxonomies that guide inferences about the distribution of biological and ecological properties." As we have seen before, only the students and, for the great part, the taxonomists use diversity-based reasoning. Instead the other groups use ecology-based reasoning and the "taxonomy constrains the likely operational range of ecological agents and causes."

We saw earlier that Atran, Medin, and Ross (chap. 4, this volume) present data that appear to falsify the thesis that folk biology is parasitic on folk psychology. On the contrary, according to other authors, the propensity to attribute human psychological properties to nonhuman agents appears much more pervasive than that to animals alone. Because the concept of *person* seems to be a primitive concept that is applied to all nonhuman intentional agents, like animals (Carey, 1985), but also to ghosts (Boyer, 1990) and gods (Barrett & Keil, 1996), these nonhuman intentional agents are represented with human psychological properties, including intentional, emotional, and affective forms. There even appears to be a tendency to treat the computer as a conversational partner, attributing it with human psychological properties and regarding it as a much more real intentional agent than we might otherwise imagine (Moon & Nass, 1996). There appears to be a fundamental level, that of personhood, on which all the other levels depends. When intentional agency appears in other domains—animal, ghost, or inanimate object—it is a result of conceptual inheritance from person.

However, how does this mind-reading function occur? There are two main conflicting theories on the subject. According to the first theory, also known as "Theory Theory," people have folk-psychological knowledge of what goes on in other people's minds and how that makes them act in particular situations. This kind of knowledge can be defined as a *theory* of other people's mental activity (Churchland, 1981; Fodor, 1987). According to the second theory, also known as "Simulation Theory," individuals try to identify with other people's mental activities, beliefs, and aims, and therefore they can infer their consequent actions and behavior (Gordon, 1986; Heal, 1986). Perner and Kühberger (chap. 6, this volume) ask how we can decide which of these two mind-reading models is genuinely active. One possibility is the different result produced by the simulation model compared with the Theory Theory when elaborating prediction. If we examine the predicted behavior of an individual faced with two options, the simulation model only allows one option to be analyzed at once, whereas the Theory Theory, in principle, also allows both conditions to be placed alongside. Empathic simulation literally means getting into the other person's mind and elaborating the choice by examining the options one at a time and then comparing them, whereas the theory regarding the behavior of the other person can blend and juxtapose the two conditions. Perner and Kühberger (chap. 6, this volume) present an experimental method, together with two experiments, that looks promising as a way of understanding in the future how the Theory of Mind (ToM) works.

In any case, understanding the behavior of other humans through the attribution of desires, beliefs, and intentions appears essential to the constitution of human society. Reading other people's minds to interpret their behavior is a crucial aspect of man's adaptation to evolutionary challenges (Tomasello, 1999). As is seen later with regard to the role of testimony and argumentation (see Sperber, chap. 7, this volume), the complexity of networks and social ties in human communities makes the possibility of mind reading, getting inside other people's minds, an essential tool to detect and track failures to cooperate and avoid the costs of cheating. This human capacity, termed by some authors the Theory of Mind (ToM), appears to emerge very early on and can already be found at the age of 9 months when the movement of a human hand is interpreted as intentional, but not that of an artifact (Woodward, 1998). As the child learns language, he tends to follow the mother's gaze to understand what is the referent for the word, therefore attributing it the intention to refer to the denotate of the term (Baldwin, 1991). Last, as Hirschfeld affirms (chap. 5, this volume), a ToM milestone in the developmental age "is the capacity to grasp that other people hold beliefs that one knows to be false."

The importance of ToM to our understanding of the social world appears to be demonstrated by the social maladjustment found in autistic children who appear to lack the ability to represent others as having beliefs and desires independent of one's own (Baron-Cohen, 1996). The fundamental level of folk psychology is also manifested in a form of folk-ontological holism that is found when we attribute intentionality to social aggregates. As Hirschfeld writes (chap. 5, this volume), "traffic jams, stampedes, riots, folie a deux (trois ou beaucoup), and other forms of 'groupthink' are aggregate phenomena that are best understood without appeal to individual persons' mental states," but ascribing to them intentions as if they had a mind of their own. According to most authors, this attribution of intentions is parasitic on folk psychology and does not constitute an independent folk sociology. Hirschfeld (chap. 5, this volume) disputes both the thesis that social understanding is largely concerned with the interactions of individual persons and their mind and the thesis that only individual persons (and other complex living organisms) are genuine intentional agents.

The understanding of the social dimension may also occur without understanding other persons' minds as postulated by ToM. We can understand another's behavior by identifying the social category to which he belongs and by foreseeing the standard and stereotypical forms of behavior resulting from this categorization. For example, if we meet an old retired general who is queuing to buy a ticket with us, we would expect him to show a low tolerance threshold to anyone failing to respect the order of precedence. If we meet a priest in the street, we would expect him to show verbal or nonverbal irritability with dissolute or shameless behavior. But, as exemplified by the case of Temple Grandin, mentioned by Hirschfeld (chap. 5, this volume), even definite cases of autism can understand the collective behavior of groups of agents (Sacks, 1995). Grandin was an autistic scientist who specialized in understanding animal psychology and raising and treating herds of domestic animals under stress. However, she was incapable of penetrating the human mind, and therefore did not possess a ToM with which to transfer intentional and affective activities to nonhuman agents like pets; her "extraordinary ability comes from her capacity to 'see' the nature of animal social experience without anthropomorphizing it." Some studies on autistic children presented by Hirschfeld (chap. 5, this volume) appear to show that, even "with significant impairment in their ability to interpret the behavior of others with respect to mental states, [they] were virtually unimpaired in their ability to interpret the behavior of others in terms of the groups of which they were members." They were able to do this by utilizing the social stereotypes, and in this way their capacity of group reasoning was independent of the capacity for person-based reasoning about behavior. This capacity for group-based reasoning independent of ToM person-based reasoning seems to emerge very early in human development. It is based on a number of cognitive and perceptive characteristics. Studies of geometric figures (Berry & Springer, 1993; Springer, Meier, & Berry, 1996) show that perceptual figures are crucial to intentional attributions. Specific patterns of motion invite people to attribute intentions to geometric figures without making any use of ToM. "Coordinated movement plus a version of spatial contiguity would thus seem an important determinant of perception of corporate individuality," namely, the attribution of intentional individuality to groups, sets, and aggregates of persons without any anthropomorphization process. To these aspects, we can add others concerning the common characteristics that supervise the social categorization of a group of individuals compared with others (e.g., physical characteristics, like skin color, hair color, or stature, or behavioral traits, like a subcultural type of dress and aesthetic identity). Therefore, the attribution of intentional individuality to groups and social aggregates is unrelated to the attribution of human psychological characteristics, such as desires, beliefs, and emotions.

In summary, for Hirschfeld, it is a question of recognizing that, together with ToM and the person as a primitive cognitive, there is another primitive cognitive represented by the social entity. Therefore, alongside folk psychology and folk biology, we must introduce a new level of lay folks' reasoning—that of folk sociology.

EVOLUTION OF SOCIAL PRACTICES
TO AVOID FALSITY

As we have seen earlier, one of the evolutionary explanations of folk psychology and the capacity for mind reading represented by ToM is the possibility of foreseeing and intercepting untruthful behavior that pretends to cooperate. The creation of social networks, organizations, and even institutions appears to be fostered by the ability to avoid the social costs of cheating behavior.

Goldman's (1999) Social Epistemology supports this veritistic aim. It identifies two goals: first, to criticize the Cartesian image of the knowledge generated by isolated thinkers with no connections; second, to launch a critical attack on those epistemological concepts of a relativistic and constructivist type that reject any truthful criterion of knowledge generation and evaluation.

On the contrary, according to Goldman (1999), social practices like communication, testimony, and argumentation are developed to help the individual pursue the goal of truth in the furthering of knowledge. Obviously, this truthful function of social procedures is not univocal, but, as Sperber (chap. 7, this volume) affirms, Goldman fails to point out that a "significant proportion of socially acquired beliefs are likely to be false beliefs and this not just as a result of the malfunctioning, but also of the proper functioning of social communication." If we analyze two means of communication—testimony and argumentation—we find that truth was not the evolutionary factor that led to the stabilization of communications. It is the causing of desirable effects on the audience that makes communication advantageous to the communicator. From this point of view, "Communication produces a certain amount of misinformation in the performance of its function, more specifically, in the performance of those aspects of its function that are beneficial to the communicator." Also when analyzed using game theory, there is no stable solution to the game between a true or false communicator and the listener who has or does not have faith in what the communicator says. Even if, in theory, the condition of the truthfulness of the communicator and the faithfulness of the listener is convenient to both, there is no stable solution to the game. Rather, it is through argumentation that evolution has developed ways of defending itself against the risk of falsehood. Contrary to animals, humans do not just communicate information, they also argue it. According to Sperber (chap. 7, this volume), argumentation has neither the general function of providing the reasons for accepting a given argument nor that, affirmed by evolutionary psychology, of "domain- and task-specific inferential mechanisms corresponding to problems and opportunities met in the environment in which a species has evolved."

Instead, in Sperber's (chap. 7, this volume) view, "there are evolutionary reasons to expect a kind of seemingly general reasoning mechanism in humans, but one that is in fact, specialized for processing communicated or to be communicated information." This mechanism does not seem to be linked to individual cognitive activity, but instead is functional to communicative activity. Communicating does not just mean testimony, as in the case of animals, but trying to cite reasons and arguments to support your own thesis. In this sense, the listener has developed various instruments to gauge the trust of the speaker. As Sperber (chap. 7, this volume) points out, the two instruments—the capacity to distinguish between behavioral signs of sincerity or insincerity and trust in relation to benevolence to the speaker—are not specifically applicable to an assessment of the argument. Above all, "coherence checking," namely focusing on the internal and external coherence of the message and what you believe in, serves as a marker for possible lies passed on by the communicator.

To be more persuasive, in their cultural evolution, humans have developed a form of argument that uses various logical terms like *if, and, or, therefore, but*, and so on. This explains, for example, as Nisbett and Masuda (chap. 2, this volume) affirm, the development of rhetoric and logic in ancient Greeks compared with the lack of this development in China. This development stemmed from the need of the Greeks, a society of merchants and individuals, to persuade their partners through the discussions and confrontations that occurred for commercial, political, religious, and later philosophical reasons. The contemporary inhabitants of China, as part of an organic society whose purpose was above all harmony and social balance, did not feel the need to affirm their reasons and tended to prefer the middle way in discussions and comparisons.

The communicator develops the argumentative capacity to persuade even if he does not always succeed; the listener develops coherence checking to assess the reliability of the communicator's arguments even if he is often wrong. The communicator develops the capacity to be considered honest and reliable in testimony even if he is not; the listener develops fallible psychological instruments to identify whether the communicator is lying. In evolution, truth and rationality, falsehood and irrationality blend, and the evolution of the social practice of communication is less univocally marked by the truthful ideal of what Goldman thinks.

UNIVERSAL AND LOCAL COGNITIVE STYLES
AND THEIR NORMATIVE CONSEQUENCES

From the experiment described by Atran, Medin, and Ross (chap. 4, this volume), it emerges that genetically inherited cognitive universals, represented by "universal taxonomic structures, centered on essence-based generic species," are likely to be present. These innate concepts could have been selected at an evolutionary level to represent important and recurrent aspects of nature.

These data seem to support the image of a human being genetically endowed with concepts and universal principles of inference. It is likely that there are not fixed irreversible cultural differences in cognition that stem from relative culturally different and fixed metaphysical and epistemological theories about the world. On the contrary, the cognitive abilities develop from universal type inferential principles that are genetically inherited. They can follow different paths of development depending on different cultural contexts. However, their diversity is reversible, and the cognitive styles are dependent on knowledge, expertise, and pragmatic needs. These factors are able to reduce and, in some cases, neutralize the cultural diversity of the cognitive abilities.

This conclusion is well known in cognitive anthropology. Education can quite easily shape cognitive attitudes, making them transculturally similar. The problem-solving ability is much stronger in real-world scenarios linked to particular pragmatic contexts and practical needs than it is in abstract tasks. The need for practical problem solving can trigger cognitive abilities that were hidden in abstract and uninteresting tasks (Boudon & Viale, 2000). Moreover, as we have seen before in summarizing the chapter by Macchi and Bagassi (chap. 9, this volume), the pragmatic dimension of the discourse involved in solving the problems of the experiments seem to strongly influence the answers. For example, many biases seem to be caused by the structure of the text than by a natural or cultural propensity to errors.

Also the analysis reported earlier on the normative aspects of probabilistic reasoning in children (Viale & Osherson, chap. 1, this volume) appears consistent with these remarks. By adopting a different normative principle of inductive judgment as the Probability Premise Principle, which seems to fit with the Bayesian theory of probability, it was seen that children from two different cultures (American and Chinese-Taiwanese) do not show any significant differences in their replies that conform to the normative standards of PPP. Before environmental differences start to influence cognitive styles, children appear to show the same inductive style irrespective of latitude and longitude.

Even Nisbett (2003) acknowledged that reversibility exists in the cognitive style of East Asians and Americans. Chinese people who have lived for a few years in America tend to adopt American cognitive styles and vice versa. In the experiments, adequate priming can significantly reduce cultural inclinations in cognitive styles. In tests of causal attribution carried out by the developmental psychologist Miller (1984; quoted in Nisbett, 2003), similar behavior can be seen between Hindu East Indian children and American children. Not until adolescence did Indians and Americans begin to diverge in causal attribution. Instead, when adults, Indians tend to explain behavior in terms of contextual factors, whereas Americans reason in terms of individual dispositions.

If, as seems to be shown by Viale and Osherson (chap. 1, this volume); Lo, Sides, Rozelle, and Osherson (2002); López et al. (1997); and Atran, Medin, and Ross (chap. 4, this volume), there do not appear to be differences in the cognitive style concerning some forms of inductive reasoning among people from different cultures, this has an important consequence for the normative justification of belief formation and revision.

The presence or otherwise of cultural differences in the cognitive style of reasoning and decision making is, according to Weinberg, Nichols, and Stich (chap. 8, this volume), a fundamental epistemological fact when understanding which epistemological strategy to adopt in justifying knowledge. Why? One of the epistemological theories most in vogue over the past few years is the internalist theory. It affirms that the sole source of normative legitimation for our beliefs is internal—inside us. With a proper process of self-exploration, we can discover the correct epistemic norms for belief formation and revision. By analogy with Romanticism in literature, Weinberg, Nichols, and Stich (chap. 8, this volume) call this approach Epistemic Romanticism. In fact, as in the case of Romanticism, only by exploring within ourselves can we make the real essence of ourselves emerge, and also in Epistemic Romanticism we are the normative source of the epistemic principles. But in what way? One of the most debated solutions is that which identifies epistemic intuitions as the main cause—namely, the spontaneous judgment about the epistemic properties of some cases. There are various examples of Intuition Driven Romanticism (IDR). The best known is the reflective equilibrium strategy of Goodman (1965), in which "a [normative] rule is amended if it yields an inference we are [intuitively] unwilling to accept [and] an inference is rejected if it violates a [normative] rule we are [intuitively] unwilling to amend" (p. 66).

The balance may occur in various forms. It may be "narrow" if we restrict the rules and inferences, for example, only to those of philosophical interest. It may be "expert" if we restrict the creation of a reflexive balance to the category of professionals of knowledge—the epistemologists, for example. Many researchers, including Laudan (1984) and Goldman (1986), support Intuition-Driven Romanticism (IDR). Rules of justification are required to justify one's own beliefs. These rules will specify permissible ways in which cognitive agents may go about the business of forming and revising their beliefs. How can we decide that a rule is correct? By appealing to a higher level, "a criterion of rightness." But how can we decide what this criterion is? Goldman (1986) affirms that the correct criterion of rightness is the one that comports with the conception that is "embraced by everyday thought and language" (p. 58). "A criterion is supported to the extent that implied judgements accord with such intuitions and weakened to the extent that they do not" (Goldman, 1986, p. 66).

Now, the validity of IDR, in its various versions, is based on a condition: Universal intuitions can be used to determine universal norms for the formation and revision of beliefs. If, on the contrary, for the same type of events and cases the intuitions were different in relation to cultural, ethnic, and social contexts, then it would not be possible to admit some form of epistemic relativism. This would reveal the impossibility of IDR strategies to generate a normative theory of knowledge.

We saw earlier that Nisbett and Masuda (chap. 2, this volume) appear to show that a difference exists between the cognitive styles of Westerners and Far Easterners. However, Viale and Osherson (chap. 1, this volume) and Atran, Medin, and Ross (chap. 4, this volume) put forward data and arguments that seem to weaken the cognitive relativism outlined by Nisbett and Masuda. Weinberg, Nichols, and Stich (chap. 8, this volume) start from Nisbett's results, and from what might be termed the moral relativism of Haidt, Koller, and Dias (1993), to verify empirically whether IDR is false and whether we are faced with a situation of epistemic relativism. To do this, they undertook a series of tests involving persons from different cultural, ethnic, and social extractions. They wanted their intuition probes—the cases that they ask subjects to judge—to be similar to cases that have actually been used in the recent literature in epistemology.

For example, a category of examples that was widely used in epistemology was the "Gettier cases" (Gettier, 1963), "in which a person has good (though, as it happens, false, or only accidentally true, or in some other way warrant-deprived) evidence for a belief which is true."

As appears to emerge from Nisbett and Masuda (chap. 2, this volume) and Norenzayan (chap. 3, this volume), the East Asians have a tendency to make categorical judgments on the basis of similarity. Instead, Westerners are more inclined to focus on causes when they have to classify things. The intuition probe that was used to explore cultural differences on Gettier cases was the following:

Bob has a friend, Jill, who has driven a Buick for many years. Bob therefore thinks that Jill drives an American car. He is not aware, however, that her Buick has recently been stolen, and he is also not aware that Jill has replaced it with a Pontiac, which is a different kind of American car. Does Bob really know that Jill drives an American car, or does he only believe it?

REALLY KNOWS   ONLY BELIEVES

The striking finding in this case is that a large majority of Ws give the standard answer in the philosophical literature, viz. 'Only Believes'. But amongst EAs this pattern is actually *reversed*! A majority of EAs say that Bob really knows.

The results from this and the other intuition probes seem to prove that East Asians and Westerners are sensitive to different features of the situation—different *epistemic vectors* as Weinberg, Nichols, and Stich call them (chap. 8, this volume). East Asians are much sensitive to communitarian, contextual factors, whereas Westerners respond to more individualistic, dispositional ones. The conclusion is that, because IDR relies on epistemic intuitions that are not universal, but local to one's own cultural and socioeconomic group, it is not able to lead to genuine normative conclusion.

CONCLUSION: OUTSIDE THE RELATIVIST CAGES

The conclusion put forward by Weinberg, Nichols, and Stich (chap. 8, this volume) appears to reinforce the thesis of epistemological relativism. If it is not possible to find an inner and universal foundation for normative principles and if we are prisoners within our local contexts, how can we not give in to relativism? However, are we really certain that no universal principle exists on which we can base the justification for our knowledge of the world?

Earlier we saw that although cultural differences do exist in cognitive styles, these are not irreversible and tend to narrow when they involve pragmatic and existential problems rather than abstract and artificial ones. The greater the adaptive meaning of a problem is, the greater the uniformity of the reply adopted. It seems likely that our conceptual cages, used in cultural learning and socialization processes, can be questioned in relation to different social and adaptive contexts.

Irrespective of the culture to which we belong, at birth we all receive the same innate endowment of principles of reasoning. The cultural differences that subsequently emerge in individuals are mainly in response to metaphysical and ontological theories and schemes for representing and interpreting the world (Gopnik & Meltzoff, 1997; Nisbett & Masuda, chap. 2, this volume). Both the metaphysical theories that dominate our cognitive styles and the physical theories on the empirical nature of the world can be altered in the light of new cultural contexts and new empirical evidence. The relative plasticity of cognitive abilities in different cultures reflects the dynamics of theory change in the little scientist hypothesis. Human cognitive abilities depend on a person's theories about the world. But these theories are not fixed, irreversibly, by his or her local sociocultural condition. They can be changed in relation to pragmatic feedback, empirical evidence, and new information derived from the environment. The relative theory change is driven by methodological norms that are effective during childhood (and we meet it again, in a similar fashion, inside the scientific community). The methodological norms of theory change appear, to a large extent, universal.

It is true that humans often fall into errors of deduction, statistical assessment, causal attribution, inductive support, and so on. These errors, both in scientific enterprise and everyday life, seem not to have a great effect on the growth of knowledge and on economic and social development. The reason for the scarce effect of biases, errors, and irrational reasoning might rely solely on the meta-inferential norms of theory change. Children, scientists, and adults make mistakes and generate false theories or empirical generalizations about the world; they produce beliefs that do not correspond to reality. However, at the same time, they are able to accept information, empirical evidence, or pragmatic feedback from the world about the reliability, legitimacy, and pragmatic utility of their hypotheses. If the theory does not work, sooner or later it will be changed and another theory will be generated. Therefore, the synchronic consequences of errors stemming from irrational reasoning are diachronically neutralized by the application of the norms of theory change.

Weinberg, Nichols, and Stich (chap. 8, this volume) are correct when they write that any epistemological internalist justification of knowledge has to cope with the cultural diversity of thinking. Boudon (1995) tackled the same problem in a different manner. If we wish to avoid the dangers of both cultural relativism and ethnocentrism, we should be able to find transcultural and transcontextual reasons for beliefs and actions. If every reason that justifies a belief or an action is relative to a given local sociocultural context and cannot be judged by others living in different contexts, then rationality will shatter into a dispersed multitude of different and incommensurable reasons. If the reasons are relative to local sociocultural contexts, but they can be judged by the inhabitants of other ethnic niches, then we can speak of transcultural reasons. An example taken from Boudon (1995) may help to explain this point. The Papago

Indios of Arizona explain any social and natural events by the will of a god living on the top of Boboquivari mountain. The place is visible to anyone in the tribe. Why does nobody see the god of the mountain? The reason is because the ants inform him when humans are coming and he hides himself. Can we accept their reasons? Obviously, according to our beliefs, knowledge, and theories of the world, their reasons seem to us completely unacceptable. But if we try to represent the theories and beliefs of the Indios, which function as the premises of their reasons, perhaps we can justify their reasons according to their theories of the world. It might be thought reasonable that they propose the ant hypothesis to justify the impossibility of seeing the god of the mountain. If this is the interpretation of the Indios' reasons, then what are the differences between this position and the relativistic one? The same exercise used in relation to the Indios' reasons can be replicated for a multitude of other ethnic niches.

The crucial point that distinguishes a normative position from a relativistic one relies, in my opinion, on using the methodology of theory change (Viale, 2001). As a thought experiment, think of a variation of the previous story. The same person who told us the story of the god of the mountain informs us that the Indios believing in the ant story are professional scientists and engineers working at the nearby nuclear power station. At this point, it is likely that our chances of justifying the believers' reasoning would greatly decrease. The justification would become almost null if, talking with them, we discovered that they share with us all our metaphysical and epistemological principles about the world. In this case, their reasons for believing the ant theory would become very unsound. A likely hypothesis is that the reason for our judgment of their irrationality relies on the following principle (i.e., an application of the methodology of theory change characteristic of the little scientist hypothesis): A given theory is maintained if a better alternative theory is not available. A theory is better when it has more empirical content and is able to solve the problems of the old one plus some others. When one has a better theory, one should use it instead of the previous one.

Faced with a new and better theory, its negative utilization can present different situations (Viale, 2001). (a) The subject may not accept the new theory that increases his ability to explain the empirical phenomena. The maintenance of the old theory may rely on traditional habits, emotional factors, theoretical support, and so on. (b) He can accept the new theory and put it in his knowledge base. But at the same time, he can continue to use the old one to generate his beliefs about the world. If the two theories are inconsistent, his cognitive behavior relies on an inconsistent set of beliefs. If the two theories are consistent, but the old one is implied by the new one, his cognitive behavior relies on a theory that has less empirical content or problem-solving ability. (c) He acquires the new theory and puts it into his knowledge base, but his previous beliefs continue to be triggered in an automatic and reflex way. They are not based on conscious reasons. They are a kind of traces of the old theory, and they do not stem from any intentional act of reasoning.

When the traditional Indios had only beliefs and knowledge stemming from their tradition, their belief in the ant theory might be judged to be reasonable because no better alternative theories were available. But when "nuclear" Indios have at their disposal alternative hypotheses to explain the social and natural events and these hypotheses are able to explain other aspects of the world, we can suppose that their belief in the ant theory might be judged as rationally unjustified.

As in the case of the Arizona Indios, also in relation to the diversity principle analyzed by Atran, Medin, and Ross (chap. 4, this volume), we can say that the knowledge and beliefs of the taxonomists would not justify their preference for an argument with more homogeneous premises that does not satisfy the diversity principle. Using the same argument, we might say that, hypothetically, the Itza', with an education on abstract taxonomy about mammals, *ceteris paribus*, would not be justified in still relying on ecology-based reasoning and not satisfying the diversity principle.

On the basis of the previous arguments, we can hold the following procedural normative principle:

> *There is reason to justify a belief of a subject that is the effect of given theories on the world when the subject has no knowledge of alternative theories that are better for their empirical content and problem-solving ability.*

It might be objected that there is no reason to try to establish normative criteria for the rational justification of beliefs. The world will go on without the need for any general normative constraint. In reality, there are many fields of human life where implicit normative criteria are applied. Education and science are important examples. Often the criteria are ad hoc and lack transparency. Other times they rely on a priori canons of rationality that find their justification in some kind of narrow social consensus by some elite set of experts. Consequently, it may be worthwhile trying to develop some general norms of epistemological justification that stem from our best real procedures of knowledge acquisition (i.e., science and developmental age). The positive features of the proposed epistemological procedural principle may be the fulfillment of the following two conditions (Viale, 2001):

It seems to meet our intuition about the reasons for accepting a belief given the actual knowledge of the subject.

It seems to be coherent with the "internalist epistemology" program: extrapolating the norms of justification from the internal cognitive procedures of theory generation and application.

In conclusion, the cultural variability of inferential styles and the errors and biases of human reasoning and decision making appear to outline an epistemological picture characterized by relativism and irrationality. This picture is countered by a number of normative factors following the internalist theory and linked to the little scientist hypothesis: the universal endowment of inferential principles that are both innate and adaptive in the sense of evolutionary psychology; the presence from birth of a method of theory and concept change based on empirical falsification, pragmatic consequences, and problem solving, which also appears to be explained, in evolutionary terms, by its capacity to promote successful environmental adaptation.

These innate principles of reasoning and the method of theory change are universal and characterize man's shared capacity, irrespective of any cultural context, to create hypotheses involving the physical, biological, psychological, and social worlds; to learn from mistakes; and to correct his theories to make them empirically and pragmatically successful.

REFERENCES

Baillargeon, R., & Hanko-Summers, S. (1990). Is the object adequately supported by the bottom object? Young infants' understanding of support relations. *Cognitive Development, 5,* 29–54.

Baldwin, D. A. (1991). Infants' contribution to the achievement of joint reference. *Child Development, 62*(5), 1875–1890.

Baron-Cohen, S. (1996). *Mindblindness: An essay on autism and theory of mind.* Cambridge, MA: MIT Press.

Barrett, J. L., & Keil, F. C. (1996). Conceptualizing a non-natural entity: Anthropomorphism in God concepts. *Cognitive Psychology, 31*(3), 1219–1247.

Berry, D. S., & Springer, K. (1993). Structure, motion, and preschoolers' perceptions of social causality. *Ecological Psychology, 5*(4), 273–283.

Boudon, R. (1995). *Le Juste et le vrai. Etudes sur l'objectivité des valeurs et de la connaissance* [The right and the true. Studies on the objectivity of values and knowledge]. Paris: Fayard.

Boudon, R., & Viale, R. (2000). Reasons, cognition and society. *Mind & Society, 1,* 80–95.

Boyer, P. (1990). *Tradition as truth and communication: A cognitive description of traditional discourse.* New York: Cambridge University Press.

Boyer, P. (1993). *The naturalness of religious ideas.* Berkeley: University of California Press.

Boyer, P. (1995). Causal understandings in cultural representations: Cognitive constraints on inferences from cultural input. In D. Sperber, D. Premack, & A. Premack (Eds.), *Causal cognition: A multidisciplinary debate* (pp. 615–649). New York: Oxford University Press.

Carey, S. (1985). *Conceptual change in childhood*. Cambridge, MA: MIT Press.

Choi, I., Nisbett, R. E., & Smith, E. E. (1997). Culture, categorization and inductive reasoning. *Cognition, 65*, 15–32.

Churchland, P. M. (1981). Eliminative materialism and the propositional attitudes. *Journal of Philosophy, 78*, 67–90.

Cosmides, L., & Tooby, J. (1996). Are humans good intuitive statisticians after all? Rethinking some conclusions from the literature on judgment under uncertainty. *Cognition, 58*, 1–73.

Fodor, J. (1987). *Psychosemantics*. Cambridge, MA: MIT Press.

Franklin, A., & Howson, C. (1984). Why do scientists prefer to vary their experiments? *Studies in the History and Philosophy of Science, 15*, 51–62.

Gelman, R. (1990). First principles organize attention to and learning about relevant data: Number and the animate/inanimate distinction as examples. *Cognitive Sciences, 14*, 79–106.

Gettier, E. (1963). Is justified true belief knowledge? *Analysis, 23*, 121–123.

Gigerenzer, G. (1991). How to make cognitive illusions disappear: Beyond "heuristics and biases." In W. Stroebe & M. Hewstone (Eds.), *European review of social psychology* (Vol. 2, pp. 83–115). Chichester, England: Wiley.

Gigerenzer, G. (1994). Why the distinction between single-event probabilities and frequencies is important for psychology (and vice versa)? In G. Wright & P. Ayton (Eds.), *Subjective probability* (pp. 129–162). Chichester, England: Wiley.

Goldman, A. (1986). *Epistemology and cognition*. Cambridge, MA: Harvard University Press.

Goldman, A. (1999). *Knowledge in a social world*. Oxford: Clarendon.

Goodman, N. (1965). *Fact, fiction and forecast*. Indianapolis: Bobbs-Merrill.

Gopnik, A., & Meltzoff, N. (1997). *Words, thoughts, and theories*. Cambridge, MA: MIT Press.

Gordon, R. M. (1986). Folk psychology as simulation. *Mind & Language, 1*, 158–171.

Gutheil, G., & Gelman, S. (1997). Children's use of sample size and diversity information within basic level categories. *Journal of Experimental Child Psychology, 64*, 159–174.

Haidt, J., Koller, S., & Dias, M. (1993). Affect, culture and morality. *Journal of Personality & Social Psychology, 65*(4), 613–628.

Heal, J. (1986). Replication and functionalism. In J. Butterfield (Ed.), *Language, mind, and logic* (pp. 135–150). Cambridge: Cambridge University Press.

Hempel, C. (1966). *Philosophy of natural sciences*. Englewood Cliffs, NJ: Prentice-Hall.

Hirschfeld, L. (1996). *Race in the making: Cognition, culture, and the child's construction of human kinds*. Cambridge, MA: MIT Press.

Horwich, P. (1982). *Probability and evidence*. Cambridge: Cambridge University Press.

Howson, C., & Urbach, O. (1993). *Scientific reasoning: The Bayesian approach*. Chicago: Open Court.

Kahneman, D., Slovic, P., & Tversky, A. (Eds.). (1982). *Judgment under uncertainty: Heuristics and biases*. Cambridge: Cambridge University Press.

Keil, F. C. (1995). The growth of causal understandings of natural kinds. In D. Sperber, D. Premack, & A. Premack (Eds.), *Causal cognition: A multidisciplinary debate* (pp. 234–267). New York: Oxford University Press.

Laudan, L. (1984). *Science and values*. Berkeley: University of California Press.

Leslie, A. M. (1988). The necessity of illusion: Perception and thought in infancy. In L. Weizkrantz (Ed.), *Thought without language* (pp. 185–210). Oxford: Clarendon.

Lo, Y., Sides, A., Rozelle, J., & Osherson, D. (2002). Evidential diversity and premise proba-bility in young children inductive judgment. *Cognitive Science, 26,* 181–206.

López, A., Atran, S., Coley, J. D., Medin, D. L., & Smith, E. E. (1997). The tree of life: Universal and cultural features of folkbiological taxonomies and inductions. *Cognitive Psychology, 32,* 251–295.

López, A., Gelman, S. A., Gutheil, G., & Smith, E. E. (1992). The development of category-based induction. *Child Development, 63,* 1070–1090.

Massey, C., & Gelman, R. (1988). Preschoolers' ability to decide whether pictured unfamiliar objects can move themselves. *Developmental Psychology, 24,* 307–317.

Miller, J. G. (1984). Culture and the development of everyday social explanation. *Journal of Personality and Social Psychology, 46,* 961–978.

Moon, Y., & Nass, C. (1996). How "real" are computer personalities? Psychological re-sponses to personality types in human–computer interaction. *Communication Research, 23*(6), 1651–1674.

Nisbett, R. E. (2003). *The geography of thought: How Asians and Westerners think differently . . . and why.* New York: The Free Press.

Nisbett, R. E., Peng, K., Choi, I., & Norenzayan, A. (2001). Culture and systems of thought: Holistic vs. analytic cognition. *Psychological Review, 108,* 291–310.

Nisbett, R. E., & Ross, L. (1980). *Human inference: Strategies and shortcomings of social judge-ment.* Englewood Cliffs, NJ: Prentice-Hall.

Osherson, D., Smith, E., Wilkie, O., López, A., & Shafir, E. (1990). Category-based induction. *Psychological Review, 97*(2), 185–200.

Sacks, O. W. (1995). *An anthropologist on Mars: Seven paradoxical tales* (1st ed.). New York: Knopf.

Spelke, E. S. (1990). Principles of object perception. *Cognitive Science, 14,* 29–56.

Spelke, E. S., Phillips, A., & Woodward, A. L. (1995). Infants' knowledge of object motion and human action. In D. Sperber, D. Premack, & A. Premack (Eds.), *Causal cognition: A multidisciplinary debate* (pp. 44–78). New York: Oxford University Press.

Sperber, D. (2000). Metarepresentations in an evolutionary perspective. In D. Sperber (Ed.), *Metarepresentations: A multidisciplinary perspective* (pp. 117–137). New York: Oxford Uni-versity Press.

Sperber, D., Premack, D., & Premack, A. (Eds.). (1995). *Causal cognition: A multidisciplinary de-bate.* New York: Oxford University Press.

Springer, K., Meier, J. A., & Berry, D. S. (1996). Nonverbal bases of social perception: Devel-opmental change in sensitivity to patterns of motion that reveal interpersonal events. *Journal of Nonverbal Behavior, 20*(4), 1199–1211.

Tomasello, M. (1999). *The cultural origins of human cognition.* Cambridge, MA: Harvard Uni-versity Press.

Viale, R. (1999). Causal cognition and causal realism. *International Studies in the Philosophy of Science, 2,* 151–169.

Viale, R. (2001). Reasons and reasoning: What comes first? In R. Boudon, P. Demeulenaere, & R. Viale (Eds.), *L'Explication des normes sociales* [The explanation of social norms] (pp. 215–236). Paris: Presses Universitaires de France.

Viale, R., & Osherson, D. (2000). The diversity principle and the little scientist hypothesis. *Foundations of Science, 5*(2), 239–253.

Woodward, A. L. (1998). Infants selectively encode the goal object of an actor's reach. *Cogni-tion, 69*(1), 1–34.

Cognitive Development, Culture, and Inductive Judgment

Riccardo Viale
Rosselli Foundation

Daniel Osherson
Princeton University

TWO VIEWS OF INTELLECTUAL DEVELOPMENT

As agents of abductive inference, children have an enviable reputation. It rests on the remarkable transition from benighted neonate to savvy and enterprising 5-year-old. During this period, children acquire a grammatical system, discover the boundaries of tolerated behavior, and begin to discern the biological and physical kinds encountered in their environment. It is no wonder that developmental psychologists often compare children's achievements to that of professional scientists embarked on their own voyage of discovery.[1] If the analogy can be sustained, it suggests that the study of cognitive development might offer clues to the successful implementation of computerized scientific activity by simulating the child's successful strategy.

Conceiving the child as scientist, however, requires more than recording her impressive achievements. Intellectual development must also be shown to derive from the kind of theory construction attributed to professional scientists. Assimilation of development to rational inquiry is precisely the view of an influential school of developmental psychology, recently defended in Gopnik and Meltzoff (1997). Abstracting away from

---

[1]See, for example, Gopnik and Meltzoff (1997), Koslowski (1996), Kuhn (1996), Keil (1989), Markman (1989), and Carey (1985). For grammar acquisition by children, see Osherson and Weinstein (1995), Gleitman and Liberman (1995), and references cited there.

differences in background knowledge and startup funds, children (like scientists) are claimed to develop a succession of theories that evolve adaptively under the impact of data. At each step, the child is supposed to have an organized corpus of belief that amounts to a scientific doctrine. The transition between theories is supposed to depend on their respective, predictive success, as well as on simplicity criteria familiar from the history of adult science. This attractive picture of cognitive growth is meant to apply to knowledge of the physical and social worlds, as well as to word meaning, mental events in other minds, and so forth.

The opposing view is Chomsky's triggering model. According to this conception, it suffices for children to come into contact with a few key data for an articulated and stable theory to leap to mind. The claim is that the child's theory enjoys not the slightest justification of a sort that makes sense to professional scientists. The process is typically described in terms of parameter setting, as is well known.[2] Let us try to isolate the different commitments of the two perspectives on development—namely, the "little scientist" view versus the triggering model of the Chomskyans. On the former account, we expect each advance in cognitive development to issue in the kinds of theories announced by scientists, for example, involving hypothetical variables related to each other in some deductive way. Such is the synchronic commitment of the little scientist view. But notice that the triggering model is equally compatible with the child having scientifically respectable theories throughout development. It need only be imagined that each parameter flip brings to the fore a prestored body of mature, scientific belief.

The two views of development are more easily distinguished diachronically, in terms of the kinds of experience that nudge the child from one theory to the next. The triggering model conceives this process in the same way that visual stimuli trigger imprinting in baby ducks. In contrast, the little scientist view assimilates the child's use of experience to theory selection on the part of a rational agent.

Clearly, the little scientist perspective is more joyous than that of the triggering model. Whereas parameter setting imposes tight limits on the kinds of theories that ordinary folk can construct about their world, little scientists can help themselves to everything accessible to modern science. Preferences notwithstanding, we must try to evaluate which of the rival perspectives is closer to the truth—or closer with respect to some particular domain of knowledge.

---

[2]See Chomsky (1986, 1988). Chomsky also entertained the view that professional science, where successful, is likewise based on blind triggering, rather than rational procedures of theory evaluation and change, as discussed in Chomsky (1975). The latter thesis merits serious consideration, but provides little assistance in designing artificial systems of induction. So we stick with the classical conception of professional science, involving rational canons of hypothesis selection.

THE CHILD AS SCIENTIST

The thesis to be evaluated in this chapter is stated in its most persuasive form by Gopnik and Meltzoff (1997). They wrote: "We want to argue that the cognitive processes that underlie science are similar to, or indeed even identical with, the cognitive processes that underlie much of cognitive development" (p. 32). These authors attempted to clarify this claim in several ways. For our part, it seems that the most straightforward reading is the following:

(1) *The little scientist thesis*: The theories that children construct of their physical and social environments result from the application of scientific method to the data that are available to them.

In this sense, children are portrayed as little scientists.[3] As a first step toward clarifying (1), we note that *scientific method* is intended here in the normative sense, not the descriptive one. In other words, it is claimed that children draw inferences the way scientists should, not the benighted way that scientists sometimes do. Of course, everyone makes mistakes, so (1) is not falsified by the occasional methodological error. Rather, what is being claimed is that, by and large, children's inductive inferences conform to proper methodology.

There are systematic inductive tendencies, however, that seem to contradict the thesis at issue. These tendencies concern the use of diverse evidence in inductive inference. We now describe the relevant psychological data and then see what can be done to make them appear less offensive to the picture of children as little scientists.

EVIDENTIAL DIVERSITY

Why did Newton's theory end up commanding so much assent? One reason is that in the presence of various background assumptions, the theory accurately predicts heterogeneous phenomena, such as the trajectories of balls thrown into the air, the behavior of gyroscopes, and the orbits of celestial bodies. At the end of the 17th century, these phenomena appeared very diverse, which forced respect for the theory despite reservations about the reliance on occult, nonmechanical entities like gravity. The potency of diverse evidence for conforming theories was subsequently rec-

---

[3]Gopnik and Meltzoff (1997) went on to say: "It is not that children are little scientists but that scientists are big children." Identity being symmetric, we allow ourselves the little scientist terminology.

ognized by philosophers of science, who often see it as a way to subject hypotheses to severe test. Now for a more modest example. Consider the hypothesis (2).

(2) Vitamin K deficiency causes neuron death in the auditory nerves of all mammals.

Even in the absence of biochemical knowledge about Vitamin K, most people find that (2) is better supported by the evidence reported in (3)a, than by that in (3)b.

(3) (a) Vitamin K deficiency causes neuron death in the auditory nerves of both tigers and elephants.
    (b) Vitamin K deficiency causes neuron death in the auditory nerves of both tigers and lions.

Indeed, preference for the tiger/elephant data was expressed by 74% of a group of 80 American college students asked to choose "which of (3)a, (3)b provides a better reason to believe the hypothesis (2)" (see Osherson, Smith, Wilkie, Lopez, & Shafir, 1990). Likewise, 80% of a sample of 58 Korean college students share the diversity intuition, as do 70% of a group of 80 Italian college students.[4] Evidential diversity makes sense of such intuitions because tigers and elephants resemble each other less than tigers and lions.

Similar results have been obtained with Korean subjects judging arguments based on social categories (see Choi, Nisbett, & Smith, 1997) and likewise in Italy (Baroni & Diamantini, 2001). For example, the latter authors asked 97 Italian college students in Milan to make a forced choice between the following two arguments, selecting the one whose premises gives better reason to believe its conclusion.

Unemployment is increasing among lawyers and notary publics.

Unemployment is increasing among all self-employed professionals.

Unemployment is increasing among lawyers and accountants.

Unemployment is increasing among all self-employed professionals.

---

[4]For the Korean data, see Choi et al. (1997). To keep the exposition simple, here and elsewhere we changed the animals and predicates used in the Korean study. For the Italian data, see Baroni and Diamantini (2001).

Among Italians, lawyers and notary publics are more similar to each other than are lawyers and accountants. For this reason, subjects were expected to perceive greater strength in the second argument compared with the first. This was the case for 84% of them. Similarly, 85% of the subjects opted for the second argument in the following pair because Italians judge bakeries and pastry shops to be more similar to each other than are bakeries and fruit vendors. Both arguments bear on a new French holiday designed to honor small businesses.

The holiday honors bakeries and pastry shops.

The holiday honors all small businesses.

The holiday honors bakers and fruit vendors.

The holiday honors all small businesses.

Of 80 secretaries working in Milan, 80% likewise judged the second argument (with more diverse premises) to give better reason to believe the conclusion than the first. So far, so good for the little scientist view because it looks as if a respectable principle of scientific methodology is present in a diverse sample of adult nonspecialists.

Trouble arises, however, in a developmental study carried out at the University of Michigan (Lopez, Gelman, Gutheil, & Smith, 1992). Two attempts were made to document an appreciation for evidence diversity in kindergartners, and both failed. The 44 five-year-olds in this study showed a mild preference for homogeneous evidence of the kind (3)b, instead of the heterogeneous (3)a, as support for (2). Similar findings are reported in Gutheil and Gelman (1997). Now, by everyone's account, the 5-year-old has already forged for himself a variety of theories about the social, physical, and linguistic worlds. It is difficult to attribute this feat to the application of scientific method if the child fails to respect elementary canons of rational inquiry such as the diversity principle, assuming it to be part of rational methodology.

It is worth underlining, in fact, the elementary character of the diversity principle. The judgment at issue has the simple form: Diverse evidence gives better reason to believe a given conclusion than does homogeneous evidence. In particular, the principle need not evoke probability for its formulation. Given the historical tardiness of the appearance of a mature conception of chance among professional scientists, we cannot expect better from children or untutored adults. That people can get mixed up about base rates and likelihoods should not count against the little scientist view.[5]

The case against the little scientist is aggravated by cross-cultural data. If children apply the scientific method, we would not expect this propensity to disappear with age (after its successful application in so many domains of mental life). We therefore expect basic, scientific intuition to be widespread across cultures. This is why we were pleased to learn that not just Americans, but also Italians and Koreans, respect the diversity principle. However, Vietnamese appear to have a different idea. Sixty-two percent of a sample of 156 college students that we queried in Ho Chi Minh City preferred the homogeneous data in (3)b as support for the hypothesis stated in (2).[6]

Similar findings are reported by Lopez, Atran, Coley, Medin, and Smith (1997) with the Itza-Mayan Indians of Central America. Referring to a disease present on an island inhabited by various animals, these investigators posed a question involving squirrels, rats, mice, and tapirs; the latter animal is a large mammal common to Central America, related to elephants and horses. Here is the question:

> Squirrels have a disease and tapirs have the same disease that squirrels do. Rats have another disease and cheek mice have the same disease that rats do. Do you think all the other animals have the same disease that squirrels have with tapirs, or the other disease that rats have with cheek mice?

Atran et al. obtained independent confirmation that squirrels and tapirs are perceived to differ from one another more than do rats and cheek mice. Michigan college students consistently judged the disease hypothesis associated with the diverse pair squirrel–tapir to be more plausible than the disease hypothesis associated with rat–mouse. In contrast, the Itza did the reverse, choosing the rat–mouse pair as giving more credibility to the universality of their disease compared to the squirrel–tapir pair.

Now consider the confirmation of a hypothesis that is less general than (2)—for example, that at line (4).

(4) Vitamin K deficiency causes neuron death in the auditory nerves of wolves.

---

[5]For the evolution of probability concepts, see Hacking (1975) and Gigerenzer, Swijtink, Porter, Daston, Beatty, and Kriger (1989). For the literature on naive probability judgment, see Baron (2000) and references given there.

[6]For the Vietnamese data, see Baroni and Diamantini (2001).

This hypothesis makes an attribution not to all mammals, but just to wolves. The difference in generality notwithstanding, we might still expect people to be more impressed with the heterogeneous evidence (3)a than with the homogeneous (3)b. Unfortunately, the diversity intuition is even weaker in this case than before. A majority of the American sample—but only 65%—believes that (4) is better supported by tiger–elephant than by tiger–lion. Sixty-three percent of the Korean sample agree with the Americans, but this is true for only 40% and 31% of the Italian and Vietnamese samples, respectively. Likewise, less than half of the kindergarten judgments in Lopez et al. (1992) concur with the diversity principle in the case of the more specific Thesis 4. Even the 9-year-olds showed preference for the homogeneous evidence.

REACTION TO THE EXPERIMENTAL DATA

Is the little scientist theory sunk by these data? Hardly. The sample sizes are small, and the range of stimuli used is narrow. In work with the Itza-Mayan, moreover, Atran et al. raised the possibility that their subjects' reasoning was influenced by specific information that gave the predicates an unintended meaning. So, considerably more research is necessary before reaching a conclusion about the prevalence of the diversity principle in children or adults. Prior to carrying out more experiments, however, it would be wise to have a closer look at the diversity principle. Is it a genuine feature of rational inquiry, hence part of the meaning of the little scientist hypothesis? Or have we missed the point about heterogeneous evidence?

The diversity variable, in fact, seems not to be related in simple fashion to argument strength even at the prescriptive level. Consider the following arguments:

>   Housecats often carry the parasite Floxum.
>   Fieldmice often carry the parasite Floxum.
>
> (5) _____
>   All mammals often carry the parasite Floxum.

>   Housecats often carry the parasite Floxum.
>   Tigers often carry the parasite Floxum.
>
> (6) _____
>   All mammals often carry the parasite Floxum.

It seems undeniable that housecats resemble tigers more than they resemble fieldmice. Yet it appears perfectly defensible to judge argument (6) to be stronger than (5), on the grounds that housecats might catch Floxum from fieldmice (their prey), whereas they have little contact with tigers.[7] We are not claiming that everyone (or even a majority of people) will think of the predator–prey reason for judging (6) to be stronger than (5). Rather, we claim that it is perfectly reasonable to make such a judgment (because of the predator–prey relation or on some other basis). In this case, reasonable judgments about strength run counter to the advice offered by the diversity principle. Hence, the latter is discredited as a basis for evaluating inductive intuition. Of course the example does not show that diversity always gives the wrong advice, only that it sometimes does. But this is enough to undermine its claim to normative status.

Perhaps it will be objected that the similarity of categories must be evaluated in light of the predicate in play. When it comes to parasites, housecats resemble fieldmice more than tigers, so the diversity principle gives the right advice after all. One difficulty with this suggestion is that it makes application of the diversity principle dependent on prior inductive inference. Before making an assessment of diversity, we must engage in substantive scientific reasoning—namely, about how similarity is to be assessed in the context of a given predicate. For example, it must be determined that animals in a predatory relation are similar when the predicate concerns parasites but not (say) color. Such determination is a scientific affair that already requires sound judgment about argument strength.[8] More generally, diversity seems to be of no greater help in evaluating hypotheses than our hypotheses are in perceiving diversity. Thus, Earman (1992) reminded us that "before the scientific revolution the motions of the celestial bodies seemed to belong to a different variety than the motions of terrestrial projectiles, whereas after Newton they seem like peas in a pod" (p. 79).[9]

In any event, it is easy to produce violations of the diversity principle even when similarity is assessed relative to a predicate. Consider *can scratch through Bortex fabric in less than 10 seconds*. The unfamiliarity of Bortex makes it impossible to tell which animals can scratch through it, al-

---

[7]Arguments (5) and (6) are inspired by an example in Lopez, Atran, Coley, Medin, and Smith (1997).

[8]This standard objection to evoking similarity in theories of reasoning is discussed in Osherson, Smith, and Shafir (1986); Shafir, Smith, and Osherson (1990); and Keil, Smith, Simons, and Levin (1998), among other places. A more favorable view of similarity in the theory of reasoning is offered by Goldstone and Barsalou (1998). The sensitivity of similarity-based reasoning to the predicate in play is documented in Heit and Rubinstein (1994). In contrast to similarity-based inference, results in Ahn, Kalish, Medin, and Gelman (1995) underline the importance of explanatory theories to adult reasoning.

[9]Another example appears in Wayne (1995), who noted that before Maxwell electromagnetic and optical phenomena were considered diverse, whereas today they are judged to be similar.

though it allows sensible inferences about the conditional probability of one animal scratching through assuming that another does. Relative to the Bortex predicate, squirrels and mice are more similar to each other than are squirrels and bears. Nonetheless, it is clear that the homogeneous premises of argument (8) convey greater strength than the diverse premises of argument (7), in contradiction to the diversity principle.

> Squirrels can scratch through Bortex fabric in less than 10 seconds.
> Bears can scratch through Bortex fabric in less than 10 seconds.
>
> (7) _____
>
> All forest mammals can scratch through Bortex fabric in less than 10 seconds.

> Squirrels can scratch through Bortex fabric in less than 10 seconds.
> Mice can scratch through Bortex fabric in less than 10 seconds.
>
> (8) _____
>
> All forest mammals can scratch through Bortex fabric in less than 10 seconds.

The only way to avoid these kinds of examples is to restrict the diversity principle to statements whose predicates are entirely empty, as in "Lions have property P." In this case, however, the discussion will have strayed so far from genuine scientific reasoning as to become irrelevant to questions about inductive methodology. Research on category-based reasoning has therefore avoided predicates like *has P* (see e.g., Osherson et al., 1990; Rips, 1975). The better solution is to formulate principles of inductive strength that are not restricted to meaningless predicates. The principle proposed below meets this condition.

We conclude that the diversity principle should not be used as a standard against which to assess the methodological soundness of children's scientific reasoning. Diverse premises often confer inductive strength, but exceptions to this rule suggest the presence of an underlying variable that mediates the impact of evidential diversity. We now attempt to identify this variable.

A PROBABILITY PRINCIPLE

There is little doubt that the premises appearing in (3)a confirm that Vitamin K deficiency causes neuron death in the auditory nerves of all mammals more than do the premises in (3)b. If diversity is not the operating variable in this difference, what is? One response comes from Bayesian probability theory interpreted as a normative account of scientific inference. The latter theory provides a systematic explanation of much scientific practice (Earman, 1992; Howson & Urbach, 1993) and has figured prominently in psychologists' assessment of adult reasoning (Kahneman & Tversky, 1996). There are certainly competing philosophies of science (e.g., Martin & Osherson, 1998; Mayo, 1996), and not all psychologists are comfortable with the Bayesian picture (Gigerenzer, 1991, 1996). But Bayesianism has the virtue of being explicit, and it offers a simple explanation for the examples discussed earlier.

Following an analysis advanced by Horwich (1982), we propose that in the kinds of arguments at issue here, it is the probability of the premises prior to accepting the conclusion that governs strength. To get the analysis off the ground, it is necessary to give a probabilistic interpretation of argument strength. Recall that an argument is strong to the extent that its premises give reason to believe its conclusion. Thus, in a strong argument, the probability of the conclusion given the premises should be greater than the probability of the conclusion alone. An argument with Premises A,B and Conclusion C should therefore be strong to the extent that $P(C/A \wedge B) > P(C)$.[10] There are many ways to quantify the extent to which $P(C/A \wedge B)$ exceeds $P(C)$. Following other authors, like Myrvold (1996), we rely on the ratio of the conditional to the unconditional probability. Officially:

Definition: Let argument A,B / C be given. Its strength is defined to be

$$\frac{P(C/A \wedge B)}{P(C)}$$

Premises confirming a conclusion thus yield strength greater than 1, and premises infirming a conclusion yield strength less than 1.

The arguments figuring in the present discussion are all general, and therefore they have the particularity that the conclusion logically implies each premise (because the same predicate occurs in all statements, and the conclusion category includes the premise categories). Under these conditions, argument strength stands in a simple relation to premise probability.

---

[10]Recall that $P(C/A \wedge B)$ denotes the conditional probability of C given A and B. The symbol "$\wedge$" denotes conjunction. The unconditional probability of the conclusion C (namely, without assuming A and B) is denoted by $P(C)$. Many authors have measured argument strength by comparing the prior probability of the conclusion with its probability given the premises (e.g., Good, 1960; Hintikka, 1968).

PREMISE PROBABILITY PRINCIPLE (PPP): Suppose that Arguments A,B / C and A1,B1 / C are given, where C logically implies A, A1, B, and B1. Then the strength of the first argument is greater than the strength of the second if and only if $P(A \wedge B) < P(A1 \wedge B1)$.

Proof: By definition, the strength of the first argument is greater than the strength of the second if and only if

$$\frac{P(C/A \wedge B)}{P(C)} > \frac{P(C/A1 \wedge B1)}{P(C)}$$

By familiar properties of conditional probability, the latter inequality holds if and only if

$$\frac{P(C \wedge A \wedge B)}{P(C) \times P(A \wedge B)} > \frac{P(C \wedge A1 \wedge B1)}{P(C) \times P(A1 \wedge B1)}$$

Because C implies A, A1, B, and B1, the last inequality holds if and only if

$$\frac{P(C)}{P(C) \times P(A \wedge B)} > \frac{P(C)}{P(C) \times P(A1 \wedge B1)}$$

which holds if and only if

$$\frac{1}{P(A \wedge B)} > \frac{1}{P(A1 \wedge B1)}$$

thus if and only if

$$P(A \wedge B) < P(A1 \wedge B1),$$

which proves the claim.

The upshot is that the less probable the premises, the stronger the argument. Diversity of premises is often (but not systematically) associated with low premise probability. For example, it seems less likely that Hippos and Hamsters have ulnar arteries than that Hippos and Rhinos do. Based on this assumption, PPP accounts for the greater strength of (3)a compared to (3)b. Likewise, given their unrelated habitats, housecats and tigers seem less likely to carry common parasites than do housecats and mice. For anyone sharing the latter judgment, PPP rules (6) to be stronger than (5). The relative probability of the premises in (7) and (8) similarly make it reasonable to judge the latter to be stronger than the former.[11]

From the proof of PPP, it can be seen that the principle applies to arguments with any predicate, blank or not (a predicate is called *blank* to the extent that its application to objects or categories cannot be determined by the reasoner). The normative status of PPP is thereby enhanced because inductive reasoning almost invariably involves meaningful predicates. Observe also that PPP is a consequence of no more than the axioms of probability along with our definition of argument strength (which could be replaced by many alternatives without altering PPP). Its normative appeal thus derives from the theory of probability, which is independently motivated (see Osherson, 1995; Skyrms, 1986, for discussion of the justification of the probability axioms). Finally, note that we have formulated PPP in terms of arguments with two premises. But the same principle holds for any number of premises, including just one.

ASSESSING CONFORMITY TO PPP

It is important to recognize that PPP imposes no specific assessments of argument strength; it merely relates strength to the probability of an argument's premises. Thus, it is no sign of methodological weakness if children do not find (9) to be stronger than (10) as described in Lopez et al. (1992):

> Cats have leukocytes inside.
> Buffalo have leukocytes inside.
>
> (9) _____
> All animals have leukocytes inside.

> Cows have leukocytes inside.
> Buffalo have leukocytes inside.
>
> (10) _____
> All animals have leukocytes inside.

They may simply take the premises of the former to be more likely than the premises of the latter (thus believing it to be more likely that cats and

---

[11]See Fitelson (1999) for measures of argument strength that are alternative to the ratio definition relied on here. (Most definitions leave PPP intact.) In the current discussion, premise diversity is taken to be a primitive concept, not defined in terms of probability and confirmation. In contrast, Myrvold (1996) and Wayne (1995), among others, attempted to reconstruct the concept of diversity in terms of probability and confirmation. Within such an analysis, diversity (as reconstructed) is constrained to be systematically related to confirmation, but this fact does not bear on the diversity principle as interpreted here. See Heit (1998) and Viale and Osherson (2000) for further discussion.

buffalo have leukocytes inside than that cows and buffalo do). However ill informed such a judgment might appear to adults, it violates no law of proper scientific methodology. Indeed, children might reasonably suppose that cows have only milk inside, which leads directly to low probability for the premises of (10), hence to high strength for (10). However, it is incompatible with PPP for children to simultaneously believe either

that the premises of (9) are less likely than those of (10) and that (10) is stronger than (9), or

that the premises of (10) are less likely than those of (9) and that (9) is stronger than (10).

More generally, consider two general Arguments X1,X2 / Z and Y1,Y2 / Z with the same conclusion Z. (Arguments 9 and 10 illustrate such a pair.) For these arguments, a reasoner respects PPP if either (a) she believes that X1 ∧ X2 is less likely than Y1 ∧ Y2 and that the first argument is stronger than the second, or (b) she believes that Y1 ∧ Y2 is less likely than X1 ∧ X2 and that the second argument is stronger than the first. Thus, respect for PPP requires no specific opinion about premise probability or about argument strength; only the relation between the opinions is at issue.

It is noteworthy that PPP appears to elicit greater respect from both college students and children than does diversity per se. Using college students as subjects, Lopez (1995) reported a strong negative correlation between premise probability and an indirect measure of argument strength. Lo, Sides, Rozelle, and Osherson (2002) reported several experiments in which American and Taiwanese preschool and elementary school children showed statistically reliable tendency to consider "surprising" premises as better "clues" to their conclusions. For example, the children in their study tended to find "Horses and mice have copper in their bodies" to be a better clue than "Horses and zebras have copper in their bodies" for the conclusion "All animals have copper in their bodies," if and only if they found the first statement to be more surprising than the second. Because surprise co-varies inversely with probability, such judgments are consistent with PPP. (Questions were posed in the context of a detective game; see Lo et al., 2002, for details.) Diversity-based reasoning (i.e., preference for horses/mice as clue regardless of surprise) was less prevalent.

CONCLUDING REMARKS

Giving content to the thesis of child as scientist requires substantive assumptions about rational inductive methodology. We have seen that the diversity principle does not serve this purpose because its normative status is open to doubt. The PPP has better credentials because it follows from the axioms of probability and a plausible definition of argument strength. Experiments in two cultures reveal tenuous but detectable conformity to PPP on the part of young children (Lo et al., 2002). If these findings are supported and extended by further experimentation, they provide one clear sense in which young children's inductive methodology can be interpreted as properly scientific.

ACKNOWLEDGMENTS

The present chapter is based on Viale and Osherson (2000) and Lo, Sides, Rozelle, and Osherson (2002).

REFERENCES

Ahn, W., Kalish, C. W., Medin, D. L., & Gelman, S. A. (1995). The role of covariation versus mechanism information in causal attribution. *Cognition, 54,* 299–352.

Baron, J. (2000). *Thinking and deciding.* New York: Cambridge University Press.

Baroni, C., & Diamantini, D. (2001). Categorizzazione concettuale e variabili sociali [Conceptual categorization and social variables]. *LASCOMES Series, 6,* 5–65.

Carey, S. (1985). *Conceptual change in childhood.* Cambridge, MA: MIT Press.

Choi, I., Nisbett, R. E., & Smith, E. E. (1997). Culture, categorization and inductive reasoning. *Cognition, 65,* 15–32.

Chomsky, N. (1975). *Reflections on language.* New York: Random House.

Chomsky, N. (1986). *Knowledge of language: Its nature, origin, and use.* New York: Praeger.

Chomsky, N. (1988). *Language and problems of knowledge: The Managua lectures.* Cambridge, MA: MIT Press.

Earman, J. (1992). *Bayes or bust? A critical examination of Bayesian confirmation theory.* Cambridge, MA: MIT Press.

Fitelson, B. (1999). The plurality of Bayesian measures of confirmation and the problem of measure sensitivity. *Philosophy of Science, 66,* S362–S378.

Gigerenzer, G. (1991). How to make cognitive illusions disappear: Beyond "heuristics and biases." In W. Stroebe & M. Hewstone (Eds.), *European review of social psychology* (Vol. 2, pp. 83–115). Chichester, England: Wiley.

Gigerenzer, G. (1996). Reply to Tversky and Kahneman. *Psychological Review, 103*(3), 592–593.

Gigerenzer, G., Swijtink, Z., Porter, T., Daston, L., Beatty, J., & Kriger, L. (1989). *The empire of chance.* Cambridge: Cambridge University Press.

Gleitman, L. R., & Liberman, M. (Eds.). (1995). *An invitation to cognitive science* (2nd ed., Vol. 1). Cambridge, MA: MIT Press.

Goldstone, R. L., & Barsalou, L. W. (1998). Reuniting perception and conception. *Cognition, 65,* 231–262.

Good, I. J. (1960). Weight of evidence, corroboration, explanatory power, information and the utility of experiments. *Journal of the Royal Statistical Society,* B22, 319–331.

Gopnik, A., & Meltzoff, A. (1997). *Words, thoughts, and theories.* Cambridge, MA: MIT Press.

Gutheil, G., & Gelman, S. (1997). Children's use of sample size and diversity information within basic level categories. *Journal of Experimental Child Psychology, 64,* 159–174.

Hacking, I. (1975). *The emergence of probability.* Cambridge: Cambridge University Press.

Heit, E. (1998). A Bayesian analysis of some forms of inductive reasoning. In M. Oaksford & N. Chater (Eds.), *Rational models of cognition* (pp. 248–274). New York: Oxford University Press.

Heit, E., & Rubinstein, J. (1994). Similarity and property effects in inductive reasoning. *Journal of Experimental Psychology: Learning, Memory, and Cognition, 20,* 411–422.

Hintikka, J. (1968). The varieties of information and scientific explanation. In B. Van Rootselaar & J. F. Staal (Eds.), *Logic, methodology and philosophy of science III.* Proceedings of the Third International Congress for Logic, Methodology and Philosophy of Science, Amsterdam 1967 (pp. 311–331). Amsterdam: North-Holland.

Horwich, P. (1982). *Probability and evidence.* Cambridge: Cambridge University Press.

Howson, C., & Urbach, P. (1993). *Scientific reasoning: The Bayesian approach.* La Salle, IL: Open Court.

Kahneman, D., & Tversky, A. (1996). On the reality of cognitive illusions. *Psychological Review, 103*(3), 582–591.

Keil, F. (1989). *Concepts, kinds, and cognitive development.* Cambridge, MA: MIT Press.

Keil, F., Smith, W. C., Simons, D. J., & Levin, D. T. (1998). Two dogmas of conceptual empiricism: Implications for hybrid models of the structure of knowledge. *Cognition, 65,* 103–135.

Koslowski, B. (1996). *Theory and evidence: The development of scientific reasoning.* Cambridge, MA: MIT Press.

Kuhn, D. (1996). Children and adults as intuitive scientists. *Psychological Review, 96*(4), 674–689.

Lo, Y., Sides, A., Rozelle, J., & Osherson, D. (2002). Evidential diversity and premise probability in young children inductive judgment. *Cognitive Science, 26,* 181–206.

Lopez, A. (1995). The diversity principle in the testing of arguments. *Memory & Cognition, 23*(3), 374–382.

Lopez, A., Atran, S., Coley, J., Medin, D., & Smith, E. (1997). The tree of life: Universal and cultural features of folkbiological taxonomies and inductions. *Cognitive Psychology, 32,* 251–295.

Lopez, A., Gelman, S. A., Gutheil, G., & Smith, E. E. (1992). The development of category-based induction. *Child Development, 63,* 1070–1090.

Markman, E. (1989). *Categorization and naming in children: Problems of induction.* Cambridge, MA: MIT Press.

Martin, E., & Osherson, D. (1998). *Elements of scientific inquiry.* Cambridge, MA: MIT Press.

Mayo, D. G. (1996). *Error and the growth of experimental knowledge.* Chicago, IL: University of Chicago Press.

Myrvold, W. C. (1996). Bayesianism and diverse evidence: A reply to Andrew Wayne. *Philosophy of Science, 63,* 661–665.

Osherson, D. (1995). Probability judgment. In D. Osherson & E. E. Smith (Eds.), *An invitation to cognitive science: Thinking* (Vol. 3, pp. 35–76). Cambridge, MA: MIT Press.

Osherson, D., Smith, E. E., & Shafir, E. (1986). Some origins of belief. *Cognition, 24,* 197–224.

Osherson, D., Smith, E. E, Wilkie, O., Lopez, A., & Shafir, E. (1990). Category-based induction. *Psychological Review, 97*(2), 185–200.

Osherson, D., & Weinstein, S. (1995). On the study of first language acquisition. *Journal of Mathematical Psychology, 39*(2), 129–145.

Rips, L. (1975). Inductive judgments about natural categories. *Journal of Verbal Learning and Verbal Behavior, 14,* 665–681.

Shafir, E., Smith, E., & Osherson, D. (1990). Typicality and reasoning fallacies. *Memory and Cognition, 18*(3), 229–239.

Skyrms, B. (1986). *Choice and chance: An introduction to inductive logic* (3rd ed.). Belmont, CA: Wadsworth.

Viale, R., & Osherson, D. (2000). The diversity principle and the little scientist hypothesis. *Foundations of Science, 5*(2), 239–253.

Wayne, A. (1995). Bayesianism and diverse evidence. *Philosophy of Science, 62*, 111–121.

2

Culture and Point of View

Richard E. Nisbett
University of Michigan

Takahiko Masuda
University of Alberta

Psychologists and philosophers have long assumed that basic processes of cognition and perception are universal—that inductive and deductive inference, attention, memory, categorization, and causal analysis are the same for everyone in every culture. Historians and philosophers of science, however, have raised the possibility that, at least for ancient Chinese and Greek scientists and philosophers, conceptions of the world and the cognitive processes used to understand it were very different (e.g., Cromer, 1993; Lloyd, 1990; Nakamura, 1964/1985). For example, although the Greeks formalized logic and made use of it for many cognitive operations, including geometry, the Chinese never formalized logic, and indeed, except for two brief periods around the third century B.C., never had much concern with logic at all (Becker, 1986). Presumably as a consequence, the ancient Chinese made little progress in geometry despite that they made great strides in arithmetic and algebra (Cromer, 1993).

Another example concerns metaphysics or fundamental assumptions about the nature of the world, together with the cognitive processes that followed from the metaphysical assumptions. The Greeks tended to focus on the object and explain its behavior with reference only to its properties and the categories to which it belonged. Aristotle explained a stone's falling when placed in water by invoking the notion that the stone had the property of "gravity," and explained a piece of wood's floating on water by reference to the wood's property of "levity." In contrast, the Chinese recognized that action always occurs in a field of forces, understood much about magnetism and acoustics, and recognized the true reason for the tides (which escaped even Galileo). The Greeks were inclined to see matter as being composed of discrete objects or atoms, whereas the Chinese were disposed to see matter as continuous substances, even as interpenetrating substances. Finally, the Greeks tended to see stability in the world (e.g., Plato's forms), whereas the Chinese saw the world as constantly changing, indeed, in line with the yin and yang of the Tao, as always being in the process of reverting to the opposite of the current state.

Nisbett and his colleagues (Nisbett, 2003; Nisbett, Peng, Choi, & Norenzayan, 2001) proposed that ancient Greek thought can be described as analytic, meaning that the focus of attention was on some salient object; the properties of the object were assessed, and the object was assigned to a category with the intention of finding the rules that governed its behavior. Relevant rules were sometimes of the most abstract kind—namely, logical rules—and the focus on the rules governing the object's behavior gave the Greeks a sense of control over the object. Ancient Chinese thought, in contrast, was holistic, meaning that the Chinese attended to the field in which a salient object was located; relationships among objects and events in the field were noticed, but specific object properties and categories were of relatively little interest. Frequently lacking explicit rules about the object's behavior, the Chinese had relatively little sense of personal agency or control. Substituting for logical rules were a variety of dialectical schemas, including finding the "middle way" between two apparently contradictory propositions and recognizing the importance of the context in making judgments about objects and individuals.

Why might the ancient Chinese and Greeks have had such different ways of thinking about the world? Various writers have proposed that the reasons have to do with the differing social practices of the two societies (e.g., Nakamura, 1964/1985; Needham, 1954). The Chinese were engaged in multiple, complex role relations with other individuals, with the extended family, the village, and the representatives of the state. The socially interdependent Chinese would always have been looking outward, trying to coordinate their actions with those of others while minimizing social friction. If, as Markus and Kitayama (1991) put it, "one perceives oneself as embedded within a larger context of which one is an interdependent part, it is likely that other objects or events will be perceived in a similar way" (p. 246). The Greeks, in contrast, were relatively independent, having fewer and less complex social relations than did the Chinese. In addition, the Greeks valued individualism and autonomy. The independence of their lives might have given them the luxury of attending to objects in light of their personal goals in relation to them and might have encouraged them to see objects, both physical and social, as distinct and separate.

If ancient Greek and Chinese philosophers differed from one another because their social systems made it natural for them to see and process the world as they did, then there would be some justification for predicting that modern East Asians (China and the cultures it strongly influenced, including Japan and Korea) might reason differently from modern Westerners (notably the people of Europe and the current and former members of the British Commonwealth). This is because there is substantial evidence that the current social practices of the East and West differ in ways that parallel those of ancient times.

The Western-style independent and largely unconnected self is hard for East Asians to comprehend. Philosopher Shih (1919) stated, "in the Confucian human-centered philosophy man cannot exist alone; all action must be in the form of interaction between man and man" (p. 116). Anthropologist Hall (1976) introduced the concept of low-context vs. high-context societies to capture differences in social relations. The Western self is composed of fixed attributes and can move from one setting or context to another without significant alteration. But for East Asians, the person is so connected to others that the self is literally dependent on the context. As philosopher Munro (1985) put it, East Asians understand themselves "in terms of their relation to the whole, such as the family, society, Tao Principle, or Pure Consciousness" (p. 17). If an important person is removed from the individual's social network, that individual literally becomes a different person.

Self-descriptions capture these differences. When asked to describe the self, Americans and Canadians tend to tell about their personality traits and attitudes more than do Japanese (Cousins, 1989; Kanagawa, Cross, & Markus, 2001). North Americans tend to overestimate their distinctiveness (Markus & Kitayama, 1991) and prefer uniqueness in themselves and their possessions (Markus & Kitayama, 1991). In one clever study, Koreans and Americans were given a choice among different colored pens to have as a gift. Americans chose the rarest color, whereas Koreans chose the most common color (Kim & Markus, 1999).

Training for independence vs. interdependence starts very early. Whereas it is common for Western babies to sleep in a different bed from their parents (or even in a different room), this is rare for Asian babies. Adults from several generations often surround the Chinese baby, and the Japanese baby is almost always with its mother. When American mothers play with their children, they tend to focus their attention on objects and their attributes ("See the truck; it has nice wheels"), whereas Japanese mothers emphasize feelings and relationships ("When you throw your truck, the wall says, 'ouch' ") (Fernald & Morikawa, 1993). Koreans are better able to judge an employer's true feelings about an employee from ratings of the employee than are Americans (Sanchez-Burks et al., 2003).

When we showed participants videos of fish, we found that Japanese were more likely to see emotions in the fish than were Americans (Masuda & Nisbett, 2001).

Surveys of businesspeople show marked differences between the East and West in terms of harmonious relationships vs. emphasis on individual performance (Hampden-Turner & Trompenaars, 1993). The differential emphasis on relationships can result in conflicts in the world of business. For example, in the mid-1970s, Japanese refiners contracted with Australian suppliers to provide them with sugar for several years at a particular set price. When, the very next year, the bottom dropped out of the world sugar market, the Japanese wanted to renegotiate the price, but to the Australians, a contract was a contract: a fixed, binding instrument that should not be subject to changes in context or by any desire to maintain a harmonious relationship with the purchasers.

If it is really the case that contemporary Asian and Western societies are different in their emphasis on relationships vs. independent action, then it might be the case that Asia and the West differ in their cognitive and perceptual habits along the lines of the holistic vs. analytic stance characteristic of ancient Chinese vs. ancient Greek science and philosophy. For the past several years, we and our colleagues have been examining this possibility in a number of domains.

COGNITIVE DIFFERENCES

Our work shows that East Asians and Westerners differ in the way they make causal attributions and predictions, in reliance on logic vs. dialectical principles, and in categorization based on rules vs. family resemblance and categorization based on shared taxonomic labels vs. relationships.

Causal Attribution and Prediction

We might expect that Westerners, like ancient Greek scientists, would be inclined to explain events by reference to properties of the object and that East Asians would be inclined to explain the same events with reference to interactions between the object and the field. There is much evidence indicating that this is the case (for reviews, see Choi, Nisbett, & Norenzayan, 1999; Norenzayan & Nisbett, 2000; Norenzayan, Choi, & Nisbett, 1999). Morris and Peng (1994) and Lee, Hallahan, and Herzog (1996) showed that Americans are inclined to explain murders and sports events, respectively, by invoking presumed traits, abilities, or other characteristics of the individual, whereas Chinese and Hong Kong citizens are more likely to explain the same events with reference to contextual factors, including historical ones. Cha and Nam (1985) and Choi and Nisbett (1998) found that East Asians used more contextual information than did Americans in making causal attributions. The same is true for predictions.

Explanations are different even for events involving animals and inanimate objects. Morris and Peng (1994) showed participants cartoon displays of an individual fish moving in relation to a group of fish in various ways. Chinese participants were more likely to see the behavior of the individual fish as being produced by external factors—namely, the other fish—than were Americans, whereas American participants were more inclined to see the behavior as being produced by factors internal to the individual fish. Peng and Knowles (2003) showed that, for ambiguous physical events involving phenomena that appeared to be hydrodynamic, aerodynamic, or magnetic, Chinese were more likely to refer to the field when giving explanations (e.g., "The ball is more buoyant than the water") than Americans were. The differences in causal attribution therefore probably reflect deep metaphysical differences that transcend specific rules about particular domains that are taught by the culture. In many of the causal attribution studies, incidentally, it could be shown that the East Asian tendency to prefer context was more likely to result in a correct analysis than was the American preference for the object.

Logic Versus Dialectics

When told that all birds have a certain property, people are more inclined to agree that eagles have the property than that penguins have the property, even though, if asked, they would of course say that penguins are birds. Norenzayan, Smith, Kim, and Nisbett (2002) showed that Korean participants were more susceptible to this so-called *typicality* effect in deduction. Koreans were also more likely than Americans to be influenced by the desirability of a proposition when judging whether it was logically consistent with propositions to which it was related deductively. A series of studies by Peng and Nisbett (1999) showed that Chinese are more comfortable with apparent contradictions than are Americans. They showed that Chinese participants had a greater preference for proverbs that contain an apparent contradiction ("too humble is half proud") than did American participants (even when the proverbs were Yiddish ones and equally unfamiliar to Americans and Chinese). They also found that the Chinese were more likely to propose "middle way" solutions to inter- and intrapersonal conflicts than were Americans, who seemed to find it necessary that one side or the other had to be correct. When presented with evidence for apparently contradictory propositions, Chinese participants tried to find truth in both, whereas Americans were more inclined to reject one proposition in favor of the other.

Categorization

East Asians have been found to classify objects and events on the basis of relationships and family resemblance, whereas Americans classify on the basis of rule-based category membership. Chiu (1972) showed triplets of objects like those in Fig. 2.1 to Chinese and American children and asked them to indicate which of the two objects went together. American children put the chicken and cow together and justified this by pointing out that "both are animals." Chinese children put the cow and grass together and justified this by saying that "the cow eats the grass." Our research group has found the same sort of differential tendency in college students given word triplets to read. Norenzayan et al. (2002) asked participants to report whether a target object like that at the bottom of Fig. 2.2 was more similar to the group of objects on the left or the group on the right. The target object bears a strong family resemblance to the group of objects on the left, but there is a rule that allows placing the object in the group on the right— namely, "has a straight stem." Figure 2.3 shows that East Asians were inclined to think that the object was more similar to the group with which it shared a family resemblance, whereas Euro-Americans were more likely to regard the object as similar to the group to which it could be assigned by application of the rule. Asian Americans, although closer to East Asians, showed no overall preference. (In several of our studies, we have included Asian Americans. They were always intermediate in their responses and most typically closer to the Euro-Americans than to the East Asians.)

FIG. 2.1.   "Which two go together?" Item from Chiu (1972) test.

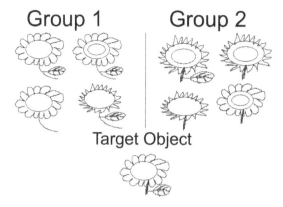

FIG. 2.2.   "Which group does the target object belong to?" Target bears a family resemblance to group on the left, but can be assigned to group on the right on the basis of a rule.

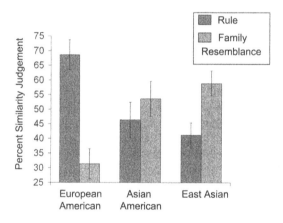

FIG. 2.3.   Percentage of participants basing similarity judgments on family resemblance vs. rule.

ATTENTION AND PERCEPTION DIFFERENCES

Differences between East Asians and Westerners extend beyond cognition to encompass many tasks that are attentional and perceptual in nature. Asians appear to attend more to the field and Westerners more to salient objects.

Detection of Covariation

If it is the case that East Asians pay more attention to the field, we would expect them to be better at detecting relationships between events. Ji, Peng, and Nisbett (2000) presented arbitrary objects like those in Fig. 2.4 to

FIG. 2.4.   Sample of arbitrary objects shown in covariation detection task.

Chinese and American participants. One of the objects on the left appeared on the left side of a split computer screen followed rapidly by one of the objects on the right appearing on the right side of the screen. The participants' task was to judge the strength of relationship between one object appearing on the left and a corresponding object appearing on the right. The actual strength ranged from zero—that is, the probability of a particular object on the right appearing was independent of which object appeared on the left—to a relationship equal in strength to a correlation of .60. The Chinese participants saw more covariation than did American participants, they were more confident about their judgments, and their confidence was better correlated with the actual degree of covariation. At any rate, all of this was true in the setup just described. When some control over the setup was given to participants by giving them a choice as to which object to present on the left and how long an interval to have before presentation of the object on the right, American performance was entirely similar to Chinese performance.

Field Dependence: Difficulty in Separating an Object From Its Surroundings

If it is the case that East Asians are inclined to focus their attention broadly on the field, we might expect them to find it more difficult to make a separation between an object and the field in which it appears. Such a tendency is called *field dependence* (Witkin et al., 1954). One of the ways to examine it is the rod and frame test presented in Fig. 2.5.

FIG. 2.5.   Rod and frame test apparatus.

The participant looks down a long box at the end of which is a rod whose orientation can be changed, and a frame around the rod can be moved independently of the rod. The participant's task is to judge when the rod is vertical. Participants are deemed field dependent to the extent that their judgments of verticality of the rod are influenced by the orientation of the frame. Ji et al. (2000) found that Chinese participants were more influenced by the position of the frame than were American participants. Although Chinese and Americans were equally confident of their judgments in the setup just described, when participants were given control in the form of being able to position the rod as they wished, the Americans became more confident than the Chinese (and the actual performance of American males improved).

Attention to the Field

We presented 20-second animated vignettes of underwater scenes to Japanese and American participants (Masuda & Nisbett, 2001). A still photo from one of the videos is presented in Fig. 2.6. After seeing each video

FIG. 2.6.   Still photo from animated underwater vignette.

twice, participants were asked to report what they had seen. The first sentence was coded as to whether a participant initially mentioned one of the salient objects (with *salience* defined as being larger, faster moving, and more brightly colored than the other objects) or the field (e.g., water color, floor of the scene, inert objects). American participants started their statements by mentioning salient objects far more frequently than Japanese participants did. In contrast, Japanese participants began by mentioning information about the field almost twice as often as Americans did. Overall, Japanese actually made 65% more observations about the field than did Americans. Japanese participants mentioned almost twice as many relations between objects and the field as did American participants.

After participants had seen 10 vignettes, they were presented with still photos of 45 objects they had seen before and 45 they had not seen. The 45 previously seen objects were shown either against the original background, no background, or a novel background, as seen in Fig. 2.7. The prediction was that, because they attend to objects in relation to the field, Japanese participants would be more thrown off by presentation of the object against the novel field than would Americans. This was, in fact, the case. Whereas American performance was literally unaffected by the background manipulation, the Japanese made substantially more errors when the object was seen against a novel background than when it was seen against the original background. (Japanese performance was significantly better for the no-background condition than for the novel background condition, but was not significantly worse for the no-background condition than for the original background condition.)

Fish with Original Background   **Fish with No Background**   **Fish With Novel Background**

FIG. 2.7.   Focal fish previously seen viewed against previously seen background (left), no background (center), or novel background (right).

Change Blindness

Perceptual psychologists have recently been studying a phenomenon called *change blindness* (Simons & Levin, 1997). When a picture of a scene and a somewhat altered version of it are presented sequentially, with just a brief pause in between, people can find it difficult to detect changes that are completely obvious when the two versions are shown side by side. This seems to be produced by an automatic tendency of the nervous system to render two highly similar scenes into a single consistent picture, something that the visual system is constantly doing to maintain a coherent view of the world. If it is the case that East Asians attend to the field more than do Westerners, then changes in the field, including relationships between objects, should be easier for them to detect. If Westerners focus more on objects and their attributes, then it should be changes in salient objects that would be easier for them to detect. Masuda and Nisbett (in press) presented Japanese and American participants with scenes like those in Figs. 2.8 and 2.9, which are stills from 20-second animated vignettes. The scene in Fig. 2.8 is intended to mimic the object salience of a Western city and that in Fig. 2.9 to mimic the field salience, complexity, and interpenetration characteristic of East Asian cities. Other vignettes included an object-salient American farm scene and a field-salient Japanese farm scene. Finally, two scenes were intended to be neutral with respect to culture: a construction scene and an airport scene.

Sensitivity to change was measured by asking participants, after they had seen two versions of the same scene that had changes in both salient foreground objects as well as in relationships between objects and less salient background objects, to tell us which aspects of the scene had changed from the first version of the vignette to the second. An example of an object change in Fig. 2.8 is a change in the front car's hubcaps. An example of a relationship change is relocation of the buildings in the background. An example of a background object change is a change in the type of buildings in the background. Figure 2.10 shows the differences in changes perceived by

FIG. 2.8. Still photo from animated "American" city vignette in change
blindness study.

FIG. 2.9. Still photo from animated "Japanese" city vignette in change
blindness study.

Americans and Japanese. It can be seen that American participants were
more likely to detect changes in salient objects than were Japanese participants, whereas Japanese participants were more likely to detect relationship and environment (context) changes than were Americans.

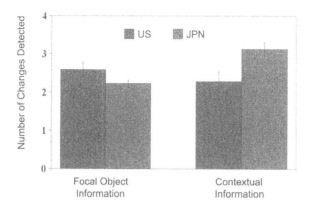

FIG. 2.10. Focal object and contextual changes detected by Americans (US) and Japanese (JPN).

"Affordances" in the Environment

As it happens, the different environments had an effect on the perception of both Americans and Japanese. As may be seen in Fig. 2.11, when the scenes were intended to resemble American environments, both Americans and Japanese found it easier to detect object changes than field changes. When the scenes were intended to resemble Japanese environments, both Americans and Japanese found it easier to detect field changes than object changes. These findings indicate that environmental factors, known as the *affordances* to perception, may contribute to people's habitual patterns of attention and perception. When the environment affords mostly salient, distinctive objects, it may be that people attend to them more closely than to the field. When objects are more numerous, more complex, and more interpenetrating, the distinction between object and field may become blurred, and relationships and background elements may become relatively salient.

Of course, these generalizations would be valid only if the scenes that we composed actually capture real differences in Eastern and Western environments. To examine this question, Miyamoto, Nisbett, and Masuda (in press) took photographs in front of, to each side of, and behind three kinds of buildings (post offices, schools, and hotels) in towns of three different sizes in Japan and America. Total populations were defined for each type of building in pairs of towns that were comparable in many respects across the two nations: New York and Tokyo, the towns of Ann Arbor, MI, and its "sister city" Hikone, Japan, and the villages of Chelsea, MI, and Torahime, Japan. Buildings were selected at random from the populations of each type. American and East Asian college students were

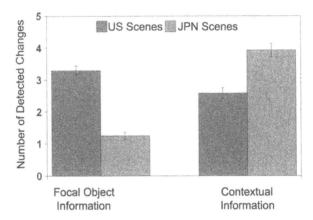

FIG. 2.11. Focal object and contextual changes detected in "American" (US) and "Japanese" (JPN) environments.

questioned about the photographs, and both groups reported finding Japanese scenes to have more objects and more ambiguous boundaries for objects. Each picture was schematized and assessed for number of objects by using the NIH IMAGE program for Macintosh. An example of a schematized picture is shown in Fig. 2.12.

The number of objects in each picture was assessed based on the number of edges: the more edges, the more objects. The average number of objects defined in this way was 32% greater for Japanese scenes than for

FIG. 2.12. Schematized rendering of a Japanese street scene for the purpose of assessing number of objects.

American scenes. The differences between Japanese and American scenes were marked at each city size.

Aesthetics East and West

Among the affordances of the environment that may influence perception are the artistic products of a culture. There are marked differences between Eastern and Western art, and we and our colleagues Richard Gonzalez and Letty Kwan have found comparable differences in the way ordinary college students draw pictures and take photographs of the environment (Masuda, Gonzalez, Kwan, & Nisbett, 2005). East Asian paintings take a very broad perspective on the scenes they represent. They tend to put the horizon high as it would be seen by a bird flying over the landscape or an artist perched on a high outcropping. Western landscapes put the horizon low, as it would be seen from the ground. Consequently, less of the landscape is seen. Eastern portrait paintings tend to diminish the size and salience of the central figure relative to Western paintings. The behavior of ordinary contemporary people duplicates these cultural trends. When college students are asked to draw a landscape showing at least a house, a tree, a person, a river, and a horizon, East Asian participants placed the horizon higher and drew more objects overall than American participants. When Japanese and American students were asked to take a photo of a person, the Japanese photos showed the person as small relative to the field. An example of the difference between a Japanese photo and an American one is shown in Fig. 2.13. Japanese literally never made photographs with the person taking up as large a fraction of

FIG. 2.13.   Photos showing different ideas of relation between central figure and environment in a portrait. (*Left*) American portrait. (*Right*) Japanese portrait.

the total space as the American photo in Fig. 2.13, but it was common for Americans to do so.

Change Versus Stability

The ancient Greeks saw stability in their worlds, and the ancient Chinese saw change. We have maintained that a contributor to this difference may have been the relative degree of focus on the object vs. the field. If one is attending primarily to a focal object and its properties, and assigning it to an abstract (and static) category, the world may appear to be stable. But if one is attending to a greater number of objects and their relationships, the world may appear to be in a constant state of change. Ji, Su, and Nisbett (2001) examined assumptions about stability vs. change in several ways. They described various current states and asked whether participants thought the state would continue or change. For example, participants were told about a relationship between a young man and a young woman and asked whether they thought it would continue in the future. For each of four events, more Chinese than American participants thought the future would be different from the past. Ji et al. also presented participants with alleged recent trends in various parameters that participants were unlikely to have direct knowledge of—for example, recent trends in global economy growth rates. Participants were shown positively and negatively accelerated growth and decay trends and were asked to make a prediction as to what the next time step would be like. For all four types of curves, Chinese participants were more likely to predict that the next time step would halt or reverse the direction of change. It may be seen in Fig. 2.14 that Chinese participants were more likely to predict reversals of trends in all but 1 of 12 cases.

Perception of Everyday Life Events

The experiments reported to this point all use materials that, to one degree or another, depart from everyday life objects and events. In a final study to be reported, Chua and Nisbett (2002) studied more naturalistic materials. They asked American and Taiwanese college students to describe some personal events (e.g., their first day of the current term), read some narratives (e.g., about a day in the life of a woman in which everything seemed to prevent her from getting to work) and then summarize what they had read, and watch videos of silent comedies and summarize them. Taiwanese were randomly selected to write either in Mandarin or English. The anticipations were that the Americans would make more mentions of the central character than would the Taiwanese; the former would also make more intentional statements expressive of control over a situation or

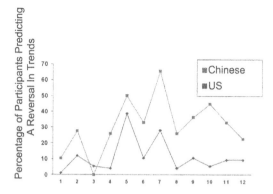

FIG. 2.14. Percentage of American and Chinese participants predicting a reversal in trends. Points 1–3, positively accelerated growth curves; points 4–6, negatively accelerated growth curves; points 7–9, positively accelerated decay curves; points 10–12, negatively accelerated decay curves.

desire to achieve control. Taiwanese were expected to make more comments about the emotional states of various characters. There were no differences in any of the variables due to whether it was personal stories, summarized narratives, or descriptions of the videos that were examined. Thus, we added all three of these together for purposes of analysis. It may be seen in Figs. 2.15 to 2.17 that all of the predictions were borne out and the results were the same whether the Taiwanese answered in Mandarin

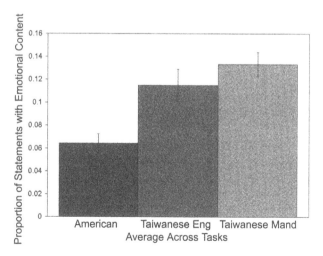

FIG. 2.15. Number of statements referring to central figures minus number of statements referring to others, by Americans and by Taiwanese tested either in English or Mandarin.

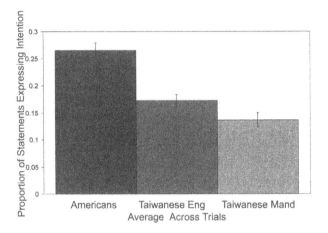

FIG. 2.16. Proportion of statements with intentional content by Americans and by Taiwanese tested either in English or Mandarin.

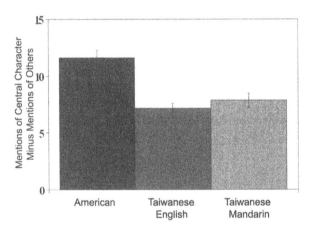

FIG. 2.17. Proportion of statements with emotional content by Americans and Taiwanese tested either in English or Mandarin.

or English. This latter finding is consistent with the results of several other studies showing that language used, and facility of Asians in English when the testing language is English, are not generally predictive of results (Norenzayan et al., 2002).

DISCUSSION

There are marked differences in the cognitive processes of East Asians and Westerners. These include categorization, causal attribution, reliance on rules, use of logic, and preference for dialectical understanding of events.

In our view, these cognitive differences derive in good part from perceptual differences—in particular, differences in what is attended to. We have shown that East Asians attend to the field more than do Westerners, and that Westerners pay more attention to focal objects. Attention to the object encourages categorization of it, application of rules to it, and causal attribution in terms of it. Attention to the field encourages noticing relationships and change, and it prompts causal attribution in terms of the context and distal forces. In addition, attention to the field could be expected to make it difficult to segregate a particular object from a field in which it is embedded.

We believe that the differences in attention, perception, and cognition that we have shown are driven by differences in social structure and social practices that prompt Asians to look to the environment and allow Westerners the luxury of attending to some focal object and their goals with respect to it. Sometimes, although not always, these differences may be caused or enhanced by economic factors. We endorse the speculation by others that East Asians emphasize role relations and social harmony as much as they do in part because, since ancient times, they have been primarily farmers, and farmers need to get along with one another (Nakamura, 1964/1985; Needham, 1954). In addition, irrigated agriculture, characteristic of much of East Asia since ancient times, requires effective hierarchies, adding more vertical constraints to the vertical and horizontal constraints within the family and village. Such an emphasis on social concerns could possibly have sustained itself, in part out of sheer inertia, for an indefinite period up to the present. The period may be briefer than one might assume, however. Our colleague Harold Stevenson quizzed the mothers of an elementary school in Beijing about their hopes for their children during a 10-year period encompassing a dramatic changeover toward a free market economy. At the beginning of the period, the mothers had primarily social concerns for their children, wanting them to be able to fit in and get along with others. At the end of the period, the mothers had shifted dramatically in the direction of hoping for their children to be ambitious and skilled in ways that would serve them in the new economic circumstances.

The economy of ancient Greece was quite different from that of East Asia. Greece, consisting substantially of mountains descending to the sea, did not lend itself to large-scale agriculture. Common occupations such as hunting, fishing, trading, and keeping kitchen gardens did not require extensive social collaboration. In the absence of substantial social concerns and constraints, attention to a focal object and one's goals in relation to it were luxuries that the Greeks could afford. Many aspects of Western industrial and postindustrial economies in the last 200 years are also characterized by relatively few social constraints, at least for those in middle-class occupations.

Thus, we believe that there is a causal chain running from social structure to social practice to attention and perception to cognition. This account does not accommodate two sets of findings, however—namely those relating to logic vs. dialectics and those relating to what appears to be the differing affordances of Eastern and Western environments, including artistic productions.

A common account of why Aristotle formalized logic is that he got tired of hearing poor arguments in the marketplace and the political assembly (Becker, 1986). Essentially, he was trying to establish that if an argument had a particular formal structure, it was a bad argument regardless of content. That the Chinese would not have formalized logic, or even have been much concerned with it, can then be explained in terms of the fact that arguments were extremely rare because of the threat they posed to the social fabric (Nisbett, 2003). That a dialectical approach to contradiction would have developed fits with this assumption: The Chinese sought the "middle way" between apparent contradictions. This account of logic vs. dialects is a direct one from social practice to cognition that does not make contact with questions of attention or perception.

That the affordances of Eastern and Western environments would differ is more of a puzzle. Part of the affordances are the artistic products that surround the individual. It may be that Asian artists show much of the field because they are capable of attending to a great deal of environmental information and prefer to do so. They may render humans and other salient objects smaller than do Westerners because these are not so focal for them. Ordinary people may make drawings and photos the way they do, and show the artistic preferences they do, in part because that is the way the artworks they are accustomed to seeing usually portray things. However, given ordinary people's habits of attending to the world, it is far from clear that the examples of artistic products are needed. It is quite possible that at least part of the field preference of ordinary East Asians, and the object emphasis of ordinary Westerners, is due to their respective customary ways of seeing the world.

It is more difficult to explain why the affordances of the built environment would be so different between East and West. One possibility seems unlikely: Eastern environments are probably not more complex simply because of greater population density. The population density of Tokyo is somewhat greater than that of New York, and the population density of Torahime is somewhat greater than that of Chelsea, but the population density of Ann Arbor is substantially greater than that of Hikone, and the East–West differences are roughly comparable for all three city sizes. Perhaps the most plausible explanation of the greater complexity of Eastern environments is that the aesthetic preferences match the perceptual focus of each group. Easterners focus broadly on the field and attend to a large number of elements, and they seem to construct environments with a large number of elements. Westerners focus more narrowly on a smaller number of elements, and they seem to prefer environments with a smaller number of elements. Our work suggests that these differences operate in such a way as to intensify each other: The environments influence perception, and the resulting perceptual preferences prompt people to produce different environments.

ACKNOWLEDGMENTS

The research reported here was supported by National Science Foundation Grants SBR 9729103 and BCS 0132074, National Institute of Aging Grant AG15047, the Russell Sage Foundation, and a John Simon Guggenheim fellowship (to R.E.N.). This contribution is part of the special series of Inaugural Articles by members of the National Academy of Sciences elected on April 30, 2002. It was previously published in the *Proceedings of the National Academy of Sciences*, September 2003, vol. 100, n. 19, pp. 11163–11170. © 2003 by The National Academy of Sciences of the USA.

REFERENCES

Becker, C. B. (1986). Reasons for the lack of argumentation and debate in the Far East. *International Journal of Intercultural Relations, 10*, 75–92.

Cha, J.-H., & Nam, K. D. (1985). A test of Kelley's cube theory of attribution: A cross-cultural replication of McArthur's study. *Korean Social Science Journal, 12*, 151–180.

Chiu, L.-H. (1972). A cross-cultural comparison of cognitive styles in Chinese and American children. *International Journal of Psychology, 7*, 235–242.

Choi, I., & Nisbett, R. E. (1998). Situational salience in the correspondence bias and in the actor-observer bias. *Personality and Social Psychology Bulletin, 24*, 949–960.

Choi, I., Nisbett, R. E., & Norenzayan, A. (1999). Causal attribution across cultures: Variation and universality. *Psychological Bulletin, 125*, 47–63.

Chua, H. F., & Nisbett, R. E. (2002, June). *Analytic and holistic thinking: Cultural influences on the perception of events and experiences*. Poster session presented at the annual meeting of the American Psychological Society, New Orleans, LA.

Cousins, S. D. (1989). Culture and self-perception in Japan and the United States. *Journal of Personality and Social Psychology, 56*, 124–131.

Cromer, A. (1993). *Uncommon sense: The heretical nature of science*. New York: Oxford University Press.

Fernald, A., & Morikawa, H. (1993). Common themes and cultural variations in Japanese and American mothers' speech to infants. *Child Development, 64*, 637–656.

Hall, E. T. (1976). *Beyond culture*. New York: Anchor.

Hampden-Turner, C., & Trompenaars, A. (1993). *The seven cultures of capitalism: Value systems for creating wealth in the United States, Japan, Germany, France, Britain, Sweden, and the Netherlands*. New York: Doubleday.

Ji, L.-J., Peng, K., & Nisbett, R. E. (2000). Culture, control, and perception of relationships in the environment. *Journal of Personality and Social Psychology, 78*, 943–955.

Ji, L.-J., Su, Y., & Nisbett, R. E. (2001). Culture, prediction, and change. *Psychological Science, 12*, 450–456.

Kanagawa, C., Cross, S. E., & Markus, H. R. (2001). "Who am I?" The cultural psychology of the concept of self. *Personality and Social Psychology Bulletin, 27*, 90–103.

Kim, H., & Markus, H. R. (1999). Deviance or uniqueness, harmony or conformity? A cultural analysis. *Journal of Personality and Social Psychology, 77*, 785–800.

Lee, F., Hallahan, M., & Herzog, T. (1996). Explaining real life events: How culture and domain shape attributions. *Personality and Social Psychology Bulletin, 22*, 732–741.

Lloyd, G. E. R. (1990). *Demystifying mentalities.* New York: Cambridge University Press.

Markus, H. R., & Kitayama, S. (1991). Culture and the self: Implications for cognition, emotion, and motivation. *Psychological Review, 98*, 224–253.

Masuda, T., Gonzalez, R., Kwan, L., & Nisbett, R. E. (2005). *Culture and aesthetic preference: Comparing the attention to context of East Asians and European Americans.* Unpublished manuscript, University of Alberta.

Masuda, T., & Nisbett, R. E. (2001). Attending holistically vs. analytically: Comparing the context sensitivity of Japanese and Americans. *Journal of Personality and Social Psychology, 81*, 922–934.

Masuda, T., & Nisbett, R. E. (in press). Culture and change blindness. *Cognitive Science.*

Miyamoto, Y., Nisbett, R. E., & Masuda, T. (in press). Culture and physical environment: Holistic versus analytic perceptual affordances. *Psychological Science.*

Morris, M. W., & Peng, K. (1994). Culture and cause: American and Chinese attributions for social and physical events. *Journal of Personality and Social Psychology, 67*, 949–971.

Munro, D. (1985). Introduction. In D. Munro (Ed.), *Individualism and holism: Studies in Confucian and Taoist values* (pp. 1–34). Ann Arbor: Center for Chinese Studies, University of Michigan.

Nakamura, H. (1964/1985). *Ways of thinking of Eastern peoples.* Honolulu: University of Hawaii Press.

Needham, J. (1954). *Science and civilisation in China* (Vol. 1). Cambridge: Cambridge University Press.

Nisbett, R. E. (2003). *The geography of thought: How Asians and Westerners think differently . . . and why.* New York: The Free Press.

Nisbett, R. E., Peng, K., Choi, I., & Norenzayan, A. (2001). Culture and systems of thought: Holistic vs. analytic cognition. *Psychological Review, 108*, 291–310.

Norenzayan, A., Choi, I., & Nisbett, R. E. (1999). Eastern and Western perceptions of causality for social behavior: Lay theories about personalities and social situations. In D. Prentice & D. Miller (Eds.), *Cultural divides: Understanding and overcoming group conflict* (pp. 239–272). New York: Sage.

Norenzayan, A., & Nisbett, R. E. (2000). Culture and causal cognition. *Current Directions in Psychological Science, 9*, 132–135.

Norenzayan, A., Smith, E. E., Kim, B. J., & Nisbett, R. E. (2002). Cultural preferences for formal versus intuitive reasoning. *Cognitive Science, 26*, 653–684.

Peng, K., & Knowles, E. (2003). Culture, ethnicity and the attribution of physical causality. *Personality and Social Psychology Bulletin, 29*, 1272–1284.

Peng, K., & Nisbett, R. E. (1999). Culture, dialectics, and reasoning about contradiction. *American Psychologist, 54*, 741–754.

Sanchez-Burks, J., Lee, F., Choi, I., Nisbett, R. E., Zhao, S., & Jasook, K. (2003). Conversing across cultural ideologies: East–West communication styles in work and non-work contexts. *Journal of Personality and Social Psychology, 85*, 363–372.

Shih, H. (1919). *Chung-kuo che-hsueh shi ta-kang* [An outline of the history of Chinese philosophy]. Shanghai: Commercial Press.

Simons, D. J., & Levin, D. T. (1997). Change blindness. *Trends in Cognitive Sciences, 1*, 261–267.

Witkin, H. A., Lewis, H. B., Hertzman, M., Machover, K., Meissner, P. B., & Karp, S. A. (1954). *Personality through perception.* New York: Harper.

3

Cultural Variation in Reasoning

Ara Norenzayan
University of British Columbia

Consider the following problem: Is the Pope a bachelor? Two approaches suggest themselves to solve this bachelor problem, each producing a different answer. One possibility is an intuitive solution: Our understanding of bachelor reflects similarity relations among people who are known to be bachelors. According to this intuitive approach, the Pope would not be seen as a bachelor. Alternatively, the concept of *bachelor* can be represented as a person who satisfies the rule, "unmarried, adult, male." Under this formal definition, the Pope, contrary to intuition, indeed would be a bachelor.

This bachelor problem illustrates an important theoretical distinction in the psychology of reasoning. According to this distinction, human thinking is guided by two separate classes of cognitive strategies that implement different computational principles. One can be described as intuitive, experience-based, or holistic, whereas the other can be described as formal, rule-based, or analytic (Evans & Over, 1996; James, 1890; Neisser, 1963; Smith, Langston, & Nisbett, 1992; Tversky & Kahneman, 1983; for a recent review of the empirical evidence for this distinction, see Sloman, 1996). The former cognitive strategies are associative or similarity based in nature, and their computations reflect temporal contiguity and statistical regularities among features. The latter strategies recruit symbolic representations, have logical structure and variables, and their computations reflect rule application. In this chapter, the terms *intuitive* and *formal* are used to refer to these two distinct reasoning systems.

In recent years, a growing number of research programs in psychology have examined these two cognitive systems under the rubric of *dual-process* theories of thinking, including deductive reasoning (Evans & Over, 1996), categorization (Rips, 1989; Smith, Patalano, & Jonides, 1998), analogical reasoning (Gentner & Medina, 1998), decision making (Tversky & Kahneman, 1983), belief formation (Gilbert, 1991), and social cognition (Chaiken & Trope, 1999). These two cognitive systems coexist in individuals, interact with each other in interesting ways (e.g., Gentner & Medina, 1998; Sloman, 1996), and occasionally may be in conflict and produce contradictory inferences, as in the previous bachelor problem. Although the intuitive system tends to dominate, the relative influence of one system versus the other on reasoning has been found to be influenced by the nature of the task, by instructions that emphasize rule following or deduction (Evans & Over, 1999; Sloman, 1996), by the particular reasoning domain (Atran, 1990; Keil, 1994), as well as by individual differences (Stanovich, 1999).

Little is known about the operation of these two systems of reasoning across diverse cultural groups. People in all cultures are likely to possess both of these reasoning systems, but cultural variation may exist in their relative accessibility and use to the extent that different values are placed on these reasoning systems. Many scholars have documented cultural differences in the intellectual outlooks of East Asian and Western cultures (Fung, 1952; Liu, 1974; Lloyd, 1996; Nakamura, 1960/1988). An *analytic* mode of thought has been held to be more prevalent in Western cultural groups. This mode involves the decoupling of the object from its context, assigning the object to categories based on necessary and sufficient features, and a preference for using rules, including the rules of formal logic, to explain and predict the object's behavior. In contrast, a *holistic* mode of thought has been held to be more prevalent in East Asian cultural groups. This mode involves attention to the context or field as a whole, a concern with relationships among objects and object–field relationships, a preference for intuitive reasoning, and dialectical reasoning, which seeks the "middle way" between conflicting propositions.

Recent evidence indicates that some of these differences in analytic versus holistic outlooks find their counterparts in the thought processes of contemporary Westerners and East Asians (for a review, see Nisbett & Norenzayan, 2002; Nisbett, Peng, Choi, & Norenzayan, 2001). For example, East Asians are more attentive to the situational context of behavior and are less prone to the *fundamental attribution error* (Ross, 1977), or the tendency to overattribute behavior to dispositions despite obvious situational constraints (Choi, Nisbett, & Norenzayan, 1999). East Asians are more *field dependent* (Witkin & Berry, 1975) than Americans, being more influenced by the position of the surrounding frame when judging the position of the rod in the rod-and-frame task (Ji, Peng, & Nisbett, 2000). East Asians have a more holistic sense of causality: They draw on a wider range of factors to explain events. As a result, East Asians show more *hindsight bias* (Fischhoff, 1975), the tendency to view events as having been inevitable in retrospect (Choi & Nisbett, 2000). East Asians also prefer *dialectical* resolutions to apparent contradictions so that a compromise or middle-way solution is sought. Americans respond to contradiction by polarizing their opinions—favoring one proposition over another (Peng & Nisbett, 1999). This chapter examines analogous cultural differences in formal and intuitive systems of reasoning.

Participants in these studies were self-identified European American, Asian American, and East Asian undergraduate students who were otherwise similar in their demographic backgrounds and intellectual abilities. In Studies 1 and 2, the East Asians were international students at the University of Michigan who were of Chinese or Korean culture, had lived in the United States for less than 4 years, had graduated from a high school in East Asia, and grew up speaking an East Asian language. In Studies 3 and 4, East Asians were Korean students at Yonsei University in Seoul, Korea. All European Americans were students at the University of Michigan. Asian Americans grew up in the United States and were of Chinese, Korean, or Japanese ethnic background. The Asian American samples were included to examine acculturation effects.

The theoretical rationale for the cultural differences was based on a simple research strategy: In each study, a cognitive conflict was activated such that formal thinking was pitted against intuitive thinking. If European Americans favor formal rules more than intuition, they should be more willing to set aside intuition and follow rules when the two are in conflict. If East Asians favor intuition more than formal rules, they should be less willing to abandon intuition in favor of formal rules.

A different prediction was made for reasoning based on intuition alone or on rules alone, with no cognitive conflict present. In these cases, responses are a function of cognitive ability, rather than a function of preference for a particular cognitive strategy. Because participants were selected in different cultures so that they were similar in cognitive abilities, no cultural differences were expected in their ability to implement a formal strategy or an intuitive strategy in the absence of a conflict between the two.

Cultural differences were examined in a variety of cognitive tasks. Study 1 was an examination of category learning. Participants were asked to apply a complex rule as a way of correctly classifying imaginary animals. Their category learning was then tested in a situation in which the complex rule conflicted with memory for previously seen animals. In Study 2, classification and similarity judgments of drawings (e.g., geometric objects, houses, flowers) were probed. These judgments admitted either a rule-based or a family-resemblance-based solution. Studies 3 and 4 went beyond immediately perceptible stimuli to examine conceptual processes. In Study 3, participants evaluated the convincingness of deductive arguments when logic conflicted with the typicality of the conclusion. Finally, in Study 4, deductive reasoning was investigated when logical structure was pitted against the believability of the conclusion. Detailed descriptions of the methods and results of these studies can be found in Norenzayan (2001) and Norenzayan, Smith, Kim, and Nisbett (2002).

STUDY 1: RULE- VERSUS EXEMPLAR-BASED CATEGORY LEARNING

If there is a cultural difference between European Americans and East Asians in formal and intuitive thinking, this difference might be apparent when categories have been learned by the formal application of rules, and when subsequent classification by rules conflicts with intuitive knowledge, such as exemplar memory. Rule-based categorization is accomplished by determining whether the novel object satisfies a rule that defines the category by its necessary and sufficient features, such as when a new neighbor is categorized as a bachelor if he satisfies the rule, "is an unmarried adult male." Exemplar-based categorization, in contrast, reflects similarity of the novel object to previously stored exemplars retrieved from memory. The more similar the new object and the retrieved exemplars are, the more likely it is that the new object belongs to the same category as the retrieved exemplars. Our new neighbor might be suspected of being a bachelor not because he satisfies some well-articulated rule, but because he is reminiscent of a bachelor relative.

Study 1 was based on a variation of a well-developed paradigm in categorization research (e.g., Allen & Brooks, 1991; Regehr & Brooks, 1993; Smith et al., 1998). Participants viewed imaginary animals on a computer screen and were told that the animals belonged to different categories, some being from Venus and others being from Saturn (Fig. 3.1). In a training phase, participants learned to categorize, with feedback, the set of animals. This was followed by a test phase, in which participants were asked to categorize new animals. Participants in the *rule condition* learned a complex rule, making categorizations based on whether the animal had three out of five specific bodily features. Critically, in the test phase of the rule condition, half of the animals were *positive matches*: They belonged to one category by the rule and also were very similar to a training exemplar from that same category. The other half of the new animals were *negative matches*: They belonged to one category as defined by the rule, but were very similar to a training exemplar from the opposite category. Thus, the negative match animals—unlike positive match ones—posed a cognitive conflict between rule-based and exemplar-based categorization.

FIG. 3.1. Examples of stimuli (Study 1). Rule: Animal lives on VENUS if it has at least three of the following five features: curly tail, hooves, antennae ears, mouth, long neck. Otherwise it lives on SATURN.

75

Unlike the rule condition, participants in the *exemplar memory condition* were not given a rule. They were asked during the training phase simply to observe a series of the cartoons and initially make guesses as to which animal belonged to which category. Feedback was given after each guess. As participants repeatedly categorized the same animals, they could rely on their memory of previous exemplars to assign the animals to their appropriate categories. The exemplar memory condition served as a control to examine whether the expected cultural differences in rule-based classification are attributable to differences in the sheer tendency to rely on exemplar memory.

Based on past findings (Allen & Brooks, 1991; Patalano, Smith, Jonides, & Koeppe, 2001; Smith et al., 1998), the anticipation was that: (a) participants would make fewer classification errors in the rule condition than in the exemplar memory condition, but take longer because of the necessity to compute the explicit rule; and (b) participants in the rule condition would make more classification errors and be slower for negative matches than positive matches—that is, when rule and exemplar memory were in conflict than when they were not.

Most important, the cultural analysis led to the prediction that (c) the difference in classification errors between positive and negative matches would be greater for East Asians than for European Americans because East Asians would be more inclined to use memory for the exemplars in the rule condition. Similarly, the difference in response times between positive and negative matches was expected to be greater for East Asians.

The results supported the prediction that a cultural difference would emerge in the extent to which memory for exemplars would interfere with rule application when the two processes were in conflict. Whereas East Asians and European Americans categorized equally well in the exemplar memory condition (see Fig. 3.2a), where no such conflict existed, in the rule condition, European Americans and Asian Americans made fewer classification errors than East Asians when conflict existed between rule- and exemplar-based categorization (Fig. 3.3a).

Similarly, no cultural differences in response times emerged in the exemplar memory condition (Fig. 3.2b). The overall lack of cultural differences in the exemplar memory condition suggests that the cultural differences in the rule condition are difficult to explain in terms of cultural differences in the sheer tendency to rely on exemplar memory in the absence of a rule.

East Asians' response times in the rule condition were overall slower than those of European Americans (Fig. 3.3b). Thus, rule application might have been harder for East Asians in a context where the rule could conflict with exemplar-based categorization for any given trial. Finally, Asian Americans responded identically to European Americans in all respects.

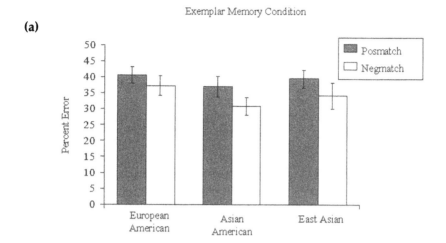

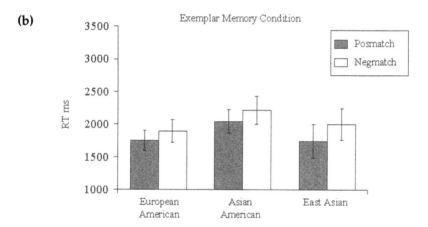

FIG. 3.2. Category learning (Study 1): (a) Classification error rates and (b) reaction times for the exemplar memory group.

STUDY 2: RULE- VERSUS FAMILY-RESEMBLANCE-BASED CLASSIFICATION AND SIMILARITY JUDGMENTS

Study 1 demonstrated that category learning based on the application of a formal rule was easier for Americans than for East Asians when the rule conflicted with exemplar memory. However, exemplar-based reasoning is only one strategy among many intuitive strategies, another being family resemblance. This strategy draws on knowledge of graded membership of exemplars within a category, such that some are believed to be more simi-

(a)

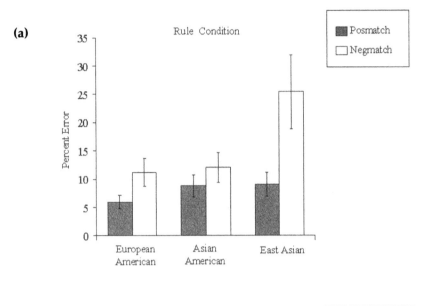

(b)

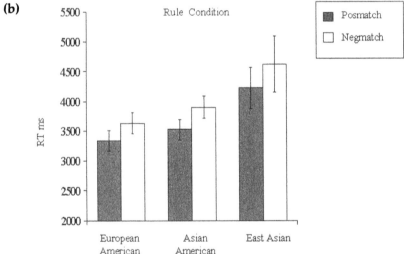

FIG. 3.3. Category learning (Study 1): (a) classification error rates and (b) reaction times for the rule group.

lar to the category than others (Rosch, 1978; Rosch & Mervis, 1975; Wittgenstein, 1953).

If cultural differences exist in rule-governed thinking and intuitive thinking, Westerners may be more tempted to spontaneously locate objects in novel categories based on a simple rule and less willing to rely on family resemblance, whereas the reverse might be true for East Asians. Study 2 tested this hypothesis.

Participants placed objects in one of two categories that could be defined on the basis of a unidimensional rule or overall similarity (Kemler-Nelson, 1984). They saw a series of presentations, each consisting of a target object beneath two groups or categories of four similar objects (Fig. 3.4). In one condition, participants were asked to decide which category the target object belonged to (*the classification condition*). Such free classification has been shown to be unidimensional as long as the stimuli allow scanning of an array of dimensionalized objects, as was the case in this study (Ahn & Medin, 1992; Medin, Wattenmaker, & Hampson, 1987). However, unlike Medin et al., where participants received items and sorted them into groups, in this study, participants were given two groups and then assigned an item to one of them. To encourage more strongly the use of an alternate family resemblance strategy, other participants were instructed to judge which category the target object was most similar to (*the similarity judgment condition*). The stimuli were constructed such that the responses driven by the rule versus family resemblance criterion led to different decisions (Fig. 3.4). Participants could rely on a unidimensional rule, deciding whether the target object shared a single feature with all category members. Alternatively, they could rely on family resemblance, judging the target object to be holistically similar to all members of a category because it shared a large number of features with them, even though no one feature characterized all members of the category. The anticipation was that East Asians would make less use of rules and more use of family resemblance than would European Americans in both conditions. As to response times, it was expected that the similarity instructions would produce faster response times than the classification instructions. However, because making judgments based on a unidimensional rule or on family resemblance are equally fast, there was no reason to expect cultural differences in reaction times in this study.

As seen in Fig. 3.5a, participants overwhelmingly preferred to classify based on the unidimensional rule rather than family resemblance, replicating past research. Contrary to predictions, all three cultural groups substantially preferred rule-based over family resemblance classification.

Matters were different when participants were asked to judge the similarity of the target object to the categories, as may be seen in Fig. 3.5b. Under these instructions, a marked cultural difference emerged. European Americans gave many more responses based on the unidimensional rule than on family resemblance (indeed, they preferred the unidimensional rule precisely to the same extent as when making classification decisions). East Asians, in contrast, gave fewer rule-based responses than family re-

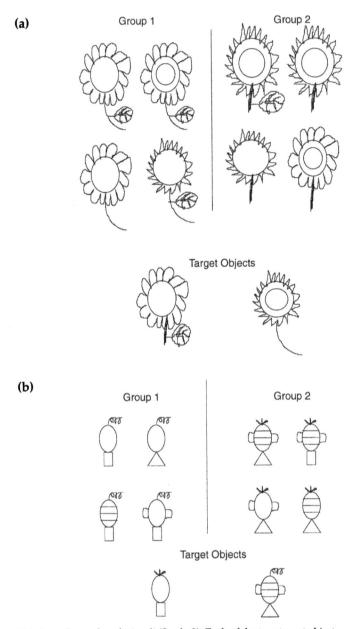

FIG. 3.4. Examples of stimuli (Study 2). Each of the two target objects was presented separately with the two groups to achieve a counterbalanced design: (a) For the flowers, the defining feature is the stem length; and (b) for the geometric figures, it is the top-most string.

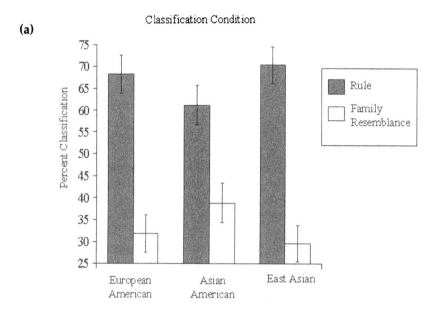

(a)

Classification Condition

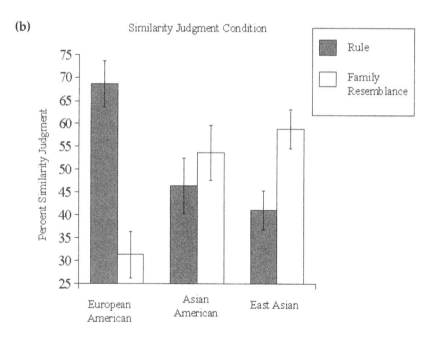

(b)

FIG. 3.5. (a) Classification and (b) similarity judgments by rule versus family resemblance (Study 2).

semblance responses. Asian Americans were intermediate, having no preference for rule versus family resemblance responses.

STUDY 3: CONCEPTUAL STRUCTURE BASED ON LOGIC VERSUS TYPICALITY

The first two studies probed categorization and similarity judgments of artificially constructed categories. In contrast, Study 3 probed the extent to which people spontaneously rely on formal rules versus intuition to mentally represent naturally occurring categories. This was done by setting logic against the typicality of category exemplars. Typicality-based reasoning relies on the similarity relations among particular exemplars of a category, with typicality judgments usually (but not always) being a function of the number of features shared by other category members (Rosch & Mervis, 1975; Smith & Medin, 1981). For example, penguins are atypical birds because of their perceptual peculiarities—large body, small wings, inability to fly—that set them apart from other members of the category *bird*. This type of reasoning is intuitive in that it relies on the perceptual features of actual category members, or on second-hand knowledge of the perceptual features of exemplars of a category.

Typicality describes a kind of intuitive reasoning distinct from *family resemblance*. Typicality refers to intuitions about the "goodness" of naturally occurring exemplars, whereas family resemblance is objectively determined as the proportion of features shared among category members, as in Study 2. Study 3 assessed how people project fictitious or unknown features from a *superordinate* category (e.g., bird) to *subordinate* categories of varying typicality (e.g., eagle, penguin; Sloman, 1993). Participants rated how convincing they found deductive categorical arguments such as:

1. All birds have ulnar arteries.
   Therefore all eagles have ulnar arteries.
2. All birds have ulnar arteries.
   Therefore all penguins have ulnar arteries.

There are two known strategies one can recruit to reason about these arguments. Reasoners following logic would "discover" the hidden premise in each argument—that "All eagles are birds" and "All penguins are birds." Once these hidden premises are exploited, the argument becomes a standard valid deductive argument. Armed with this knowledge, participants should be equally convinced by the typical and atypical arguments.

But the typicality of the conclusion category can make the arguments more convincing to the extent that reasoning is guided by intuitive strategies rather than logic. When participants evaluate both typical and atypical arguments, a *typicality effect* is found—that is, participants are less convinced of atypical arguments than typical ones (Sloman, 1993).

Study 3 examined this typicality effect cross-culturally. The phenomenon was evaluated both within groups (when typicality is salient) and between groups (when typicality is not salient). If East Asians rely on intuition more than European Americans, the typicality effect should be stronger for East Asians, particularly when typicality is not salient.

First, a different group of European American and Korean students rated the typicality of the conclusion categories as a manipulation check. The typicality manipulation was successful. All typical conclusions were rated as more typical than their atypical counterparts, for both European Americans and Koreans.

As can be seen in Fig. 3.6a, when typicality was nonsalient, the typicality effect was stronger for Koreans than European Americans, and it was marginally stronger for Koreans than Asian Americans. European Americans and Asian Americans did not differ statistically. However, the cultural differences were most revealing when the typicality effect was evaluated separately for each cultural group. As expected, a large typicality effect emerged for Koreans. This effect was marginally significant for Asian Americans. Most tellingly, European Americans did not show any typicality effect. Instead, their responses were consistent with logic, being equally convinced by the two arguments. When typicality was salient (Fig. 3.6b), no cultural differences were found: the typicality effect was observed for all.

STUDY 4: LOGIC VERSUS BELIEF
IN DEDUCTIVE REASONING

Evidence presented in Studies 1 to 3 indicates that there are cultural differences in the ways individuals living in East Asian and Western cultural contexts categorize and organize concepts. In Study 4, the consequences of this cultural difference were examined for reasoning based on logical structure versus belief. Unlike Study 3, which did not directly manipulate the logical structure of arguments, Study 4 included an orthogonal variation of both the logical structure of arguments and the intuitive content of the conclusions.

In Study 4, a cognitive conflict was created between the logical structure of a deductive argument and the empirical plausibility of the argument's conclusion. Participants evaluated the logical validity of a series of categorical syllogisms and conditional arguments that were either valid or invalid and had conclusions that were either believable or nonbelievable

(a)

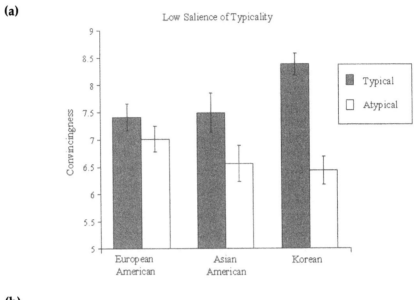

(b)

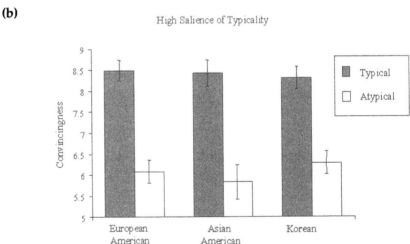

FIG. 3.6.   Convincingness of deductive arguments with (a) nonsalient and
(b) salient typical versus atypical conclusions (Study 3).

(Table 3.1). Moreover, at the end of the task, the same argument forms
were presented in an abstract version so as to assess logical reasoning independent of content (for these abstract arguments, believability was irrelevant). Finally, a separate group of participants rated the believability
of each conclusion as a manipulation check and to establish the functional
equivalence of the believability manipulation across cultures.

TABLE 3.1
Selected Arguments in Study 4

Valid/Believable
  Premise 1:   No police dogs are old.
  Premise 2:   Some highly trained dogs are old.
  Conclusion: Some highly trained dogs are not police dogs.
Valid/Nonbelievable
  Premise 1:   All things that are made of plants are good for the health.
  Premise 2:   Cigarettes are things that are made of plants.
  Conclusion: Cigarettes are good for the health.
Invalid/Believable
  Premise 1:   All tall athletes have large foot size.
  Premise 2:   Famous basketball players have large foot size.
  Conclusion: Famous basketball players are tall athletes.
Invalid/Nonbelievable
  Premise 1:   If a country is a member of the European Community, it is permitted to
              apply for loans from the European Bank.
  Premise 2:   India is not permitted to apply for loans from the European Bank.
  Conclusion: India is a member of the European Community.

To the extent that one's reasoning is guided by intuitive knowledge, the believability of the conclusion may interfere with logical evaluations. As a result, valid arguments with implausible conclusions may be mistakenly thought to be invalid, and invalid arguments with plausible conclusions may be mistakenly thought to be valid. This is known as the *belief bias effect* in psychology (Evans, Barston, & Pollard, 1983; Newstead, Pollard, Evans, & Allen, 1992; Oakhill & Johnson-Laird, 1985; Revlin, Leirer, Yop, & Yop, 1980). However, to the extent that one's reasoning strategy favors logic, one should be willing or able to decontextualize—that is, separate form from content. This study was a first investigation into possible cultural differences in the belief bias effect. It was expected that Koreans would show a stronger belief bias than European Americans. Furthermore, it was investigated whether this cultural difference in belief bias would remain holding logical reasoning ability constant, as measured by performance on the abstract arguments.

First, a different group of European American and Korean students rated the believability of the conclusions as a manipulation check for believability. The results showed that the believability manipulation was successful for both cultures.

Figure 3.7 presents the results for the abstract arguments. There was evidence for response bias, such that Koreans were overall less likely to respond "yes." Nevertheless, the rate of accurately detecting valid arguments was the same in the two cultural groups. Thus, any cultural differences found in belief bias cannot be attributed to differences in logical reasoning ability.

Abstract Arguments

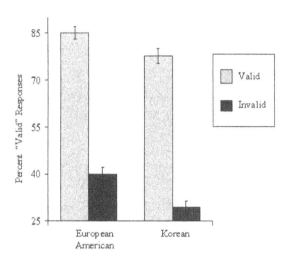

FIG. 3.7. Deductive reasoning with abstract arguments: percent "valid" responses (Study 4).

Koreans, relative to European Americans, were expected to evaluate the arguments as valid when the conclusion was believable and less likely to do so when the conclusion was nonbelievable. Different results emerged for valid and invalid arguments. Therefore, the belief bias effect was thus examined separately for valid and invalid arguments. It was found that the belief bias effect emerged across both cultural groups. However, for valid arguments, Koreans showed a stronger belief bias effect than Americans (see Fig. 3.8a). Contrary to predictions, no cultural differences in belief bias were detected for invalid arguments (see Fig. 3.8b).

In summary, Koreans showed a stronger belief bias effect than European Americans, although only for valid arguments. Because European Americans and Koreans showed the same degree of logical reasoning for the abstract arguments, it can be concluded that the stronger belief bias of Koreans was not due to differences in reasoning ability, but rather to differing tendencies to decontextualize the content of an argument from its logical structure.

GENERAL DISCUSSION

The present research investigated cultural variation in formal and intuitive reasoning. Formal reasoning is rule-based, emphasizes logical inference, represents concepts by necessary and sufficient features, and over-

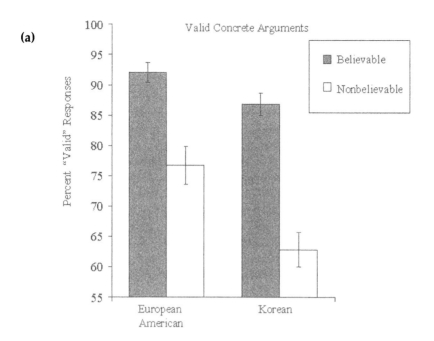

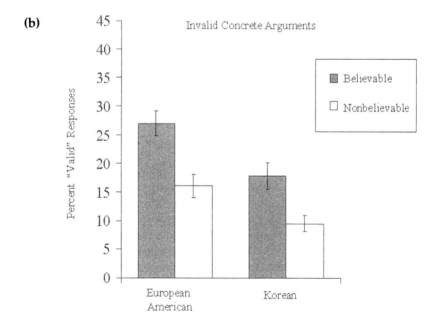

FIG. 3.8. Deductive reasoning with concrete (a) valid and (b) invalid arguments: percent "valid" responses (Study 4).

looks sense experience when it conflicts with rules or logic. Intuitive reasoning is experience-based, resists decontextualizing or separating form from content, relies on sense experience and concrete instances, and overlooks rules and logic when they are at odds with intuition.

The reasoning of European American, Asian American, and East Asian university students was compared under conditions where a cognitive conflict was activated between formal and intuitive strategies of thinking. The central hypothesis was that European Americans would be more willing to set aside intuition and follow rules than East Asians. Overall the results were consistent with the hypothesis.

Although in each study an effort was made to rule out obvious methodological artifacts, it is possible that each individual finding could be subject to an alternative explanation. For this reason, each specific cultural difference should be interpreted with caution. However, the strategy adopted in this chapter of seeking converging evidence from four rather different paradigms, using different sets of instructions, tasks, stimuli, and cultural samples, suggests that the best explanation for the cognitive differences that emerged in these studies is that there are different cultural preferences for the use of cognitive strategies to solve the same problem.

Two alternative explanations for the overall pattern of cultural differences are considered. First, it is possible that East Asians are less practiced than Americans with experimental situations such as these and, as a result, performed less well on such cognitive tasks that happened to favor rule-following. Because the presumed difference in familiarity applies to the experimental situation in general, cultural differences should have emerged in all tasks and conditions. However, this was clearly not the case. Differences emerged only when formal and intuitive strategies were in conflict. European Americans and East Asians performed similarly when there was no conflict between the two strategies (positive matches in the Rule Condition of Study 1), when they were instructed simply to implement an intuitive strategy (Exemplar Memory Condition in Study 1), or a formal strategy (abstract deductive reasoning in Study 4).

The second possibility is that the cultural groups did not differ in reasoning tendencies, but perhaps they differed in the way they interpreted the experimental setting (Orne, 1962). That is, European Americans and East Asians had different hypotheses regarding the experimenter's expectations about what is a preferable mode of reasoning, and the cultural differences reflected different patterns of hypothesis guessing. Although this consideration cautions us about extending these findings to other settings, this explanation is unlikely to account for the entire pattern of results. In two of the studies, participants were clearly and explicitly instructed to use a formal strategy (Studies 1 and 4). Therefore, European American and East Asian participants presumably had similar awareness of the experimenter's expectation that the formal strategy is the appropriate one to use. Nevertheless, significant cultural differences were found in the extent to which the intuitive strategy interfered with the formal strategy.

Why are Western and East Asian participants biased toward different modes of reasoning? The attempt to answer this important question must of course be speculative at this time because it involves complex sociological and historical issues beyond the scope of this chapter and is left open for the future. Here three factors are mentioned that have been identified by philosophers, ethnographers, and social historians (for a fuller discussion, see Nisbett et al., 2001). First, the practice of *adversarial debate* prevalent in Western cultures, as opposed to the practice of consensus-based decision making prevalent in East Asia, has been linked to analytic versus holistic cognitive orientations, respectively (e.g., Lloyd, 1990; Ohbuchi & Takahashi, 1994). Second, *pedagogical practices* emphasizing critical thinking in Western classrooms, as opposed to experience-based learning in Chinese classrooms, appear to encourage differing modes of thinking in Western and East Asian societies (On, 1996; for a review, see Tweed & Lehman, 2002). Third, many historians of science and philosophy both Western and East Asian have reported important cultural differences in the dominant *philosophical traditions* that have influenced the intellectual practices in the West and East. Early Greek and Chinese philosophy, science, and mathematics were quite different in their strengths and weaknesses. Many Greek philosophers looked for universal rules to explain events and were concerned with categorizing objects with precision and respect to their "essences." There was a marked distrust of intuition. Chinese philosophers, especially Taoists, were more pragmatic and intuitive, and they were distrustful of formal logic and rational distinctions (Fung, 1952; Liu, 1974; Lloyd, 1990, 1996; Nakamura, 1960/1988; Needham, 1954; Russell, 1945; for a discussion of the evidence, see Nisbett, 2003; Norenzayan, 2001; Norenzayan & Nisbett, 2000).

Cognitive differences were found in reasoning that to some degree mirror differences in philosophical traditions. As provocative as this congruence may be, it cannot be known at this time whether these traditions are actually implicated in such reasoning processes. Whether there is psychological continuity between these philosophical traditions and reasoning processes remains an open question. The findings reported in this chapter and elsewhere (see Nisbett et al., 2001) can serve as one starting point for such interdisciplinary investigation.

A general point about analytic and holistic thinking is that each mode of thought produces a mixed bag of normative and non-normative outcomes. For example, in deductive reasoning, analytic thinkers tend to respond more logically than holistic thinkers, but in causal attribution, the former more readily commit the fundamental attribution error than the latter. Conversely, holistic thinkers are more accurate in covariation detection (Ji et al., 2000), yet they are more vulnerable to hindsight bias (Choi & Nisbett, 2000). Thus, neither the analytic nor the holistic mode guarantees accuracy in reasoning.

In two studies presented here, the East Asian reliance on intuitive processes led to less accurate responses than the American reliance on rule-based approaches. In Study 1, East Asians made more errors when asked to categorize the negative matches—for which a conflict existed between rule- and exemplar-based judgments. Note, however, that under other task conditions, intuitive responses could lead to *more* accurate responses than would formal processes. In fact many life circumstances present us with poorly structured cognitive problems that may favor intuitive strategies. This can occur when a rule is poorly defined or only partially predictive. For example, in the category learning procedure of Study 1, suppose the rule were made only partially predictive of the categories, such that it would accurately predict category membership for positive match animals, but would predict the *wrong* category for negative match animals. In such a situation, it has been shown that switching to an exemplar-based strategy leads to superior overall performance than continuing to use the rule (e.g., Allen & Brooks, 1991, Experiment 4), and East Asians might perform more accurately than European Americans (a proposal that remains to be tested).

East Asians also made more errors in Study 4, in which they were explicitly asked to judge the logical validity of the concrete arguments, as opposed to their plausibility or convincingness. Although this is an error, and undoubtedly one that would have been acknowledged by the participants given their performance with fully abstract materials, it is the result of a bias that does not always yield less reasonable conclusions than the rationalistic bias of Westerners. Indeed, many East Asian scholars have noted that in East Asian cultures logic does not enjoy the normative status that it does in the West. In Japanese culture, for example, "to argue with logical consistency is thus discouraged, and if one does so continuously one may not only be resented but also be regarded as immature" (Nagashima, 1973, p. 96). Liu (1974) made a similar point about China when he wrote, "it is precisely because the Chinese mind is so rational that it refuses to become rationalistic and [. . .] refuses to separate form from content" (p. 325). Consistent with these assertions, recent evidence indicates that Koreans rank "being an intuitive person" to be important for work success more than Americans, whereas the opposite is true for "being a logical person" (Buchtel & Norenzayan, 2005). Furthermore, in recent research, European Americans have been shown to make errors, in their efforts to be logically consistent, that actually result in judgments that are *incoherent* in the sense that one judgment actually follows from the opposite of the other (Peng & Nisbett, 1999). These errors were avoided by East Asian participants, who, however, made logical errors of their own in their attempts to reconcile opposing views.

CONCLUSION: CULTURAL VARIATIONS IN REASONING

Far from being a blank slate, the human mind is equipped with basic cognitive primitives that constitute the raw building blocks that guide cultural learning (Atran & Sperber, 1991; Pinker, 1997). People everywhere are likely to possess cognitive processes such as the ones that realize exemplar-based categorization, formal reasoning, and so on. Evidence is also accumulating that core aspects of domain-specific competencies that guide mechanical reasoning, folk-biological reasoning, and folk-psychological reasoning are universal (Hirschfeld & Gelman, 1994; Pinker, 1997). However, the universality of these basic processes does not preclude the possibility that there are important avenues through which cultural variation shapes cognition (see Norenzayan & Heine, 2005).

There may be *accessibility differences* in cognitive processes. Societies differ in the cultural practices they promote, affording differential expertise in the use of a cognitive strategy. The result is that a given cognitive process may be equally available in principle, but differentially accessible in different cultures. Thus, East Asian reasoning is less likely than Western reasoning to resist exemplar interference in rule-based category learning (as found in Study 1), less likely to decontextualize deductive arguments (as found in Study 4), and more likely to explain behavior situationally (Choi, Nisbett, & Norenzayan, 1999).

Different cultural contingencies or affordances may result in more significant *functional differences*, in that people may habitually rely on qualitatively different cognitive strategies to solve the same problems of everyday life even if these processes are in principle cognitively available across cultures. Thus, even if all cultures were able to draw from similar cognitive toolkits, the tools of choice for the same problem may be altogether different. In many studies comparing American and East Asian reasoning, the same problem often triggered qualitatively distinct cognitive responses. For example, under identical conditions, American similarity judgments were driven by a simple unidimensional rule, in contrast to East Asian judgments, which were driven by family resemblance (Study 2). A functional difference was also found in Study 3, in which the convincingness of arguments was affected by formal logic versus typicality in different cultures (see Nisbett et al., 2001, for additional examples).

Finally, *existential differences* may emerge across cultures, such that actual availability of particular cognitive processes may differ across cultures. Through invention and tinkering, complex ways of thinking have achieved widespread distribution in societies throughout history. It is in this sense that culture-specific complex cognitive structures can emerge out of universal primitive ones (Dennett, 1995). The inventions of symbolic systems such as calendars, number-naming conventions, pictographic writing, alphabetic writing, Arabic numerals, and formal logic provide examples. Beginning in the West in the 17th century, statistical, methodological, and cost-benefit rules having applicability to scientific reasoning as well as to policy analysis and everyday judgment and decision making began to be developed. There is great variation even today in the degree of understanding and use of these rules. Similarly, Chinese philosophy developed the ancient Taoist notions of *yin* and *yang* into sophisticated ways of reasoning about change, moderation, relativism, and multiple viewpoints that are now widespread in Chinese-influenced cultures and rare in other populations.

If there are culturally diverse ways to go about the business of cognition, and if there are culturally diverse systems of justification for cognitive processes, then it is vital to illuminate the ways by which cultural affordances and reasoning tendencies mutually shape each other. In this spirit, the philosopher Stich (1990) said that "there are no intrinsic epistemic virtues [. . .] cognitive mechanisms or processes are to be viewed as tools or policies and evaluated in much the same way that we evaluate other tools or policies" (p. 24). The reasonable epistemic stance then would be to evaluate thinking in terms of the local standards of justification, as well as specific goals and task requirements (Stich, 1990; see also Resnick, 1994). This is not to say that it is unreasonable to criticize specific inferential practices, even by the standards of another culture, but that criticism must be cognizant of inferential goals and cultural context.

ACKNOWLEDGMENTS

This research is based on a doctoral dissertation authored by Ara Norenzayan and submitted to the University of Michigan. A different version of this chapter appeared in *Cognitive Science*, 2002 (26), pp. 653–684, and has been reprinted with the permission of the Cognitive Science Society.

REFERENCES

Ahn, W., & Medin, D. L. (1992). A two-stage model of category construction. *Cognitive Science, 16*, 81–121.

Allen, S. W., & Brooks, L. R. (1991). Specializing in the operation of an explicit rule. *Journal of Experimental Psychology: General, 120,* 3–19.

Atran, S. (1990). *Cognitive foundations of natural history.* New York: Cambridge University Press.

Atran, S., & Sperber, D. (1991). Learning without teaching. Its place in culture. In L. Tolchinsky-Landsmann (Ed.), *Culture, schooling, and psychological development* (pp. 39–55). Norwood, NJ: Ablex.

Buchtel, E., & Norenzayan, A. (2005). *Who is rational? Cultural differences in normative evaluations of reasoning.* Unpublished manuscript, University of British Columbia.

Chaiken, S., & Trope, Y. (Eds.). (1999). *Dual-process theories in social psychology.* New York: Guilford.

Choi, I., & Nisbett, R. E. (2000). The cultural psychology of surprise: Holistic theories and recognition of contradiction. *Journal of Personality and Social Psychology, 79,* 890–905.

Choi, I., Nisbett, R. E., & Norenzayan, A. (1999). Causal attribution across cultures: Variation and universality. *Psychological Bulletin, 125,* 47–63.

Dennett, D. (1995). *Darwin's dangerous idea.* New York: Simon & Schuster.

Evans, J. B. T., Barston, J. L., & Pollard, P. (1983). On the conflict between logic and belief in syllogistic reasoning. *Memory and Cognition, 11,* 295–306.

Evans, J. B. T., & Over, D. E. (1996). *Rationality and reasoning.* Hove: Psychology Press.

Fischhoff, B. (1975). Hindsight's foresight: The effect of outcome knowledge on judgment under uncertainty. *Journal of Experimental Psychology: Human Perception and Performance, 1,* 288–299.

Fung, Y. L. (1952). *A history of Chinese philosophy* (Vol. 1; D. Bodde, Trans.). Princeton, NJ: Princeton University Press.

Gentner, D., & Medina, J. (1998). Similarity and the development of rules. *Cognition, 65,* 263–297.

Gilbert, D. T. (1991). How mental systems believe. *American Psychologist, 46,* 107–119.

Hirschfeld, L. A., & Gelman, S. A. (Eds.). (1994). *Mapping the mind: Domain specificity in cognition and culture.* New York: Cambridge University Press.

James, W. (1890). *The principles of psychology.* New York: Dover.

Ji, L., Peng, K., & Nisbett, R. E. (2000). Culture, control, and perception of relationships in the environment. *Journal of Personality and Social Psychology, 78,* 943–955.

Keil, F. (1994). The birth and nurturance of concepts by domains: The origins of concepts of living things. In L. Hirschfeld & S. Gelman (Eds.), *Mapping the mind: Domain specificity in cognition and culture* (pp. 234–254). New York: Cambridge University Press.

Kemler-Nelson, D. G. (1984). The effect of intention on what concepts are acquired. *Journal of Verbal Learning and Verbal Behavior, 23,* 734–759.

Liu, S. H. (1974). The use of analogy and symbolism in traditional Chinese philosophy. *Journal of Chinese Philosophy, 1,* 313–338.

Lloyd, G. E. R. (1990). *Demystifying mentalities.* New York: Cambridge University Press.

Lloyd, G. E. R. (1996). Science in antiquity: The Greek and Chinese cases and their relevance to the problems of culture and cognition. In D. R. Olson & N. Torrance (Eds.), *Modes of thought: Explorations in culture and cognition* (pp. 15–33). Cambridge: Cambridge University Press.

Medin, D. L., Wattenmaker, W. D., & Hampson, S. E. (1987). Family resemblance, conceptual cohesiveness, and category construction. *Cognitive Psychology, 19,* 242–279.

Nagashima, N. (1973). A reversed world: Or is it? In R. Horton & R. Finnegan (Eds.), *Modes of thought: Essays on thinking in Western and non-Western societies* (pp. 92–111). London: Faber & Faber.

Nakamura, H. (1960/1988). *The ways of thinking of Eastern peoples.* New York: Greenwood.

Needham, J. (1954). *Science and civilization in China* (Vol. 1). Cambridge: Cambridge University Press.

Neisser, U. (1963). The multiplicity of thought. *British Journal of Psychology, 54,* 1–14.

Newstead, S. E., Pollard, P., Evans, J. B. T., & Allen, J. L. (1992). The source of the belief bias effects in syllogistic reasoning. *Cognition, 45,* 257–284.

Nisbett, R. E. (2003). *The geography of thought.* New York: The Free Press.

Nisbett, R. E., & Norenzayan, A. (2002). Culture and cognition. In D. L. Medin (Ed.), *Stevens' handbook of experimental psychology: Cognition* (3rd ed., pp. 561–597). New York: Wiley.

Nisbett, R. E., Peng, K., Choi, I., & Norenzayan, A. (2001). Culture and systems of thought: Holistic vs. analytic cognition. *Psychological Review, 108,* 291–310.

Norenzayan, A. (2001). Rule-based and experience-based thinking: The cognitive consequences of intellectual traditions. *Dissertation Abstracts International, 62,* 6B. (University Microfilms No. 2992)

Norenzayan, A., & Heine, S. J. (2005). Psychological universals across cultures: What are they and how can we know? *Psychological Bulletin, 135,* 763–784.

Norenzayan, A., & Nisbett, R. E. (2000). Culture and causal cognition. *Current Directions in Psychological Science, 9,* 132–135.

Norenzayan, A., Smith, E. E., Kim, B., & Nisbett, R. E. (2002). Cultural preferences for formal versus intuitive reasoning. *Cognitive Science, 26,* 653–684.

Oakhill, J. V., & Johnson-Laird, P. N. (1985). The effects of belief on the production of syllogistic conclusions. *Quarterly Journal of Experimental Psychology, 37A,* 553–569.

Ohbuchi, K. I., & Takahashi, Y. (1994). Cultural styles of conflict management in Japanese and Americans: Passivity, covertness, and effectiveness of strategies. *Journal of Applied Psychology, 24,* 1345–1366.

On, L. W. (1996). The cultural context of Chinese learners: Conception of learning in the Confucian tradition. In D. A. Watkins & J. B. Biggs (Eds.), *The Chinese learner: Cultural, psychological, and contextual influences* (pp. 25–42). Hong Kong: Comparative Education Research Centre.

Orne, M. T. (1962). On the social psychology of the psychological experiment: With particular reference to demand characteristics and their implications. *American Psychologist, 17,* 776–783.

Patalano, A. L., Smith, E. E., Jonides, J., & Koeppe, R. A. (2001). PET evidence for multiple strategies of categorizations. *Cognitive, Affective, & Behavioral Neuroscience, 1,* 360–370.

Peng, K., & Nisbett, R. E. (1999). Culture, dialectics, and reasoning about contradiction. *American Psychologist, 54,* 741–754.

Pinker, S. (1997). *How the mind works.* New York: Norton.

Regehr, G., & Brooks, L. R. (1993). Perceptual manifestations of an analytic structure: The priority of holistic individuation. *Journal of Experimental Psychology: General, 122,* 92–114.

Resnick, L. B. (1994). Situated rationalism: Biological and social preparation for learning. In L. A. Hirschfeld & S. A. Gelman (Eds.), *Mapping the mind: Domain specificity in cognition and culture* (pp. 474–493). Cambridge: Cambridge University Press.

Revlin, R., Leirer, V., Yop, H., & Yop, R. (1980). The belief-bias effect in formal reasoning: The influence of knowledge on logic. *Memory and Cognition, 8,* 584–592.

Rips, L. J. (1989). Similarity, typicality, and categorization. In S. Vosniadou & A. Ortony (Eds.), *Similarity and analogical reasoning* (pp. 21–59). Cambridge: Cambridge University Press.

Rosch, E. (1978). Principles of categorization. In E. Rosch & B. B. Lloyd (Eds.), *Cognition and categorization* (pp. 27–48). Hillsdale, NJ: Lawrence Erlbaum Associates.

Rosch, E., & Mervis, C. B. (1975). Family resemblances: Studies in the internal structure of categories. *Cognitive Psychology, 7,* 573–605.

Ross, L. (1977). The intuitive psychologist and his shortcomings. In L. Berkowitz (Ed.), *Advances in experimental social psychology* (Vol. 10, pp. 173–220). New York: Academic Press.

Russell, B. (1945). *A history of Western philosophy.* New York: Simon & Schuster.

Sloman, S. (1993). Feature-based induction. *Cognitive Psychology, 25,* 231–280.

Sloman, S. (1996). The empirical case for two systems of reasoning. *Psychological Bulletin, 119*, 30–32.

Smith, E. E., Langston, C., & Nisbett, R. E. (1992). The case for rules in reasoning. *Cognitive Science, 16*, 1–40.

Smith, E. E., & Medin, D. L. (1981). *Categories and concepts*. Cambridge, MA: Harvard University Press.

Smith, E. E., Patalano, A. L., & Jonides, J. (1998). Alternative strategies of categorization. *Cognition, 65*, 167–196.

Stanovich, K. E. (1999). *Who is rational? Studies of individual differences in reasoning*. Mahwah, NJ: Lawrence Erlbaum Associates.

Stich, S. P. (1990). *Fragmentation of reason*. Cambridge, MA: MIT Press.

Tversky, A., & Kahneman, D. (1983). Extensional versus intuitive reasoning: The conjunction fallacy in probability judgment. *Psychological Review, 90*, 293–315.

Tweed, R. G., & Lehman, D. R. (2002). Learning considered within a cultural context: Confucian and Socratic approaches. *American Psychologist, 57*, 89–99.

Witkin, H. A., & Berry, J. W. (1975). Psychological differentiation in cross-cultural perspective. *Journal of Cross Cultural Psychology, 6*, 4–87.

Wittgenstein, L. (1953). *Philosophical investigations*. New York: Macmillan.

Thinking About Biology: Modular Constraints on Categorization and Reasoning in the Everyday Life of Americans, Maya, and Scientists

Scott Atran
*Centre National de la Recherche Scientifique
and University of Michigan*

Douglas L. Medin
Northwestern University

Norbert Ross
Vanderbilt University

What follows is a discussion of four sets of experimental results that deal with various aspects of biological understanding among American and Maya children and adults. The first set of experiments shows that Yukatek Maya children do not have an anthropocentric understanding of the biological world; that is, children do not universally reason about nonhuman living kinds by analogy to human kinds. The fact that urban (but not rural) American children do show an anthropocentric bias appears to owe more to a difference in cultural exposure to nonhuman biological kinds than to a basic causal understanding of folk biology per se. The second set of experiments shows that by the age of 4 to 5 years (the earliest age tested in this regard), rural Maya children as well as urban Brazilian (and American) children employ a concept of innate species potential, or underlying essence, as an inferential framework for projecting known and unknown biological properties to organisms in the face of uncertainty. Together, the first two sets of experiments indicate that folk psychology cannot be the initial source of folk biology. They also suggest that to understand modern biological science, people must *unlearn* universal dispositions to view species essentialistically and to see humans as fundamentally different than other animals.

The third set of results shows that the same taxonomic rank is cognitively preferred for biological induction in two diverse populations: people raised in the Midwestern United States and Itza' Maya of the Lowland Mesoamerican rainforest. This is the generic species—the level of *oak* and *robin*. These findings cannot be explained by domain-general models of similarity because such models cannot account for why both cultures prefer species-like groups in making inferences about the biological world, given that Americans have relatively little actual knowledge or experience at this level. In fact, general relations of perceptual similarity and expectations derived from experience produce a basic level of recognition and recall for many Americans that corresponds to the superordinate life-form level of folk-biological taxonomy—the level of *tree* and *bird*. Still Americans prefer generic species for making inductions about the distribution of biological properties among organisms and for predicting patterns in the face of uncertainty. This supports the idea of the generic-species level as a partitioning of the ontological domains of *plant* and *animal* into mutually exclusive essences that are assumed (but not necessarily known) to have unique underlying causal natures.

The fourth set of experiments shows that adult Maya, as well as American college students and various groups of biological experts (landscapers, parks workers, birdwatchers, professional taxonomists), spontaneously order generic species into taxonomies with higher and lower levels. Only the college students, however, consistently use their taxonomies to reason as science suggests they should: Given a property found in two organisms (e.g., a turkey and an eagle), it is reasonable to generalize that property to all and only those organisms that fall within the smallest taxon containing the original pair of organisms (e.g., birds). Moreover, only college students consistently project biological properties across taxa in accordance with similarity-based typicality or central tendency.

The implication from these experiments is that folk biology may well represent an evolutionary design: Universal taxonomic structures, centered on essence-based generic species, are arguably routine products of our "habits of mind," which may be in part naturally selected to grasp relevant and recurrent "habits of the world." The science of biology is built on these domain-specific cognitive universals: Folk biology sets initial cognitive constraints on the development of macrobiological theories, including the initial development of evolutionary theory. Nevertheless, the conditions of relevance under which science operates diverge from those pertinent to folk biology.

For the Maya, and arguably for others who subsist owing to their knowledge of the living world, folk-biological taxonomy works to maximize inductive potential relative to human interests. Here, folk-biological taxonomy provides a well-structured but adaptable framework. It allows people to explore the causal relevance to them, including the ecological relevance, of the natural world. Historically, for pragmatic reasons, the West's development of a worldwide scientific systematics involved disregard of ecological relationships, and of the colors, smells, sounds, tastes, and textures that constitute the most intimate channels of ordinary human recognition and access to the surrounding living world. For scientific systematics, the goal is to maximize inductive potential regardless of human interest. The motivating idea is to understand nature as it is "in itself," independently of the human observer (as far as possible). From this standpoint, the species concept, like teleology, should arguably be allowed to survive in science more as a regulative principle that enables the mind to establish a regular communication with the ambient environment than as an epistemic principle that guides the search for nomological truth.

Finally, these experiments suggest that standard undergraduate populations in major North American (or European) universities are often the "odd group out" in cross-cultural research on basic cognitive processes of biological categorization and reasoning. This has troubling implications for theoretical and methodological generalizations that are often based exclusively on such populations. This is especially problematic for claims about what is universal and what is not.

FOUR POINTS OF GENERAL CORRESPONDENCE BETWEEN FOLK BIOLOGY AND SCIENTIFIC SYSTEMATICS

In every human society, people think about plants and animals in the same special ways (Atran, 1998). These ways of thinking, which can be described as *folk biology*, are basically different from the ways humans ordinarily think about other things in the world, such as stones, tools, or even people. The science of biology also treats plants and animals as special kinds of objects, but applies this treatment to humans as well. Folk biology, which is present in all cultures, and the science of biology, whose origins are particular to Western cultural tradition, have corresponding notions of living kinds. Consider four corresponding ways in which ordinary folk and biologists think of plants and animals as special.

First Point

People in all cultures classify plants and animals into species-like groups that biologists generally recognize as populations of interbreeding individuals adapted to an ecological niche. We call such groups—like *redwood*, *rye*, *raccoon*, or *robin*—"generic species." Generic species often correspond to scientific genera (e.g., oak) or species (e.g., dog), at least for the most phenomenally salient organisms, such as larger vertebrates and flowering plants. Generic species may also be the categories most easily recognized, most commonly named, and most easily learned by children in small-scale societies (Stross, 1973). Indeed, ethnobiologists who otherwise differ in their views of folk taxonomy tend to agree that one level best captures discontinuities in nature and provides the fundamental constituents in all systems of folk-biological categorization, reasoning, and use (Bartlett, 1940; Berlin, Breedlove, & Raven, 1973; Bulmer, 1974; Ellen, 1993; Hunn, 1982). Ethnobiologists, historians of systematics, and field biologists mostly agree "that species come to be tolerably well defined objects [. . .] in any one region and at any one time" (Darwin, 1883 [1872], p. 137) and that such local species of the common man are the heart of any natural system of biological classification (Diamond & Bishop, 1999).

The term *generic species* is used here, rather than *folk genera/folk generic* or *folk species/folk species*, because a principled distinction between biological genus and species is not pertinent to most people around the world. For humans, the most phenomenally salient species (including most species of large vertebrates, trees, and evolutionarily isolated groups such as palms and cacti) belong to monospecific genera in any given locale. Closely related species of a polytypic genus may be hard to distinguish locally, and often no readily perceptible morphological or ecological "gap" can be discerned between them (Diver, 1940).[1]

Generic species are usually as obvious to a modern scientist as to local folk. Historically, the generic-species concept provided a pretheoretical basis for scientific explanation of the organic world in that different theories, including evolutionary theory, have sought to account for the apparent constancy of "common species" and the organic processes that center on them (Wallace, 1901 [1889]).

Second Point

There is a commonsense assumption that each generic species has an underlying causal nature or essence that is uniquely responsible for the typical appearance, behavior, and ecological preferences of the kind. People in

---

[1]In a comparative study of Itza' Maya and rural Michigan college students, we found that the great majority of mammal taxa in both cultures correspond to scientific species, and most also correspond to monospecific genera: 30 of 40 (75%) basic Michigan mammal terms denote biological species, of which 21 (70%, or 53% of the total) are monospecific genera; 36 of 42 (86%) basic Itza' mammal terms denote biological species, of which 25 (69%, or 60% of the total) are monospecific genera (López, Atran, Coley, Medin, & Smith, 1997). Similarly, a Guatemalan government inventory of the Itza' area of the Peten rainforest indicates that 69% (158 of 229) are monospecific (AHG/APESA, 1992), the same percentage of monospecific tree genera (40 of 58) as in our study of the Chicago area (Medin et al., 1997).

diverse cultures consider this essence responsible for the organism's identity as a complex, self-preserving entity governed by dynamic internal processes that are lawful even when hidden. This hidden essence maintains the organism's integrity even as it causes the organism to grow, change form, and reproduce. For example, a tadpole and frog are the same animal, although they look and behave very differently and live in different places. Western philosophers, such as Aristotle and Locke, attempted to translate this commonsense notion of essence into some sort of metaphysical reality, but evolutionary biologists reject the notion of essence as such (Ghiselin, 1981). Nevertheless, biologists have traditionally interpreted this conservation of identity under change as due to the fact that organisms have separate genotypes and phenotypes.

Third Point

In addition to the spontaneous division of local flora and fauna into essence-based species, such groups have "from the remotest period in [. . .] history [. . .] been classed in groups under groups. The structure of these hierarchically included groups, such as *white oak/oak/tree* or *mountain robin/robin/bird*, is referred to as 'folkbiological taxonomy.' " Especially in the case of animals, these nonoverlapping taxonomic structures can often be scientifically interpreted in terms of speciation (related species descended from a common ancestor by splitting off from a lineage).

In all societies that have been studied in depth, folk-biological groups, or taxa, are divided into hierarchically organized ranks. Most folk-biological systems have between three and six ranks (Berlin, 1992). Taxa of the same rank are mutually exclusive and tend to display similar linguistic, biological, and psychological characteristics. Ranks and taxa, whether in folk-biological or scientific classification, are of different logical orders, and confounding them is a category mistake. Biological ranks are second-order classes of groups (e.g., species, family, kingdom) whose elements are first-order groups (e.g., lion, feline, animal). Folk-biological ranks vary little across cultures as a function of theories or belief systems. Ranks are intended to represent fundamentally different levels of reality, not convenience.[2]

---

[2]Generalizations across taxa of the same rank thus differ in logical type from generalizations that apply to this or that taxon. *Termite, pig,* and *lemon tree* are not related to one another by a simple class inclusion under a common hierarchical node, but by dint of their common rank—in this case, the level of generic species. A system of rank is not simply a hierarchy as some suggest (Carey, 1996; Rosch, 1975). Hierarchy—that is, a structure of inclusive classes—is common to many cognitive domains, including the domain of artifacts. For example, *chair* often falls under *furniture,* but not *vehicle,* and *car* falls under *vehicle,* but not *furniture.* But there is no ranked system of artifacts: No inferential link or inductive framework spans both *chair* and *car,* or *furniture* and *vehicle,* by dint of a common rank, such as the artifact *species* or the artifact *family.*

Fourth Point

Such taxonomies not only organize and summarize biological information; they also provide a powerful inductive framework for making systematic inferences about the likely distribution of organic and ecological properties among organisms. For example, given the presence of a disease in robins, one is automatically justified in thinking that the disease is more likely present among other bird species than among nonbird species. In scientific taxonomy, which belongs to the branch of biology known as *systematics*, this strategy receives its strongest expression in "the fundamental principle of systematic induction" (Bock, 1973; Warburton, 1967). On this principle, given a property found among members of any two species, the best initial hypothesis is that the property is also present among all species that are included in the smallest higher order taxon containing the original pair of species. For example, finding that the bacteria *Escherichia coli* shares a hitherto unknown property with robins, a biologist would be justified in testing the hypothesis that all organisms share the property. This is because *E. coli* links up with robins only at the highest level of taxonomy, which includes all organisms. This or any general-purpose system of taxonomic inference for biological kinds is grounded in a universal belief that word naturally divides into the limited causal varieties we commonly know as (generic) species.

These four principles provide the backbone and background for studying the role of culture and experience in cognizing nature. That is, they suggest candidates for universals as well as variations that may derive from limited contact with plants and animals or from different cultural lenses for perceiving biological kinds. In the next sections of this chapter, we review four case studies that illustrate these themes.

FOLK BIOLOGY DOES NOT COME FROM FOLK PSYCHOLOGY: EXPERIMENT 1

One influential model of conceptual development in folk biology is Carey's (1985) notion that young children's understanding of living things is embedded in a folk-psychological, rather than a folk-biological, explanatory framework, and that until age 10, it is based on their understanding of humans. Carey reported three major findings to bolster the claim that children's conceptions of the biological world are anthropocentric. First, projections from humans are stronger overall than projections from other living kinds. The other two findings are consequences of this difference in induction potential. The second result is that there are asymmetries in projection: Inferences from humans to mammals are stronger than from mammals to humans. Third, children violate projections according to similarity: Inferences from humans to bugs are stronger than from bees to bugs. Together these findings suggest that humans are the preferred base for children's inferences about the biological world.

This research has had a powerful impact on psychological theory and educational practice, but it suffers from a serious limitation. It has been conducted almost exclusively with individuals from North American, urban, technologically advanced populations. In the few studies that go beyond this sample (e.g., studies by Inagaki and Hatano in Japan), the focus is still on urban, majority culture children from advanced societies. Thus, it is not clear which aspects of children's naive biology are likely to be universal and which depend critically on cultural conceptions and conditions of learning.

Human-centered reasoning patterns might reflect lack of knowledge about nonhuman living things, rather than a radically different construal of the biological world. Indeed there is evidence that the onset of the industrial revolution was associated with a sharp and continuing drop in cultural interest in and support for learning about biological kinds (e.g., Wolff, Medin, & Pankratz, 1999), at least in industrialized nations. Over the past few years, we have been testing the generality of Carey's finding. We have examined biological induction in rural U.S. majority culture children, rural U.S. Native American children, and in Yukatek Maya children living in rural Mexico. Here we concentrate on our findings in Mexico (see Atran et al., 2001, for full details).

Our participants were nearly 100 Yukatek Maya-speaking children (ages 4–5 and 6–7) and adults from rural villages in southcentral Quintana Roo, Mexico. By and large, younger children were monolingual, older children had begun learning Spanish, and almost all of the adults understood Spanish as a second language. All testing was done in Yukatek Maya.

Detailed color drawings of objects represented base and target categories. Four bases were used: Human, Dog, Peccary, and Bee. Targets were divided into two sets. Each set included a representative of the categories Human (man, woman), Mammal (coatimundi, deer), Bird (eagle, chachalaca), Reptile (boa, turtle), Invertebrate (worm, fly), Tree (kanan, gumbolimbo), Stuff (stone, mud), Artifact (bicycle, pencil), and Sun (included in both sets).

Children were shown a picture of one of the bases and taught a new property about it. For example, the experimenter might show the dog picture and say, "Now, there's this stuff called andro. Andro is found inside some things. One thing that has andro inside is dogs. Now, I'm going to show you some pictures of other things, and I want you to tell me if you think they have andro inside like dogs do." Participants were then shown each of the targets and asked: "Does it have andro inside it, like the

[base]?" Properties were unfamiliarly internal substances of the form "has X inside." A different property was used for each base, and bases and targets were presented in random order for each participant.

The first result of interest is that humans were not the only useful inductive base for the young children. All groups show generalization as a function of biological affinity (similarity) between base and target for bases like dog, bee, and peccary. Furthermore, the young children were actually more likely to generalize from dog to other animals than to generalize from humans to other animals.

With humans as a base, 4- to 5-year-olds generalize broadly in an undifferentiated manner—they show no reliable effect of similarity. In contrast, adults show characteristically sharp gradients with humans as a base. The 6- to 7-year-olds show a very weak similarity gradient. In short, the clearest developmental change is in determining the role of humans in the folk-taxonomic system (see Fig. 4.1a). A second major result is that the children did not show reliable human–animal asymmetries. For inferences involving the bases Human and Dog, the data are inconsistent with Carey because only adults show the asymmetry favoring Human to mammal over Dog to human (see Figs. 4.1a–4.1d).

Using the same experimental setup as in the Yucatán, Ross, Medin, Coley, and Atran (2003) studied projection patterns for over 200 U.S. chil-

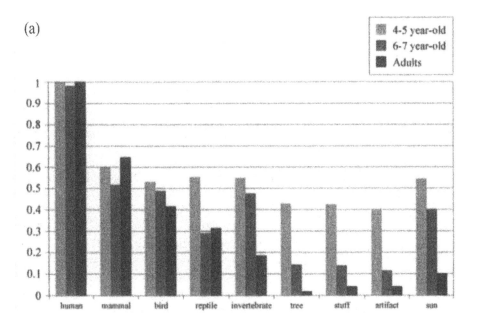

FIG. 4.1.   (Continued)

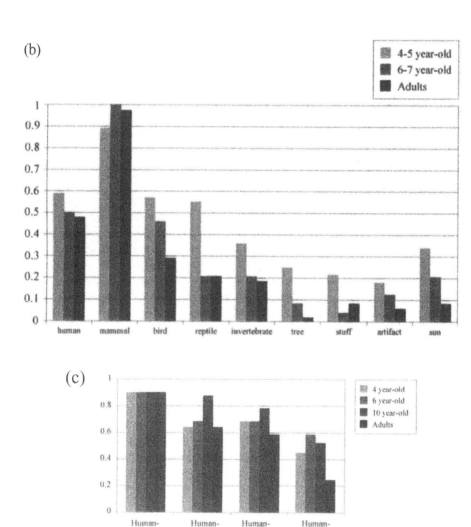

(b)

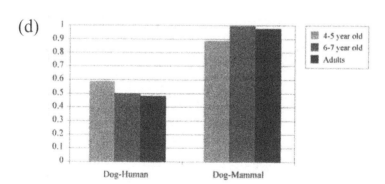

(c)

(d)

FIG. 4.1. (a) Maya projections from human. (b) Maya projections from dog. (c) U.S. projections from human (after Carey, 1985). (d) U.S. projections from dog (after Carey, 1985).

dren from the urban Boston area and from rural Wisconsin. They found that the young urban children generalized in a broad, undifferentiated manner, and the only clear trend was greater generalization from a human base to a human target than to other targets. Older urban children generalized in terms of biological affinity, but showed a strong asymmetry in reasoning between humans and other animals. Overall, these data from urban children provide a rough replication of Carey's original results.

Studies with rural children revealed a different pattern. The youngest children showed the mature pattern of generalizing in terms of biological affinity. Interestingly, both they and older rural children showed asymmetries in reasoning between humans and animals and often justified a failure to extend a property from an animal to humans on the grounds that "people are not animals." This observation implies that the asymmetry does not derive from humans being conceptualized as the "prototypic" animal. Instead, seeing humans as animals may be something of a developmental achievement, as Johnson, Mervis, and Boster (1992) suggested.

Young Yukatek Maya children and young rural American children do not show commitment to an anthropocentric understanding of the living world. This suggests that folk psychology is not a necessary or universal source for folk biology. Carey's results may derive from the fact that humans are the only animal that urban children know much about and so they generalize from them. Consistent with this view, Inagaki (1990) presented evidence that experience influences children's biological reasoning (cf. Inagaki & Hatano, 1991). She found that kindergartners who raised goldfish were more likely than their counterparts who did not raise goldfish to reason about a novel aquatic animal (a frog) by analogy to goldfish rather than by analogy to humans.

CHILDHOOD CONCEPTIONS OF SPECIES
ESSENCES: EXPERIMENT 2

Young individuals have the potential to develop certain adult characteristics before those characteristics appear. The origins of these characteristics can be explained in two broadly different ways: nature and nurture. Some characteristics seem likely to develop from birth because they are essential to the species to which the individual belongs, such as a squirrel's ability to jump from tree to tree and hide acorns. Other characteristics are determined by the environment in which the individual is reared, such as a squirrel's fear or lack of fear of human beings.

Gelman and Wellman (1991) argued that young children predict category-typical characteristics of individual animals based on the innate potential of the animal (i.e., the species of its birth parent), rather than the environment in which it was raised (i.e., the species of its adoptive parent). Using an adoption study, they showed that 4-year-old children judge that a baby cow raised by pigs will have the category-typical characteristics of cows (*moos, straight tail*) rather than pigs (*oinks, curly tail*). They interpret the results as showing that preschoolers believe that the innate potential or essence of species determines how an individual will develop, even in contrary environments.

This study has been criticized for two reasons. First, before the children in the study predicted the adult properties of the adopted baby, they were shown a drawing of the baby animal and told its species identity. Because the experimenters told the child that the baby and mother were of the same species, it does not address the question of how the children identify to which species the baby belongs in the first place (Johnson & Solomon, 1997).

Second, the study explored only known facts about species and their associated properties. It did not examine whether children use the concept of species essence or biological parentage as an inferential framework for interpreting and explaining hitherto unknown facts. It may be that a child has learned from experience, and, as a matter of fact, that a calf is a cow because it was born to a cow. Still, the child may not know that being a member of a certain species *causes* a cow to *be* a cow (Carey, 1996).

Hickling and Gelman (1995) addressed this criticism in a later experiment; our focus has been on evaluating the generality of their results. Our studies are designed to test the extent to which children's assumptions about innate species potential govern projection of both known and unknown properties, and to avoid the problems noted earlier. Our research team has studied children and adults in rural Wisconsin, Brazil, and Mexico. Here we concentrate on our results in Mexico and Brazil (for details, see Atran et al., 2001), but our findings are quite general.

Participants in Mexico were some 100 Yukatek Maya-speaking children and adults. All testing was done in Yukatek Maya. In a forced-choice task, children were asked whether an adult animal adopted at birth would resemble its adoptive parent (e.g., cow) or birth parent (e.g., pig) on four different individual traits: known behaviors (e.g., *moo/oink*), known physical features (e.g., *straight/curly tail*), unknown behaviors (e.g., *looks for chachalacas/looks for pigeons*), and unknown physical features (e.g., *heart gets flatter/rounder when it is sleeping*). Known traits were context-free, category-typical features that the children readily associated with species, whereas unknown traits were chosen to minimize any possibility of factual or prelearned associations of traits with categories. Each unknown trait within a set was attributed to the birth parent for half the participants and to the adoptive parent for the other half. This ensured that projection patterns of the unknown traits were not based on prior associations.

The stories were accompanied by sketches of each parent. Sketches were designed to unambiguously represent a particular species of animal with minimum detail. In addition, sketches of known physical features (e.g., a sketch of a curly or straight tail), unknown physical features (e.g., flat vs. round heart), and relevant aspects of unknown behavioral contexts (e.g., closed vs. open eyes, mahogany vs. cedar tree) were shown to participants. The sketches did not indicate the species to which the traits belonged. Subjects chose birth or adoptive parent species in response to the probes by pointing to the relevant parent sketch.

The story was followed by two comprehension controls: a birth control (*Who gave birth to the baby? Go ahead and point out the drawing of who gave birth to the baby*) and a nurture control (*Who did the baby grow up with?*). Children were then presented with the four experimental probes. For example: *The cow mooed and the pig oinked. When the baby is all grown up will it moo like a cow or oink like a pig?* For each set, the four probes (counterbalanced in order across children) were followed by a bias control in which the participant was asked: *When the baby was growing up did it eat with animals that looked like X or animals that looked like Y?*

Overall, the results show a systematic and robust preference for attributions from the birth parent (Table 4.1a). This preference was observed for all age groups and for known and unknown behavior and physical properties. The trend is somewhat stronger in older children and adults and slightly stronger for known than unknown properties. Means for all probes were significantly different from chance. The low mean on the bias control probe for all groups indicates that the method of the current experiment did not bias participant responses toward the birth parent.

A similar study with over 100 urban Brazilian children and adults revealed almost the same pattern of results (Sousa, Atran, & Medin, 2002). One minor difference was that several of the 6- to 7-year-old Brazilian children based their responding on an explicit analogy with the Disney movie, *Tarzan*, which was widely shown at the time of the study (Table 4.1b). They evinced a marginally weaker birth bias than did 4- to 5-year-olds, consistent with Tarzan's mixed human/ape characteristics.

Summary

Results of these studies indicate that Yukatek Maya children and adults, as well as urban Brazilian children and adults, reliably assume that members of a species share an innate causal potential that largely determines category-typical behavioral and physical properties even in conflicting environments. Projection of properties to the birth parent in the face of uncertainty and novelty implies that even young Maya and Bra-

TABLE 4.1a
Percent Birth Parent Choice for Each Probe Type
for Each Age Group (Rural Maya)

Group	Known		Unknown		Bias Control (Food)
	Behavior	Physical Feature	Behavior	Physical Feature	
4- to 5-year-olds	0.74**	0.68*	0.69**	0.68*	0.06***
6- to 7-year-olds	0.96***	0.97***	0.82***	0.83***	0.01***
Adults	1.00***	0.96***	0.90***	0.93***	0.00***

*$p < .05$. **$p < .01$. ***$p < .001$.

TABLE 4.1b
Percent Birth Parent Choice for Each Probe Type
for Each Age Group (Urban Brazil)

Group	Known		Unknown		Bias Control (Play)
	Behavior	Physical Feature	Behavior	Physical Feature	
4- to 5-year-olds	0.90***	0.92***	0.78***	0.85***	0.06***
6- to 7-year-olds	0.77***	0.85***	0.75***	0.79***	0.00***
Adults	1.00***	1.00***	0.83***	0.87***	0.00***

*$p < .05$. **$p < .01$. ***$p < .001$.

zilian children use the notion of underlying essence as an inferential framework for understanding the nature of biological species. These findings, together with Gelman and Wellman's (1991) earlier results for urban American children, suggest that such an essentialist bias in children is universal. Bloch, Solomon, and Carey (2001) reported an apparent counterexample among (older) Zafimaniry children, but they did not counterbalance properties across birth and adoptive parents (and birth and adoptive parents differed markedly in social status), so it is difficult to assess their findings.

ESSENCE (GENERIC SPECIES) VERSUS APPEARANCE (BASIC LEVELS) IN FOLK BIOLOGY: EXPERIMENT 3

In a justly celebrated set of experiments, Rosch and her colleagues set out to test the validity of the notion of a psychologically preferred taxonomic level (Rosch, Mervis, Grey, Johnson, & Boyes-Braem, 1976). Using a broad array of converging measures, they found that there is indeed a basic level

in category hierarchies of "naturally occurring objects," such as "taxonomies" of artifacts as well as living kinds. For artifact and living kind hierarchies, the basic level is where: (a) many common features are listed for
categories, (b) consistent motor programs are used for the interaction with
or manipulation of category exemplars, (c) category members have similar enough shapes so that it is possible to recognize an average shape for
objects of the category, and (d) the category name is the first name to come
to mind in the presence of an object (e.g., "table" vs. "furniture" or
"kitchen table").

There is a problem, however. The basic level that Rosch, Mervis, Grey,
Johnson, and Boyes-Braem (1976) hypothesized for artifacts was con-
firmed (e.g., *hammer, guitar*). Yet the hypothesized basic level for living
kinds (e.g., *maple, trout*), which Rosch initially assumed would accord
with the generic-species level, was not. For example, instead of *maple* and
trout, Rosch et al. found that *tree* and *fish* operated as basic-level categories
for American college students. Thus, Rosch's basic level for living kinds
generally corresponds to the life-form level, which is superordinate to the
generic-species level (see Zubin & Köpcke, 1986, for supporting evidence
involving the German language). In short, the level assumed to be psychologically salient based on ethnobiological studies, generic species, did not
prove to be privileged for Berkeley undergraduates. How can one reconcile these differences?

To explore the apparent discrepancy between preferred taxonomic levels in small-scale and industrialized societies, and the cognitive nature of
ethnobiological ranks in general, we used inductive inference. Inference
allows us to test for a psychologically preferred rank that maximizes the
strength of any potential induction about biologically relevant information, and whether this preferred rank is the same across cultures. If a preferred level carries the most information about the world, then categories
at that level should favor a wide range of inferences about what is common among members (for detailed findings under a variety of lexical and
property-projection conditions, see Atran, Estin, Coley, & Medin, 1997;
Coley, Medin, & Atran, 1997).

The prediction is that inferences to a preferred category (e.g., *white oak*
to *oak*, *tabby* to *cat*) should be much stronger than inferences to a superordinate category (*oak* to *tree*, *cat* to *mammal*). Moreover, inferences to a
subordinate category (*swamp white oak* to *white oak*, *short-haired tabby* to
tabby) should not be much stronger than or different from inferences to a
preferred category. What follows is a summary of results from one representative set of experiments in two very diverse populations: Midwestern
American adults and lowland Maya elders. The Itza' are Maya Amerin-
dians living in the Petén rainforest region of Guatemala. Until recently,
men devoted their time to shifting agriculture, hunting, and silviculture,

whereas women concentrated on the myriad tasks of household maintenance. The Americans were college students, self-identified as people
raised in Michigan, and recruited through an advertisement in a local
newspaper.

Based on extensive fieldwork, we chose a set of Itza' folk-biological categories of the kingdom (K), life-form (L), generic-species (G), folk-specific
(S), and folk-varietal (V) ranks. We selected three plant life forms (*che'* =
tree, *ak'* = vine, *pok~che'* = herb/bush) and three animal life forms
(*b'a'al~che' kuxi'mal* = "walking animal"—i.e., mammal, *ch'iich'* = birds including bats, *käy* = fish). Three generic-species taxa were chosen from each
life form; each generic species had a subordinate folk specific, and each
folk specific had a salient varietal.

The properties chosen for animals were diseases related to the "heart"
(*puksik'al*), "blood" (*k'ik'el*), and "liver" (*tamen*). For plants, diseases related to the "roots" (*motz*), "sap" (*itz*), and "leaf" (*le'*). Properties were chosen according to Itza' beliefs about the essential, underlying aspects of
life's functioning. Properties used for inferences had the form, "is susceptible to a disease of the <root> called <X>." For each question, "X" was replaced with a phonologically appropriate nonsense name (e.g., "eta") to
minimize the task's repetitiveness.

All participants responded to a list of over 50 questions, in which they
were told that all members of a category had a property (the premise) and
were asked whether "all," "few," or "no" members of a higher level category (the conclusion category) also possessed that property. The premise
category was at one of four levels, either life-form (e.g., L = bird), generic-
species (e.g., G = vulture), folk-specific (e.g., S = black vulture), or varietal
(e.g., V = red-headed black vulture). The conclusion category was drawn
from a higher level category—either kingdom (e.g., K = animal), life-form
(L), generic-species (G), or folk-specific (S). Thus, there were 10 possible
combinations of premise and conclusion category levels. For example, a
folk-specific to life-form (S→L) question might be, "If all black vultures are
susceptible to the blood disease called eta, are all other birds susceptible?" If
a participant answered "no," the follow-up question would be, "Are some
or a few other birds susceptible to disease eta, or no other birds at all?"

The corresponding life forms for the Americans were: mammal, bird,
fish, tree, bush, and flower (on flower as an American life form, see
Dougherty, 1979). The properties used in questions for the Michigan participants were "have protein X," "have enzyme Y," and "are susceptible
to disease Z." These were chosen to be internal, biologically based properties intrinsic to the kind in question, but abstract enough so that rather
than answering what amounted to factual questions participants would
be likely to make inductive inferences based on taxonomic category
membership.

Figure 4.2a summarizes the results from all Itza' informants for all life forms and diseases and shows the proportion of "all" responses (black), "few" responses (checkered), and "none" responses (white). For example, given a premise of folk-specific (S) rank (e.g., red squirrel) and a conclusion category of generic-species (G) rank (e.g., squirrel), 49% of responses indicated that "all" squirrels, not just "some" or "none," would possess a property that red squirrels have. Results were obtained by totaling the proportion of "all or virtually all" responses for each kind of question (e.g., the proportion of times respondents agreed that if red oaks had a property, all or virtually all oaks would have the same property). A higher

(a)

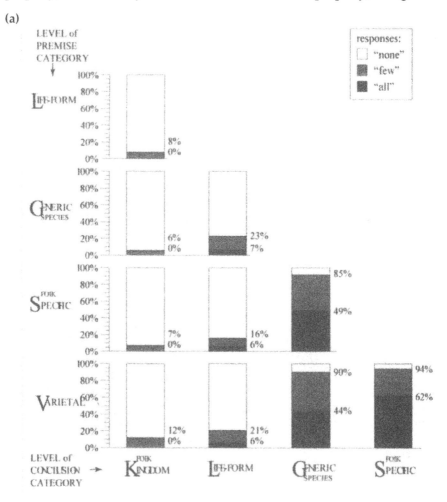

FIG. 4.2.   *(Continued)*

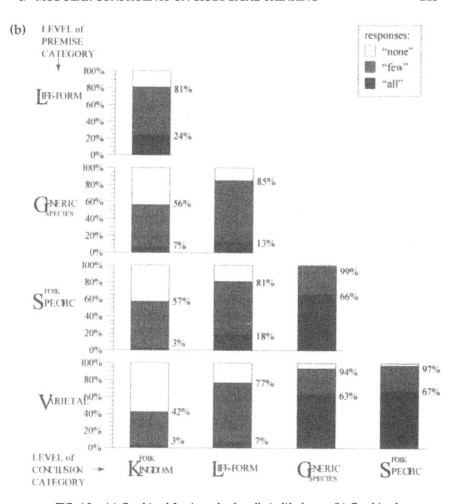

FIG. 4.2. (a) Combined Itza' results for all six life forms. (b) Combined Michigan results for all six life forms.

score represented more confidence in the strength of the inductive inference. Figure 4.2b summarizes results of Michigan response scores for all life forms and biological properties.

Following the main diagonals of Figs. 4.2a and 4.2b refers to changing the levels of both the premise and conclusion categories while keeping their relative level the same (with the conclusion one level higher than the premise). Induction patterns along the main diagonal indicate a single inductively preferred level. Examining inferences from a given rank to the adjacent higher order rank (i.e., V→S, S→G, G→L, L→K), we find a sharp

decline in strength of inferences to taxa ranked higher than generic species, whereas V→S and S→G inferences are nearly equal and similarly
strong. Notice that for "all" responses, the overall Itza' and Michigan patterns are nearly identical.

Moving horizontally within each graph corresponds to holding the
premise category constant and varying the level of the conclusion.[3] We
find the same pattern for "all" responses for both Itza' and Americans as
we did along the main diagonal. However, in the combined response
scores ("all" + "few"), there is evidence of increased inductive strength for
higher order taxa among Americans versus Itza'. Both Americans and
Itza' show the largest break between inferences to generic species versus
life forms, but only American subjects also show a consistent pattern of
rating inferences to life-form taxa higher than to taxa at the level of folk
kingdom: G→K versus G→L, S→K versus S→L, and V→K versus V→L.

These results indicate that both the ecologically inexperienced Americans and the ecologically experienced Itza' prefer taxa of the generic-
species rank in making biological inferences. These findings cannot be
explained by appeals either to cross-domain notions of perceptual "similarity" or to the structure of the world "out there," as most
ethnobiologists contend (Berlin, 1992; Boster, 1991; Hunn, 1976). If inferential potential were a simple function of perceptual similarity, then
Americans should prefer life forms for induction (in line with Rosch et
al.). Yet Americans prefer generic species as do Maya. Unlike Itza', however, Americans perceptually discriminate life forms more readily than
generic species (although one might expect that having less biodiversity
in the American environment allows each species to stand out more from
the rest). This lack of convergence between knowledge and expectation
on the part of the U.S. participants may represent devolution associated
with diminished contact with nature. If this view is correct, evidence that
biological experts treat the generic-species level as privileged on perceptual, feature-listing, and naming tasks (e.g., Johnson & Mervis, 1997;
Tanaka & Taylor, 1991) may represent the natural byproduct of experience with nature. In other words, performance of people in less industrialized contexts and U.S. experts may reflect "normal development" with
so-called "U.S. nonexperts" reflecting the cognitive consequences of diminished contact with nature. In this sense, it is all the more remarkable
that our nonexpert U.S. adults privileged the generic-species level on the

---

[3]Moving vertically within each graph corresponds to changing the premise while holding
the conclusion category constant. This allows us to test another domain-general model of
category-based reasoning: the Similarity-Coverage Model (Osherson et al., 1990). In this
model, the closer the premise category is to the conclusion category, the stronger induction
should be. Our results show only weak evidence for this general reasoning heuristic, which
fails to account for the various "jumps" in inductive strength that indicate absolute privilege.

induction task.[4] We see that as reflecting the robust presumption of essence focused on this level.

The findings suggest that root categorization and reasoning processes in folk biology owe to domain-specific conceptual presumptions and not exclusively to domain-general, similarity-based (e.g., perceptual) heuristics. To be sure, language may signal an expectation that little or poorly known generic species are more biologically informative than better known life forms for Americans (e.g., via common use of binomials, such as *oak/red oak*). Our experiments, however, still show reliable results in the absence of clear linguistic cues (e.g., *oak/white oak/swamp white oak* vs. *dog /poodle/toy poodle*).

CULTURAL AND EXPERTISE EFFECTS
IN TAXONOMIC INFERENCE

An important function of taxonomic classification is enabling generalizations between categories. Osherson, Smith, Wilkie, López, and Shafir (1990) identified a set of phenomena that characterize category-based inferences in adults, and they formalized a model that predicts the strength of those inferences. Consider Argument 1:

(1) Hyenas have an ileal vein.
   Cows have an ileal vein.
   Wolves have an ileal vein.

This argument is strong to the extent that belief in the premises leads to belief in the conclusion. There are two components to Osherson, Smith, Wilkie, López, and Shafir's (1990) similarity-coverage model (SCM). Participants may infer that wolves have an ileal vein because they are similar to hyenas, or they may infer it because they have inferred that all mammals share the property given that hyenas and cows do. Thus, the first component of the model, *similarity*, calculates the maximum similarity of the premise categories to the conclusion category; the greater this similarity, the stronger the argument. In this example, hyenas are more similar to wolves than cows are, hence similarity is calculated for hyenas. The second component—*coverage*—calculates the average maximum similarity of premise categories to members of the "inclusive category"—the lowest category that includes both premise and conclusion categories. For Argument 1, the in-

---

[4]In nature walks, undergraduates at Northwestern University and the University of Michigan identify the overwhelming majority of trees and birds they encounter as simply "tree" or "bird"—that is, at the life-form level. In contrast, Itza' Maya identify the overwhelming majority of trees and birds at the generic-species level (cf. Bailenson et al., 2002; Coley et al., 1999).

clusive category is presumably *mammal*. In our research, the inclusive category is simply the conclusion category. The greater the coverage of the inclusive category by the premise categories, the stronger the argument.

For present purposes, we focus on the phenomenon of diversity. Diversity is a measure of category coverage. The diversity phenomenon predicts that an argument will be inductively strong to the degree that categories mentioned in its premises are similar to different instances of the conclusion category. For example, consider Arguments 2a and 2b:

(2a) Jaguars have protein Y.
     Leopards have protein Y.
     All mammals have protein Y.
(2b) Jaguars have protein Y.
     Mice have protein Y.
     All mammals have protein Y.

The SCM predicts that the categories mentioned in the premise of Argument 2b provide greater *coverage* of the conclusion category *mammal* (i.e., are more similar to more mammals) than the categories mentioned in the premises of Argument 2a, thus making Argument 2b the stronger argument. Indeed most subjects agree that Argument 2b is stronger than Argument 2a (Osherson et al., 1990). Diversity predicts that an argument with more diverse premises will be evaluated as stronger than an argument with more similar premises.

López, Atran, Coley, Medin, and Smith (1997) used the similarity-coverage model to investigate inductive reasoning about mammals among U.S. college students and Itza' Maya elders. They found that the groups differed markedly in the extent of their use of diversity. U.S. participants demonstrated powerful diversity effects, whereas the Itza' were reliably below chance in the selection of arguments with more diverse premises. Itza' reasoned on the basis of specific knowledge of the species in question, which was often ecological in nature.

Consider the following scenario: Suppose we know that River Birch and Paper Birch trees can get some new disease A and that White Pine and Weeping Willow can get some new disease B. Which disease is more likely to be able to affect all kinds of trees? According to the "diversity principle" that underlies taxonomic sampling and inference in science, one would choose disease B on the grounds that White Pines and Weeping Willows are more different (diverse) than River Birch and Paper Birch. Undergraduates overwhelmingly pick the argument with the more diverse premises as stronger. Taxonomists show diversity, but not nearly to the extent of undergraduates. Landscapers show even less diversity, whereas parks maintenance workers show *negative* diversity (Proffitt,

Medin, & Coley, 2000). Justifications for judgments reveal these tree experts engaging in causal/ecological reasoning. For instance, in the earlier example, 13 of 14 parks maintenance personnel selected the disease associated with birches. Their reasoning was as follows: "Birches are found all over the place and incredibly susceptible to disease so that if one of them gets it, they all will get it. Then there will be many opportunities for the disease to spread."

American birdwatchers and Itza' Maya also show causal/ecological reasoning and relatively little diversity-based responding (Bailenson, Shum, Atran, Medin, & Coley, 2002). By contrast, American undergraduates, who are relative novices with respect to the birder expertise of the other two groups, again appear to be the "odd group out." Novices relied very heavily on familiarity or typicality as the basis of their choices on both the typicality and diversity trials (Table 4.2). Neither the Itza' nor the U.S. experts *ever* gave typicality as a justification for either type of probe. Instead, they used knowledge about birds that the novices did not possess. For example, both the Itza' and U.S. experts frequently mentioned the geographical range of birds, an explanation that the novices rarely produced. This is a truly striking qualitative difference.

Work in progress in Wisconsin shows a similar focus on causal and ecological relations among freshwater fishermen (Medin, Ross, Atran, Burnett, & Blok, 2002). Only when there is clear disregard for ecological context (from relative ignorance in the case of college students, from a scientific tradition of decontextualized comparisons in the case of taxonomists) do taxonomic inductions follow the diversity principle. In short, although people may use folk taxonomies in reasoning, there are often more compelling

TABLE 4.2
Summary of Reliable Main Effects Found for Typicality
and Diversity Trial Justifications in Bird Study

Justification Category	Typicality Trials		Diversity Trials	
	Subject Type	Stimulus Set	Subject Type	Stimulus Set
Typicality	N > E, I	US > TIK	N > E, I	n.s.
Behavioral	I > N, E	n.s.	I > N, E	n.s.
Ecological	I > N, E	n.s.	I > N, E	n.s.
Geographical range	E, I > N	n.s.	E, I > N	n.s.
Number	N > E, I	n.s.	n.s.	n.s.
Evolutionary age	n.s.	n.s.	n.s.	n.s.
Diversity	—	—	N > I	n.s.

Note. Subject groups are represented by U.S. nonexperts (N), U.S. experts (E), and Itza' (I). Subject type effects are listed in the first subcolumn. Stimulus set effects are listed in the second subcolumn and indicate a difference between justifications based on whether the American (US) or Itza' (TIK) stimulus set was used.

strategies linked to ecological relations. Only novices appear to resort to abstract, similarity-based reasoning strategies on a consistent basis.

Only U.S. novices (i.e., undergraduates) show patterns of judgment consistent with current models of category-based taxonomic inference and universal claims about similarity-based notions of diversity and typicality in natural categorization and reasoning. This has troubling implications given that U.S. undergraduates comprise the one subject pool in the literature that is consistently and overwhelmingly relied on for making psychological generalizations—not only with respect to folk biology, but also virtually every aspect of human cognition. It is hard to imagine a more culturally limited subject pool as a basis for generalization to humankind as a whole.

Take the case of typicality. In our reasoning studies, typicality strategies are also reliably used only by U.S. nonexperts (undergraduates). Consequently, models invoking such principles may apply solely to situations where novices are reasoning about stimuli with which they have limited knowledge. Those models tend to support the view that similarity-based structures (e.g., central tendency, family resemblance) are the primary predictors for typicality in taxonomic categories, in general, and folk-biological categories, in particular (Barsalou, 1985; Rosch & Mervis, 1975). In this view, the mind's similarity judgments about typicality and the world's correlational structure are closely linked: Typical members of categories capture the correlational structure of identifiable features in the world better than do atypical members. This capacity to recognize correlated similarity structures in the world, such as other species types, seems to be a built-in part of human and well as nonhuman species (Brown & Boysen, 2000; Cerella, 1979; Herrnstein, 1984; Lorenz, 1966; cf. Smith & Medin, 1981). From these considerations, Boster (1988) predicted a biological, cognitive and cultural universal: "Passerines appear to be densely and continuously spread through the bird similarity space [. . .] non-passerines are more sparsely and discontinuously distributed, leading to the choice of passerines as both more typical and more difficult to categorize than non-passerines" (p. 258). But for Itza' Maya, passerines are not very typical at all.

Work on direct typicality judgments among Itza' shows that inductively useful notions of typicality may be driven more by notions of idealness than central tendency (Atran, 1999). In each case for which we have direct Itza' ratings, the truest or most representative living kind categories are large, perceptually striking, culturally important, and ecologically prominent. The dimensions of perceptual, ecological, and cultural salience all appear necessary to a determination of typicality, but none alone appears to be sufficient. For example, the three most highly rated mammals are the jaguar (also called "The Lord of the Forest"), the mountain lion (the jaguar's principal rival), and the tapir (also called "The Beast of

All Seven Edible Kinds of Flesh"). The three most highly related snakes are the large and deadly fer-de-lance (*Bothrops asper*, also called "The True Snake") and its companions, the large and venomous tropical rattlesnake (*Crotalus durissus*) and the smaller but deadly coral (*Micrurus* sp.). The three most representative birds are all large, morphologically striking, and highly edible Galliformes (wild fowl): ocellated turkey, crested guan, and great curassow.

Consistent with these results, Lynch, Coley, and Medin (2000) found that tree experts based their typicality judgments on ideals (e.g., height, absence of undesirable characteristics), and that central tendency was uncorrelated with judgments. They found no effects of type of expertise. The fact that U.S. experts and Itza' both show effects of ideals undermines concerns about the wording of the typicality instructions in Itza' Maya somehow conveying a different notion of typicality. Lynch et al. used instructions that followed verbatim those by Rosch and Mervis (1975) in their original studies showing central-tendency-based typicality effects.[5] Bailenson et al. (2002) also found that typicality judgment was correlated with central tendency only among novices.

No doubt similarity structures and similarity-based typicality and diversity are important determinants in natural categorization and reasoning. Our findings suggest that, at least for American undergraduates, these may be dominant factors. But for our relative experts (U.S. experts and Itza'), who have substantial knowledge, goals, and activities about the items they classify and reason with, information other than that derived from perceptual clustering and similarity judgment is relevant to understanding natural biodiversity. Behavior and ecology, for example, appear to be crucial to the deeper and broader understanding of nature that scientists and birdwatchers seek. For example, Bailenson et al. (2002) found that Itza' Maya rely less on passerines than do U.S. informants on reasoning tasks. American subjects tended to pick small songbirds as generalizing to the population of all birds, whereas Itza' preferred larger, more perceptually striking birds. Given the prominent role of the larger game birds in the behavioral ecology of Mayaland, and the more interactive goals of Itza' in monitoring their ecology, the information provided by their ideal birds would be more relevant to environmental understanding and management than information provided by songbirds. Itza' preferentially monitor those species in their ecosystem (e.g., game birds as opposed to passerines) that provide the most relevant information about the interaction of human needs with the needs of the forest. For Americans,

---

[5]Barsalou (1985) argued that idealness rather than central tendency predicts typicality in goal-derived categories (e.g., foods not to eat on a diet, things to take from home during a fire, camping equipment), although central tendency still supposedly predicts typicality in "taxonomic" categories (furniture, vehicles), including folk-biological categories (birds).

whose interest in, and interaction with, behavioral ecology is of a much reduced and different order (game birds are not considered palpably crucial
to survival of the human habitat), correlated perceptual information may
be more relevant by default.

Such concerns may also be critical to the way the Maya and perhaps
other peoples in small scale manage to live and survive with nature. If so,
it is practically impossible to isolate folk-ecological orientation from other
aspects of cultural knowledge. Thus, previous studies indicate that Itza'
share with other cultural groups (e.g., Spanish-speaking Ladino immigrants, highland Q'eqchi' Maya immigrants) an identical habitat and a
similar taxonomic understanding of its flora and fauna. Nevertheless,
these different cultural groups cognitively model species relationships
(including humans) and socially interact with the same local ecology in
fundamentally different ways (Atran et al., 1999, 2002). Such findings
strongly simply that culture-specific cognitions and practices—and not
just biotic, demographic, or other material features of the environment—
reliably determine population differences in ecological orientation and
folk-biological understanding.

Most compellingly, we found patterns of expertise in natural categorization and reasoning that selectively transcend cultural boundaries: Itza'
Maya and U.S. experts employ causal and ecological reasoning more than
do U.S. novices, and the Maya and U.S. experts are better at discriminating
one another's natural environments than the novices are at discriminating
their own. One implication is that rich interaction with the environment
and relative expertise is the evolutionarily determined default condition for
the operation of folk biology. Trying to understand the structure of folk biology by focusing exclusively on relatively unknowledgeable college students may be akin to an attempt to understand the structure of language by
concentrating entirely on feral children.

THE GENERAL-PURPOSE NATURE
OF FOLK-BIOLOGICAL TAXONOMY

These experimental results in two very different cultures—an industrial
Western society and a small-scale tropical forest society—indicate that people across cultures organize their local flora and flora in similarly structured
taxonomies. Yet they may reason from their taxonomies in systematically
different ways. With their ranked taxonomic structures and essentialist understanding of species, it would seem that no great cognitive effort is additionally required for the Itza' or U.S. experts to recursively essentialize the
higher ranks as well, adopt the diversity principle, and thereby avail themselves of the full inductive power that ranked taxonomies provide. But con-

trary to earlier assumptions (Atran, 1990), our studies show this is not the case. Itza' and probably other traditional folk do not essentialize ranks: They do not establish causal laws at the intermediate or life-form levels, and they do not presume that higher order taxa share the kind of unseen causal unity that their constituent generic species do.

There seems, then, to be a sense to Itza' "failure" in turning their folk taxonomies into one of the most powerful inductive tools that humans may come to possess. To adopt this tool, Itza' would have to suspend their primary concern with ecological and morphobehavioral relationships in favor of deeper, hidden properties of greater inductive potential. But the cognitive cost would probably outweigh the benefit (Sperber & Wilson, 1996). For this potential, which science strives to realize, is to a significant extent irrelevant, or only indirectly relevant, to local ecological concerns. The only U.S. experts to consistently show diversity effects are those with a great deal of training in scientific taxonomy. For expertise organized around more practical goals, it is seldom necessary to go above the level of family.

Scientists use diversity-based reasoning to generate hypotheses about global distributions of biological properties so that theory-driven predictions can be tested against experience and the taxonomic order subsequently restructured when prediction fails. For scientific systematics, the goal is to maximize inductive potential regardless of human interest. The motivating idea is to understand nature as it is "in itself" independently of the human observer (as far as possible). For Itza', people from other small-scale societies and practical experts, folk-biological taxonomy works to maximize inductive potential relative to human interests. Here, folk-biological taxonomy provides a well-structured but adaptable framework. It allows people to explore the causal relevance to them—including the ecological relevance—of the natural world. Maximizing the human relevance of the local biological world—its categories and generalizable properties—does not mean assigning predefined purposes or functional signatures to it. Instead, it implies providing a sound conceptual infrastructure for the widest range of human adaptation to local cultural and environmental conditions.

For scientific systematics, folk biology may represent a ladder to be discarded after it has been climbed. But for an increasingly urbanized and formally educated people, who are often unwittingly ruinous of the environment, no amount of cosmically valid scientific reasoning skill may be able to compensate the local loss of ecological awareness on which human survival may ultimately depend. Because folk in industrialized societies often lack aspects of folk-biological knowledge as well as scientific theory, reliance on diversity-based induction and other scientific strategies at the expense of ecologically based folk-biological strategies may discourage, rather than encourage, better understanding of the world.

SCIENCE AND COMMON SENSE

Much of the history of systematics has involved attempts to adapt locally relevant principles of folk biology to a more global setting, such as the taxonomic embedding of biodiversity, the primacy of species, and the teleo-essentialist causality that makes sense of taxonomic diversity and the life functions of species. This process has been far from uniform (e.g., initial rejection of plant but not animal life forms, recurrent but invariably failed attempts to define essential characters for species and other taxa, intermittent attempts to reduce teleological processes to mechanics, etc.; Atran, 1990).

Historical continuity between universal aspects of biological common sense and the science of biology should not be confounded with epistemic continuity or use of folk knowledge as a learning heuristic for scientific knowledge. Scientists have made fundamental ontological shifts away from folk understanding in the construal of species, taxonomy, and underlying causality. For example, biological science today rejects fixed taxonomic ranks, the primary and essential nature of species, teleological causes for the sake of species' existence, and phenomenal evidence for the existence of taxa (e.g., trees do not constitute a scientifically valid superordinate plant group, but bacteria almost assuredly should).

Nevertheless, from the vantage point of our own evolutionary history, it may be more important that our ordinary concepts be adaptive than true. Relative to ordinary human perceptions and awareness, evolutionary and molecular biology's concerns with vastly extended and minute dimensions of time and space have only marginal value. The ontological shift required by science may be so counterintuitive and irrelevant to everyday life as to render inappropriate and maladaptive uses of scientific knowledge in dealing with ordinary concerns. Science cannot wholly subsume or easily subvert folk-biological knowledge.

CONCLUSION: CULTURAL EMERGENCE
IN AN EVOLUTIONARY LANDSCAPE

We have provided evidence for structural and functional autonomy of folk biology in human cognition. First, our cross-cultural experiments on children's inductions from human to animals and vice versa indicated that humans are not the prototype that organizes the domain of animals. Second, young children from diverse cultures, who were tested on inheritance and adoption tasks, showed evidence for understanding the concept of underlying biological essence as determining the innate potential of species. Together with previous research by other investigators, the data suggest that folk biology does not come from folk psychology. Third, induction experiments regarding the basic level indicated that folk-biological taxonomies are universally anchored on the generic-species level, where inductive potential is greatest. Fourth, our category-based induction experiments showed that people from diverse societies build topologically similar biological taxonomies that guide inferences about the distribution of biological and ecological properties. Just how the taxonomies are used may vary across groups. For undergraduates, the taxonomy is a stand-in for ideas about the likely distribution of biologically related properties (e.g., diseases). For the Itza' (and other knowledgeable groups), the taxonomy constrains the likely operational range of ecological agents and causes.

These universal tendencies are most salient outside the center of industrialized societies, but nonetheless discernable everywhere. Our observations provide a cautionary tale: At least in the case of folk biology, standard populations may be nonstandard and vice versa. For example, it was only when we confronted the custom of taking undergraduates as the base or standard that we began to see their reasoning strategies as a response to a lack of relevant domain knowledge.

Different cognitive scientists have offered distinctly different notions of modules, so we will take a few paragraphs to provide a definition and characterization of modules. We consider that there are roughly two classes of evolved cognitive modules: perceptual and conceptual. A *perceptual module* has automatic and exclusive access to a specific range of sensory inputs. It has its own proprietary database and may not draw on information produced by other conceptual modules or processes. A perceptual module is usually associated with fairly fixed neural architecture and fast processing that is not accessible to conscious awareness. Examples may be modules for facial recognition, color perception, identification of object boundaries, and morpho-syntax (Fodor, 1983).

A *conceptual module* works on a privileged, rather than a strictly proprietary, database that is provided by other parts of the nervous system (e.g., sensory receptors or other modules) and that pertains to some specific cognitive domain (Atran, 1990).[6] Examples include folk mechanics, folk

---

[6]Virtually any game (e.g., chess) or routine activity (e.g., car driving) relies on a restricted database that gives it privileged access to a certain range of input. This would seem to trivialize the notion of modularity and rob it of any descriptive or explanatory force. Indeed, according to Fodor (2000), the best case that can be made for the computational theory of mind (i.e., the view that all conceptual processes are Turing-like computations over syntactic-like representational structures) is in terms of conceptual modularity. However, because conceptual modularity "is pretty clearly mistaken," a computational theory of mind would not tell us very much about conceptual categorization and reasoning. For Sperber (2001), Fodor's pessimism is unwarranted because it ignores the fact that privileged access to an input set *depends on the competition for mental resources.* Evolutionary task demands competitively favor certain naturally selected modular structures for processing certain types of input (*ceteris paribus*), although contingent circumstances can occasionally favor other ways of functionally processing the same inputs.

biology, and folk psychology. The argument for conceptual modules involves converging evidence from a number of venues: functional design (analogy), ethology (homology), universality, precocity of acquisition, independence from perceptual experience (poverty of stimulus), resistance to inhibition (hyperactivity), and cultural transmission. None of these criteria may be necessary, but the presence of all or some is compelling, if not conclusive (Atran, 2001). Consider these criteria of evidence for modularity in the case of folk biology:[7]

Functional Design.   Natural selection may account for the appearance of complexly well-structured biological traits that are designed to perform important functional tasks of adaptive benefit to organisms. In general, naturally selected adaptations are structures functionally "perfected for any given habit" (Darwin, 1883 [1872], p. 140), having "very much the appearance of design by an intelligent designer [. . .] on which the wellbeing and very existence of the organism depends" (Wallace, 1901 [1889], p. 138). The universal appreciation of generic species may be one such functional evolutionary adaptation. Moreover, the pigeonholing of generic species into a hierarchy of mutually exclusive taxa arguably allows the incorporation of indefinitely many species and biological properties into an inductively coherent system that can be extended to any habitat whatsoever, thus facilitating adaptation to any habitat (a hallmark of *Homo sapiens*). Hence,

> From the most remote period in the history of the world organic beings have been found to resemble each other in descending degrees, so that they can be classed into groups under groups. This classification is not arbitrary like the grouping of stars in constellations. (Darwin, 1859, p. 431)

Ethology.   One hallmark of adaptation is a phylogenetic history that extends beyond the species in which the adaptation is perfected. For example, ducklings crouching in the presence of hawks, but not other kinds of birds, suggests dedicated mechanisms for something like species recognition. But there is no a priori reason for the mind to always focus on categorizing and relating species *qua* species unless doing so served some adaptive function. For example, it makes little sense to know the individual differences between lions that can eat you and bananas you can eat,

---

[7]Griffiths (2002) argued that because the items on any such symptomatic list do not necessarily co-occur in any given case, and cannot unequivocally demonstrate innateness, notions of innateness are inherently confused and should be discarded. The same could be said against modularity. But the list represents only an evidential claim, not a causal claim about innateness or modularity. It provides a family of heuristics, rather than a causal diagnosis.

but a lot of sense to know that *lions* can eat you and *bananas* you can eat (cf. Eldredge, 1986).

Universality. Ever since the pioneering work of Berlin and his colleagues, evidence from ethnobiology and experimental psychology has been accumulating that all human societies have similar folk-biological structures (Atran, 1990, 1999; Berlin, 1992; Berlin et al., 1973; Brown, 1984; Hays, 1983; Hunn, 1977). These striking cross-cultural similarities suggest that a small number of organizing principles universally define folk-biological systems.

Ease of Acquisition. Acquisition studies indicate a precocious emergence of essentialist folk-biological principles in early childhood that are not applied to other domains (Atran et al., 2001; Gelman & Wellman, 1991; Hatano & Inagaki, 1999; Keil, 1995).

Independence From Perceptual Experience. Experiments on inferential processing show that humans do not make biological inductions primarily on the basis of perceptual experience or any general similarity-based metric, but on the basis of imperceptible causal expectations of a peculiar, essentialist nature (Atran et al., 1997; Coley et al., 1997).

Inhibition and Hyperactivity. One characteristic of an evolved cognitive disposition is evident difficulty in inhibiting its operation (Hauser, 2000). Consider beliefs in biological essences. Such beliefs greatly help people explore the world by prodding them to look for regularities and to seek explanations of variation in terms of underlying patterns. This strategy may help bring order to ordinary circumstances, including those relevant to human survival. But in other circumstances, such as wanting to know what is correct or true for the cosmos at large, such intuitively ingrained concepts and beliefs may hinder more than help.

Because intuitive notions come to us so naturally they may be difficult to unlearn and transcend. Even students and philosophers of biology often find it difficult to abandon commonsense notions of species as classes, essences or natural kinds in favor of the concept of species as a logical individual—a genealogical branch whose endpoints are somewhat arbitrarily defined in the phyletic tree and whose status does not differ in principle from that of other smaller (variety) and larger (genus) branches. Similarly, racism—the projection of biological essences onto social groups—seems to be a cognitively facile and culturally-universal tendency (Hirschfeld, 1996). Although science teaches that race is biologically incoherent, racial or ethnic essentialism is as notoriously difficult to suppress as it is easy to incite (Gil-White, 2001).

Cultural Transmission. Human cultures favor a rapid selection and stable distribution of those ideas that: (a) readily help to solve relevant and recurrent environmental problems, (b) are easily memorized and processed by the human brain, and (c) facilitate the retention and understanding of ideas that are more variable (e.g., religion) or difficult to learn (e.g., science) but contingently useful or important. Folk-biological taxonomy readily aids humans to orient themselves and survive in the natural world. Folk-biological taxonomy serves as a principled basis for transmission and acquisition of more variable and extended forms of cultural knowledge, such as certain forms of religious and scientific belief (Atran, 1990, 2002).

In summary, the sort of cultural information that is most susceptible to modular processing is the sort of information most readily acquired by children, most easily transmitted from individual to individual, most apt to survive within a culture over time, and most likely to recur independently in different cultures and at different times. Critically, it is also the most disposed to cultural variation and elaboration. It makes cultural variation comprehensible. This evolutionarily constrained learning landscape can be viewed from two complementary perspectives. On the one hand, it is forgiving enough to allow strikingly different folk-ecological cognitions and behaviors among distinct cultural groups living in the same habitat. On the other hand, it also provides sufficient structure to allow us to understand these self-same contrasts as variations on a pan-human theme of interactions between people and generic species.

Folk biology plays a special role in cultural evolution in general, and particularly in the development of totemic tribal religions and Western biological science. To say an evolved mental structure is "innate" is not to say that every important aspect of its phenotypic expression is "genetically determined." The particular organisms observed, actual exemplars targeted, and specific inferences made can vary significantly from person to person. Much as mountain rain will converge to the same mountain-valley river basin no matter where the rain falls, so each person's knowledge will converge on the same cognitive "drainage basin" (Sperber, 1996; Waddington, 1959). This is because: (a) inputs naturally cluster in causally redundant ways inasmuch as that is the way the world is (e.g., where there are wings there are beaks or bills, where there are predators there are prey, where there are fruit-eating birds there are fruit-bearing trees, etc.), and (b) dedicated mental modules selectively target these inputs for processing by domain-specific inferential structures (e.g., to produce natural taxonomies).

In this way, the mind is able to take fragmentary instances of a person's experience (relative to the richness and complexity of the whole data set) and spontaneously predict (project, generalize) the extension of those scattered cases to an indefinitely large class of intricately related cases (of larger relevance to our species and cultures). Thus, many different people, observing many different exemplars of dog under varying conditions of exposure to those exemplars, all still generate more or less the same general concept of *dog*. Within this evolutionary landscape of medium-sized objects that are snapshot in a single lifespan of geological time, biologically poised mental structures channel cognitive development, but do not determine it. Cultural life, including religion and science, can selectively target and modify parts of this landscape, but cannot simply ignore or completely replace it.

The full expression of the folk-biology module may require natural environmental triggering conditions (akin to those of ancestral environments) and cultural support perhaps lacking for certain groups in industrialized societies, including the usual subjects in most cognitive psychology experiments. These subjects, then, would be prime candidates for studies of knowledge devolution—at least in the domain of folk biology.

ACKNOWLEDGMENTS

This chapter was previously published in *Mind & Society*, 6(3), 2002, pp. 31–63. The studies reported were funded by NSF (SBR 93-19798, SBR 97-07761, SES-9981762) and the French Ministry of Research and Education (Contrat CNRS 92-C-0758). Participants in this project on biological thinking across cultures include: Norbert Ross, Elizabeth Lynch, Elizabeth Proffitt, Ross Burnett, Serge Blok and Michael Shum (Psychology, Northwestern University), Jeremy Bailenson (Research Center for Virtual Environments and Behavior, University of California, Santa Barbara), Alejandro López (Psychology, Max Planck), John Coley (Northeastern University), Ximena Lois (Institut Jean Nicod, Paris), Valentina Vapnarsky (CNRS-EREA, Villejuif, France), Edward Smith and Paul Estin (Psychology, University of Michigan), Michael Baran and Paolo Sousa (Anthropology, University of Michigan), Brian Smith (Biology, University of Texas, Arlington), and Edilberto Ucan Ek' (Herbolaria Maya, Yucatán).

REFERENCES

AHG/APESA. (1992). *Plan de desarollo integrado de Petén: Inventario forestal*. Convenio Gobiernos Alemania y Guatemala, Santa Elena, Petén (SEGEPLAN).

Atran, S. (1990). *Cognitive foundations of natural history: Towards an anthropology of science*. Cambridge: Cambridge University Press.

Atran, S. (1998). Folkbiology and the anthropology of science. *Behavioral and Brain Sciences*, 21, 547–609.

Atran, S. (1999). Itzaj Maya folk-biological taxonomy. In D. Medin & S. Atran (Eds.), *Folk biology* (pp. 119–204). Cambridge, MA: MIT Press.

Atran, S. (2001). The case for modularity: Sin or salvation? *Evolution and Cognition, 7,* 46–55.

Atran, S. (2002). *In gods we trust: The evolutionary landscape of religion.* New York: Oxford University Press.

Atran, S., Estin, P., Coley, J., & Medin, D. (1997). Generic species and basic levels: Essence and appearance in folk biology. *Journal of Ethnobiology, 17,* 22–45.

Atran, S., Medin, D., Lynch, E., Vapnarsky, V., Ucan Ek', E., & Sousa, P. (2001). Folkbiology doesn't come from folkpsychology: Evidence from Yukatek Maya in cross-cultural perspective. *Journal of Cognition and Culture, 1,* 3–42.

Atran, S., Medin, D., Ross, N., Lynch, E., Coley, J., Ucan Ek', E., & Vapnarsky, V. (1999). Folkecology and commons management in the Maya lowlands. *Proceedings of the National Academy of Sciences U.S.A., 96,* 7598–7602.

Atran, S., Medin, D., Ross, N., Lynch, E., Vapnarsky, V., Ucan Ek', E., Coley, J., Timura, C., & Baran, M. (2002). Folk ecology, cultural epidemiology, and the spirit of the commons. A garden experiment in the Maya lowlands, 1991–2001. *Current Anthropology, 43,* 421–450.

Bailenson, J., Shum, M., Atran, S., Medin, D., & Coley, J. (2002). A bird's eye view: Biological categorization and reasoning within and across cultures. *Cognition, 84,* 1–53.

Barsalou, L. (1985). Ideals, central tendency, and frequency of instantiation as determinants of graded structure of categories. *Journal of Experimental Psychology: Learning, Memory, and Cognition, 11,* 629–654.

Bartlett, H. (1940). History of the generic concept in botany. *Bulletin of the Torrey Botanical Club, 47,* 319–362.

Berlin, B. (1992). *Ethnobiological classification.* Princeton: Princeton University.

Berlin, B., Breedlove, D., & Raven, P. (1973). General principles of classification and nomenclature in folk biology. *American Anthropologist, 74,* 214–242.

Bloch, M., Solomon, G., & Carey, S. (2001). An understanding of what is passed on from parents to children: A cross-cultural investigation. *Journal of Cognition and Culture, 1,* 43–68.

Bock, W. (1973). Philosophical foundations of classical evolutionary taxonomy. *Systematic Zoology, 22,* 275–392.

Boster, J. (1988). Natural sources of internal category structure: Typicality, familiarity, and similarity of birds. *Memory & Cognition, 16,* 258–270.

Boster, J. (1991). The information economy model applied to biological similarity judgment. In L. Resnik, J. Levine, & S. Teasely (Eds.), *Perspectives on socially shared cognition* (pp. 203–225). Washington, DC: American Psychological Association.

Brown, C. (1984). *Language and living things: Uniformities in folk classification and naming.* New Brunswick, NJ: Rutgers University Press.

Brown, D., & Boysen, S. (2000). Spontaneous discrimination of natural stimuli by chimpanzees (*Pan troglodytes*). *Journal of Comparative Psychology, 114,* 392–400.

Bulmer, R. (1974). Folk biology in the New Guinea highlands. *Social Science Information, 13,* 9–28.

Carey, S. (1985). *Conceptual change in childhood.* Cambridge, MA: MIT Press.

Carey, S. (1996). Cognitive domains as modes of thought. In D. Olson & N. Torrance (Eds.), *Modes of thought* (pp. 187–215). New York: Cambridge University Press.

Cerella, J. (1979). Visual classes and natural categories in the pigeon. *Journal of Experimental Psychology: Human Perception and Performance, 5,* 68–77.

Coley, J., Medin, D., & Atran, S. (1997). Does rank have its privilege? Inductive inferences in folkbiological taxonomies. *Cognition, 63,* 73–112.

Coley, J., Medin, D., Lynch, E., Proffitt, J., & Atran, S. (1999). Inductive reasoning in folkbiological thought. In D. Medin & S. Atran (Eds.), *Folk biology* (pp. 205–232). Cambridge, MA: MIT Press.

Darwin, C. (1859). *On the origins of species by means of natural selection.* London: Murray.

Darwin, C. (1883 [1872]). *On the origins of species by means of natural selection* (6th ed.). New York: Appleton.

Diamond, J., & Bishop, D. (1999). Ethno-ornithology of the Ketengban people, Indonesian New Guinea. In D. Medin & S. Atran (Eds.), *Folk biology* (pp. 17–46). Cambridge, MA: MIT Press.

Diver, C. (1940). The problem of closely related species living in the same area. In J. Huxley (Ed.), *The new systematics* (pp. 303–328). Oxford: Clarendon.

Dougherty, J. (1979). Learning names for plants and plants for names. *Anthropological Linguistics, 21,* 298–315.

Eldredge, N. (1986). Information, economics, and evolution. *Annual Review of Ecology and Systematics, 17,* 351–369.

Ellen, R. (1993). *The cultural relations of classification.* Cambridge: Cambridge University Press.

Fodor, J. (1983). *Modularity of mind.* Cambridge, MA: MIT Press.

Fodor, J. (2000). *The mind doesn't work that way: The scope and limits of computational psychology.* Cambridge, MA: MIT Press.

Gelman, S., & Wellman, H. (1991). Insides and essences. *Cognition, 38,* 214–244.

Ghiselin, M. (1981). Categories, life, and thinking. *Behavioral and Brain Sciences, 4,* 269–313.

Gil-White, F. (2001). Are ethnic groups biological "species" to the brain? *Current Anthropology, 42,* 515–554.

Griffiths, P. (2002). What is innateness? *The Monist, 85,* 70–85.

Hatano, G., & Inagaki, K. (1999). A developmental perspective on informal biology. In D. Medin & S. Atran (Eds.), *Folk biology* (pp. 321–354). Cambridge, MA: MIT Press.

Hauser, M. (2000). *Wild minds: What animals really think.* New York: Henry Holt.

Hays, T. (1983). Ndumba folkbiology and general principles of ethnobotanical classification and nomenclature. *American Anthropologist, 85,* 592–611.

Herrnstein, R. (1984). Objects, categories, and discriminative stimuli. In H. Roitblat, T. G. Bever, & H. S. Terrace (Eds.), *Animal cognition* (pp. 233–261). Hillsdale, NJ: Lawrence Erlbaum Associates.

Hickling, A., & Gelman, S. (1995). How does your garden grow? Evidence of an early conception of plants as biological kinds. *Child Development, 66,* 856–876.

Hirschfeld, L. (1996). *Race in the making.* Cambridge, MA: MIT Press.

Hunn, E. (1976). Toward a perceptual model of folk biological classification. *American Ethnologist, 3,* 508–524.

Hunn, E. (1982). The utilitarian factor in folk biological classification. *American Anthropologist, 84,* 830–847.

Inagaki, K. (1990). The effects of raising animals on children's biological knowledge. *British Journal of Developmental Psychology, 8,* 119–129.

Inagaki, K., & Hatano, G. (1991). Constrained person analogy in young children's biological inference. *Cognitive Development, 6,* 219–231.

Johnson, K., & Mervis, C. (1997). Effects of varying levels of expertise on the basic level of categorization. *Journal of Experimental Psychology: General, 126,* 248–277.

Johnson, K., Mervis, C., & Boster, J. (1992). Developmental changes within the structure of the mammal domain. *Developmental Psychology, 28,* 74–83.

Johnson, S., & Solomon, G. (1997). Why dogs have puppies and cats have kittens: The role of birth in young children's understanding of biological origins. *Child Development, 68,* 404–419.

Keil, F. (1995). The growth of causal understandings of natural kinds. In D. Sperber, D. Premack, & A. Premack (Eds.), *Causal cognition: A multidisciplinary debate* (pp. 234–267). New York: Oxford University Press.

López, A., Atran, S., Coley, J., Medin, D., & Smith, E. (1997). The tree of life: Universals of folk-biological taxonomies and inductions. *Cognitive Psychology, 32,* 251–295.

Lorenz, K. (1966). The role of gestalt perception in animal and human behavior. In L. White (Ed.), *Aspects of form* (pp. 157–178). Bloomington: Indiana University Press.

Lynch, E., Coley, J. D., & Medin, D. L. (2000). Tall is typical: Central tendency, ideal dimensions and graded category structure among tree experts and novices. *Memory & Cognition, 28,* 41–50.

Medin, D., Lynch, E., Coley, J., & Atran, S. (1997). Categorization and reasoning among tree experts: Do all roads lead to Rome? *Cognitive Psychology, 32,* 49–96.

Medin, D., Ross, N., Atran, S., Burnett, R., & Blok, S. (2002). Categorization and reasoning in relation to culture and expertise. In B. Ross (Ed.), *The psychology of learning and motivation: Advances in research and theory* (Vol. 41, pp. 1–41). New York: Academic Press.

Osherson, D., Smith, E., Wilkie, O., López, A., & Shafir, E. (1990). Category-based induction. *Psychological Review, 97,* 85–200.

Proffitt, J., Medin, D., & Coley, J. (2000). Expertise and category-based induction. *Journal of Experimental Psychology: Learning, Memory and Cognition, 26,* 811–828.

Rosch, E. (1975). Universals and cultural specifics in categorization. In R. Brislin, S. Bochner, & W. Lonner (Eds.), *Cross-cultural perspectives on learning* (pp. 177–206). New York: Halstead.

Rosch, E., & Mervis, C. (1975). Family resemblances: Studies in the internal structure of categories. *Cognitive Psychology, 7,* 573–605.

Rosch, E., Mervis, C., Grey, W., Johnson, D., & Boyes-Braem, P. (1976). Basic objects in natural categories. *Cognitive Psychology, 8,* 382–439.

Ross, N., Medin, D., Coley, J., & Atran, S. (2003). Cultural and experiential differences in the development of folkbiological induction. *Cognitive Development, 18,* 35–47.

Smith, E., & Medin, D. (1981). *Concepts and categories.* Cambridge, MA: Harvard University Press.

Sousa, P., Atran, S., & Medin, D. (2002). Folkbiological essentialism: Further evidence from Brazil. *Journal of Cognition and Culture, 2,* 195–203.

Sperber, D. (1996). *Explaining culture: A naturalistic approach.* Oxford: Blackwell.

Sperber, D. (2001, November). *In defense of massive modularity.* Paper presented to the Innateness and Structure of the Mind Workshop, University of Sheffield.

Sperber, D., & Wilson, D. (1996). *Relevance* (2nd ed.). Oxford: Blackwell.

Stross, B. (1973). Acquisition of botanical terminology by Tzeltal children. In M. Edmonson (Ed.), *Meaning in Mayan languages* (pp. 107–141). The Hague: Mouton.

Tanaka, J. M., & Taylor, M. (1991). Object categories and expertise: Is the basic level in the eye of the beholder? *Cognitive Psychology, 23,* 457–482.

Waddington, C. (1959). Canalisation of development and the inheritance of acquired characteristics. *Nature, 183,* 1654–1655.

Wallace, A. (1901 [1889]). *Darwinism* (3rd ed.). London: Macmillan.

Warburton, F. (1967). The purposes of classification. *Systematic Zoology, 16,* 241–245.

Wolff, P., Medin, D., & Pankratz, C. (1999). Evolution and devolution of folkbiological knowledge. *Cognition, 73,* 177–204.

Zubin, D., & Köpcke, K.-M. (1986). Gender and folk taxonomy. In C. Craig (Ed.), *Noun classes and categorization* (pp. 139–180) [Proceedings of a symposium on categorization and noun classification, Eugene, Oregon, October 1983]. Amsterdam: John Benjamins.

Who Needs a Theory of Mind?

Lawrence A. Hirschfeld
New School for Social Research

Two notions shape a broad range of psychological theories that explore the ways lay folk understand and predict social behavior. The first is the assumption that social understanding is largely concerned with the interactions of individual persons and their minds. The second, a corollary of the first, is the confidently held conviction that only individual persons (and other complex, living organisms) are genuine intentional agents. (When other entities—computers, ghosts, or typhoons—are treated as intentional agents, such treatments are analogies or metaphorical extensions of a quality that properly applies only to humans.) Both assumptions, I suggest, although self-evident to psychologists, strike other social scientists, especially those with interest in aggregate phenomena, as, at the very least, controversial.

I approach the issue from the purchase of research on Theory of Mind, the proposal that humans (and possibly other primates) possess a complex knowledge structure that affords interpretations of others' behavior in terms of mental states such as belief and desire. I take dispositions and traits—enduring cognitive and affective propensities characteristic of an individual—to be parasitic on Theory of Mind (henceforth ToM), in the vein of Wellman's (1990) proposal that dispositions and traits are essentially the developmental crystallization of beliefs and desires. There are several reasons for taking ToM as a point of departure—and to some extent a touchstone throughout this discussion. Research in ToM is vibrant and rich, particularly in the convergence of findings from cognitive, neurocognitive, evolutionary, comparative, developmental, and cultural research. ToM is often viewed as the foundation of all social cognition. Indeed, to some it is *the* area of social cognition relevant to cognitive scientists.

That ToM is a theory about the social seems to follow uncontroversially from the fact that we are interested in and capable of developing beliefs about other people's beliefs and desires because we as humans are concerned with being able to effectively interact with other people. Knowing that they are doing what they are doing because they have intentions, beliefs, desires, and so on is extremely informative for how we should engage and interact with them. That is, intentions, beliefs, and desires are plausibly tethered to specific and co-occurring behaviors. (This confidence aside, there is considerable research indicating that the route from mental states to action is often poorly understood.) ToM is not a way to understand beliefs and desires per se, but the way that mental states are believed to precede and motivate particular behaviors.

ToM capacities are both early emerging and robust. Consider the following achievements made by infants and young toddlers: By 9 months, infants interpret an action performed by a human hand as intentional, but interpret the same movements performed by an artifact as not intentional (Woodward, 1998). Prelinguistic 14-month-old infants, when imitating a goal-directed action performed by a model, do not simply reenact (emulate) the behavior they observe, but seek the most "rational" strategy to achieve the model's goal (Gergely & Harold Kiraly, 2002; Meltzoff & Brooks, 2001). The language-learning infant, in its turn, follows its mother's gaze, rather than relying on its own line of sight when matching a referent to a novel word (Baldwin, 1991). A ToM milestone is the capacity to grasp that other people hold beliefs that are recognized as false; by 4 years, preschoolers generally understand this. (For example, when shown a candy box that actually has pencils inside, most 3-year-olds predict that a person who has not looked inside the box will expect to find pencils inside. Five-year-olds understand that the person will incorrectly expect to find candy.) Given that all these capacities contribute significantly to the infant's and child's developing understanding of the world, the title question hardly seems serious.

A ToM is something every human needs and all intact humans precociously develop. Baldwin and Baird (2001) offered the following thought experiment:

> Imagine for a moment failing to grasp the idea that people act in large part to fulfill intentions arising from their beliefs and desires. As you watch people move about the world, you register their motions yet lack a sense of any purpose to these motions. This means that for you, a doctor's diverse actions

of offering advice, administering an injection, and performing out-patient surgery are as different as tooth-brushing is from driving a car, because an intention to heal is all that makes these distinctly dissimilar movement patterns cohere conceptually. (p. 171)

Later I revisit what life would be like without a ToM. For the moment, let us share Baldwin & Baird's confidence that persons lacking the ability to mindread would be radically disabled. Indeed, there is a good deal of evidence that this is the case. Children whose ToM capacities are limited *are* profoundly impaired (see e.g., Baron-Cohen, 1996).

The title question, however, is serious if recast in the admittedly less attention-grabbing version: "How *much* do we need a ToM?" In other words, do we need a ToM to the degree that the literature suggests? I propose the following:

1. We need a ToM less than one might conclude on the basis of existing psychological literature;
2. much of the emphasis on ToM derives less from empirical or theoretical considerations than from a propensity by psychologists to take as their mandate the explication of how individual minds process information about other individual minds;
3. the psychological literature further supposes that ToM is a theory about people's minds, rather than a theory about individuals (which may be persons, but not necessarily so) whose actions are best understood using notions like "intention," "believe," "desire," and so on; and
4. to the extent that ToM is a theory of people's minds, it is insufficient to account for many of the inferences humans (and other primates) readily and reliably draw about social entities and their behavior.

To anticipate a point developed later: Not all social individuals are individual persons. Understanding a crowd (say during a stampede) is best achieved by ascribing it intentions. These ascriptions are not cumulative: A crowd's intentions are not the sum total of the intentions of the individual persons who constitute it. Traffic jams, stampedes, riots, folie à deux (trois ou beaucoup), and other forms of "groupthink" are aggregate phenomena that are best understood without appeal to individual persons' mental states (both under folk and scientific theories). The fundamental question is whether the notion that a crowd "has a mind of its own" is a metaphor. Many social scientists have argued that it is not. When economists speak of capital, anthropologists of culture, Marxists of class, and Foucauldians of regimes of truth, and some linguists of language (Katz, 1981), it cannot be assumed that they are using figures of speech.

Suppose that the laws of economics hold because people have the attitudes, motives, goals, needs, strategies, etc., that they do [. . .] it doesn't begin to follow that the typical predicates of economics can be reduced to the typical predicates of psychology [. . .] I think it fair to say that there is no reason to suppose [. . .] that they cannot. (Fodor, 1975, p. 16)

This, of course, is a claim about explanatory reductionism, not meta-physics. My concern here is essentially with folk metaphysics, but I believe that the *easy appeal* of nonreductionist explanations derives in part from folk habits of thought. Atran (1990) offered something of a parallel argument for the easy mappings between folk-biological taxonomies and formal systematics (and for the way folk biology inhibited the evolution of formal systematics).

To be sure, not all accounts of making sense of behavior in psychology assume the primacy of ToM. Proposed psychological reductions involve stimulus and response as much as they do belief and desire. Still much cognitive and developmental psychology over the past two decades has focused on higher level phenomena, particularly mental states like belief and desire. In this work, the individual person is a fundamental building block, and ToM is a fundamental capacity. In its nascent form (e.g., the infant's capacity for and contribution to joint attention), ToM facilitates and shapes basic patterns of social interaction as well as other developmental tasks, including language acquisition (Baldwin, 1991). In slightly older children, it enables toddlers to transparently take meaning from interactions that would otherwise be opaque, such as pretense (Leslie, 1987). Impairment in a slightly later-emerging dimension of ToM (i.e., deficit in the ability to represent others as having beliefs and desires independent of one's own), in Baron-Cohen's (1996) apt phrase autistic *mindblindness*, causes severe social dysfunction (Leslie, 1991; Perner, Frith, Leslie, & Leekam, 1989).

The question of whether all individuals are persons would arguably not come up if ToM were solely about psychological processes. But a number of researchers have argued, as Baldwin and Baird did earlier, that ToM is closely linked to the very nature of human society. It has been proposed, for example, that ToM represents an evolutionary adaptation to the specific challenges of human social existence (e.g., Tomasello, 1999). This is not implausible. Humans inhabit particularly complex networks of social relations, unlike those of any other species. Many species are social, and many evince altruistic behaviors. But human societies are uniquely multilayered, fluid, and imagined (as opposed to perceived). Enduring social relations in which reciprocity is often delayed and indirect are subject to unique risks. For example, given the costs of cheating, sophisticated cooperation could evolve only if participants were able to detect and track failures to cooperate. The more complex cooperative endeavors became, the more important was the ability to represent others' behaviors as a function of their states of mind.

Cooperative endeavors are social by definition, and the emergence of ToM is theoretically identified with the emergence of human sociality (Byrne & Whiten, 1988; Premack, 1991), such that ToM becomes central to human social endowment: "The mindreading system is part of the social module [. . .] in that mindreading is by definition a system for use with the social environment" (Baron-Cohen, 1996, p. 96). Tomasello (1999) contended that culture itself is a function of emergent ToM capacities:

> this single adaptation [. . .] transformed such basic primate phenomena as communication, dominance, exchange, and exploration into the human cultural institutions of language, government, money and science—without any additional genetic events. (p. 209)

Conceptualizing ToM as a function of social experience seems sensible. Without social experience, ToM is inconceivable. ToM is about mental representations of *another's* mental states. Seeing the social as a function of ToM may, however, be more problematic. The kind of experience necessary to enable ToM is social in the weakest sense of social. We do not have to interact with others or even encounter them to imagine that they have mental states. No actual social interaction is necessary. A delusional person's attributions of beliefs and desires to a voice in her head, a person with multiple personality disorder attributing beliefs and desires in the mind of one of his alters, and a Dobuan Islander's attribution of beliefs and desires to the spirits that cause a canoe to drift off to sea are all representations of another's beliefs and desires. Still, on the face of it, it seems odd to call them social in that none involves social *interaction*, but rather social imagination.

We need not turn to the exotic or rare to see that people don't always rely on ToM in making sense of the social world. A little introspection—a parallel thought experiment to Baldwin and Baird's—helps make this clear. It is necessary in the course of everyday life to predict what others will do. We do this when paying for food at a checkout counter or determining who goes where and when while driving. Yet typically we do not do much in the way of mentally representing mental representations in such situations. Much of our daily life is heavily constrained by social topography: We pay the cashier, we stop at red lights, we go on green, and we anticipate that others will do the same. Now, we could, of course, anticipate what others do so because we attribute to them beliefs and desires, but there is no reason to believe that we do it all that much. When did you last think about the cashier's *desires*? Similarly, we do not believe that cashiers have a disposition to take money or are endowed with a personality trait that makes them well suited for being a cashier. People do what they do because their position and activities in a social field are a function of roles taken by individuals whose motives for action flow from their social status, not their states of mind. We may acknowledge that a person might not be *happy* at what they are doing, but except in exceptional cases (which I return to in a moment) this has little effect on how we interpret and predict how they actually will act.

It might be objected that we may not use belief/desire psychology all the time, in the sense of actually forming representations online of other people's beliefs and desires, but we *could* recruit it if need be. I am not challenging this. As noted, ToM deficit has a massive effect, and although a fairly effective, although manifestly odd, social existence can derive from a database of expectations based on empirical generalizations (as the daily lives of high-functioning Asperger patients make clear), a detriment in ToM has dramatic consequences (Sacks, 1995).

The question remains, however, how often do typically endowed folk actually use the potential power of ToM representations? One possibility is that when ordinary schema, scripts, or whatever we want to call unreflective expectations about social interaction fail, ToM reasoning is triggered. In other words, perturbations in the normal course of events cause us to shift into ToM gear, seeking out hypotheses about the beliefs and desires of those with whom we interact. I am not convinced of this, nor is most of social psychology if the role that largely incorrigible processes like illusory correlation, stereotyping, and other social heuristics play in inhibiting awareness of perturbations in the social landscape. Consider driving a car. When someone violates the expectations that the social typography otherwise supports (say, turning left from the right-hand lane), what do we do (beside modifying the motion of our car to avoid an accident)? Do we start to consider the beliefs of the other driver, searching for possible mental causes of the violation? Does the individual's mental state become particularly relevant? Perhaps occasionally. More often, I suggest, we seek out a category explanation that involves an interpretation grounded in social positioning. Predictions about behavior are based on the premise that the person involved is a token of a type. Women drivers who have not mastered the requisite skills or habits, elderly drivers who have lost these skills, or entitled Republicans in their Mercedes who believe themselves above needing them.

EXPLAINING PEOPLE AND THEIR ACTIONS

Humans activities, like those of all social animals, are shaped by the wealth of aggregations that constitute the social environment. Who an individual is—how he or she is likely to interact with others—is conditioned on the particular group affiliation that is most relevant in a given situation. It is not surprising that human cognition is organized in ways that facilitate group living through development of rich capacities to identify and remember the relevant groups in a particular social universe, to identify and remember the individuals affiliated with these groups, and to use these detection skills to compute and track, among other things, risk and advantage.

A rich literature in social psychology demonstrates that humans spontaneously, and typically nonconsciously, scan the social landscape for evidence of group membership. They use this information to ascribe behavioral likelihoods (Hilton & von Hippel, 1996). Generally interpreted to be a function of individual information processing *about* individual persons and their attributes, this sort of cognition can just as persuasively be interpreted as information processing *about the social environment*. Human behavior lends itself to this kind of interpretation when it involves actual, single-purpose aggregations. In such a case, groups are manifest. Examples include teams in sports, congregations during religious services, and self-selecting social convergence (such as race, gender, or class-based groupings during a middle-school lunch hour). More frequently, however, groups are recognized through inference. Individuals are encountered, and we infer from appearance, behavior, the situation, and so on what group affiliations are most relevant to understanding that individual.

The kind of groups to which an individual belongs shapes the kind of group-based interpretations such memberships evoke. Some groups—race, gender, and age among others—support many inferences that go far beyond what is given by experience. Social psychologists have tried to determine which particular kinds of groups are inferentially rich in this way, suggesting that some groups are conceptualized as more entity-like (entitative) than others:

> the individual person is not the only stable cause that perceivers can invoke [. . .] group memberships and social roles represent other candidates. [. . .] Group membership may constitute a suitable causal factor in order to interpret the observed behavior. Moreover, our data confirm the importance of entitativity in the attribution process. Whenever a group of people is perceived to be entitative, observers tend to interpret the members' behaviors more in terms of a dispositional feature than in terms of situational forces. (Yzerbyt, Castano, Leyens, & Paladino, 2000, pp. 15–16)

More important, the predominant view in social psychology is that reasoning about groups is a function of a single set of psychological mechanisms: "Forming an impression of an individual and developing a conception of a group are, in fact, governed by the same fundamental information-processing system" (Hamilton & Sherman, 1996, p. 336). Yzerbyt, Rogier, and Fiske (1998) made the same claim: "Perceivers deal with meaningful social entities very much like they handle information about individual targets" (p. 1090). On this view, groups are essentially "big people."

Of course groups are not *literally* big people, nor are they simply a mapping of processes of person perception to aggregates. For one thing, the semantics of groups and persons are interestingly different. For example, the transitivity of personhood does not hold for groups. A part of a part of a person is a part of a person (e.g., my stomach is part of my digestive system, which is part of my body, and my stomach is also part of me). The same is not true of a group (e.g., my stomach is part of my body, but is not part of my race).[1] Similarly, a person is a person unless there is a basic insult to his or her integrity (like death physically or slavery socially). A confederation (or other cohesive induction-promoting group) is not a confederation *tout court*, but a confederation in virtue of some social context.

Still, with respect to attributions of mental states, groups and their members are strikingly similar: The activities of both are interpretable in terms of belief, desires, and intentions (even if it appears that the seat of a group's mental state is problematic). Groups might be big people because whatever *causes* people to have intentions and dispositions is the thing that *causes* groups to have them. In both cases, on folk belief, groups and people are what they are and do what they do largely in virtue of having hidden essences. According to Medin (1989), people act as if the identity of things and their underlying natures are a function of an unseen essence, which causes development to occur in predictable and typical ways. Medin called this mode of thought *psychological essentialism*. Much research on psychological essentialism focuses on the domain of folk biology. However, Susan Gelman and her colleagues (Gelman, 1992; Heyman & Gelman, 2000a; see also Yuill, 1992) have shown that children also treat behavioral dispositions and traits as if they were essences.

For example, Heyman and Gelman (2000b) found that 3- and 4-year-olds used information about traits to make novel psychological infer-

---

[1] I thank Dan Sperber for bringing this to my attention. Discussions with him have been crucial in working out the logic of my argument in this section. Chomsky (1965) noted that this is a formal universal of semantics:

> There is no logical necessity for names or other "object words" to meet any condition of spatiotemporal contiguity or to have other Gestalt qualities [that persons do], and it is a nontrivial fact that they apparently do, insofar as the designated objects are of the type that can actually be perceived (for example, it is not true of [social entities like] "United States" . . .). Thus there is no logical grounds for the apparent nonexistence in natural languages of words such as . . . "HERD," like the collective "herd" except that it denotes a single scattered object with cows as parts, so that "a cow lost a leg" implies "the HERD lost a leg," etc. (p. 201)

ences, even when the trait information conflicted with other dimensions of similarity. In another study, they demonstrated that young children believed that two children who share a similar personality trait (e.g., being shy) were more likely to share an unfamiliar property (e.g., likes to play jimjam) than two children who closely resemble each other in appearance, but did not share the personality trait. Trait labels in this instance function much as Gelman (1988) found living kind category labels to function in promoting inferences about novel properties; namely, they seem to be embedded in theory-like constructs the causal relations of which derive from underlying essences.

Yzerbyt and his colleagues (Yzerbyt et al., 2000; Yzerbyt, Rogier, & Fiske, 1998) have similarly linked adult disposition and trait attributions to essentialist reasoning (see also Haslam, Rothschild, & Ernst, 2000):

> there is an unmistakable tendency of social perceivers to call on the trait of honesty to account for a person's bringing in a lost wallet to the police station. In other words, the essentialistic assumption—that some dispositional property of the actor or some essential feature at the heart of an event—can be seen as a central aspect of social perception. (Yzerbyt et al., 1998, p. 1089)

Not all groups support essentialism to the same degree, and hence the extent to which a group can be seen as having traits and dispositions can also vary. Groups have dispositions when they are perceived as individual entities—as having the property, to use Campbell's (1958) inelegant term, *entitativity*.[2] The more entitative a group is, the more likely people will believe that it has an underlying essence. Entitative groups and persons are *individuals*. Still, given a choice, psychologists generally assume that persons are the standard of intentional agents—the prototype or proper intentional agent. The proper domain of intentionality, on this account, is the individual, not the type of individual an agent may be. Both groups and persons are individuals, and thus potential intentional agents. They are different types of individuals. Groups are corporate individuals, and persons are individual (or moral) individuals (of which there might be several subtypes).

The idea that group perception might merit investigation independent of person perception is not new to social psychology (Thibaut & Kelley, 1959). But the notion has not been influential. As Dasgupta, Banaji, and Abelson (1999) observed, "[d]espite the early emphasis on group perception, social psychological research did not focus long on this most basic

---

[2]"Entitativity: the degree of being entitative. The degree of having the nature of an entity, of having real existence" (Campbell, 1958, p. 17). According to Campbell, groups that are entitative are perceived as having a common fate, being constituted of a similar type, and engaged in a good deal of face-to-face interaction (which Campbell called *proximity*).

unit of social perception—the social group" (p. 991). There are a number of reasons that this might be the case, the most blatant of which is the ontological dilemma it raises. If not in their members, where do group dispositions and intentions reside? If group perception is grounded in person perception, this dilemma disappears. A second objection turns on Occam's razor: PERSON is clearly a conceptual primitive (Keil, 1979; Miller & Johnson-Laird, 1976), and several studies have shown that nonhuman intentional agents—be they dogs (Carey, 1985), ghosts (Boyer, 1990), or God (Barrett & Keil, 1996)—are modeled on persons and their putatively unique psychological properties. There is broad, but largely implicit, agreement that these nonhuman intentional agents inherit their intentionality from the more primitive entity—person.

Neither of these objections, however, excludes the possibility I propose. Indeed, both objections cut two ways. PERSON is a conceptual primitive, but so is OBJECT. Persons are objects and share properties with all other objects (e.g., if they are unsupported they fall, they have spatial contiguity, they obey constraints on numerosity, etc.). In principle, then, PERSON could be a conceptual primitive and so could OBJECT, despite that they span the same phenomenal domain. The conceptual primitive evoked in any given situation is contingent on a variety of contextual factors, including the causal framework deemed most relevant. There may well be contexts in which the causal framework favors GROUP over PERSON, a possibility I return to later. Second, it has been proposed that persons are the model for reasoning about ghosts and God (i.e., reasoning about ghosts and God are constrained by reasoning about persons). What has actually been demonstrated is that "individual intentional agent most like a person in relevant dimensions" seems to be the model on which reasoning about ghosts and God (and, as we see, computers) is based.

I am not suggesting that GROUP could replace PERSON as the "authentic" domain of intentional agency (although Durkheim did in 1915). Rather I propose that the notion of INDIVIDUAL encompasses both. In truth, I am less concerned here with identifying the proper domain than I am with identifying the input conditions to the mental device that triggers the attribution of intentional agency. Social groups, on this view, would be a kind of corporate individual, whereas persons would be a kind of (moral) individual.

COGNITIVE ARCHITECTURE AND MODES
OF CONSTRUAL

My goal here is to untangle the relationship between a number of phenomena: agency and individual, group and person, and so on. A critical question in this effort is to ask what properties adhere to the various phenomena. For example, can groups have agency? Can aggregate phenomena be conceptual individuals? What causal properties are attributed to agents, either person or corporate? I suggest that much discussion has been inhibited by the commitment to the notion that agency, and particularly intentional agency, is inextricably linked to the notion of person. If we scream at our computers for what they have done to our lives, we are not really attributing malign agency to semiconductor-based artifacts. We simply treat artifacts by analogy as if they were living, sentient creatures. Presumably this is a function of cognitive miserliness: There are limited numbers of ways to construe the nature of things, and analogical transfer saves cognitive energy the way category-based induction over novel circumstances does.

Consider folk psychology, the umbrella structure under which ToM emerges. Folk psychology holds that observable behavior is a function of nonobvious mental states. Further it specifies a causal theory explaining *how* mental states lead to behavior. I understand Susie's reaching for the cookie jar because I believe that (a) Susie is hungry, (b) she believes that cookies are stored in the cookie jar, and (c) she believes that satiating her hunger can be accomplished by eating a cookie. The conventional wisdom is that other seemingly similar attributions of nonobvious states like intention, desire, and belief to nonperson agents are derivative of person-based folk psychology. The reason (sometimes implied) is that person-based folk psychology is self-evidently more fundamental than these other intentional attributions.

The argument that person-based intentional attribution is more fundamental presumes that intentional agency is proprietary of one domain. Yet there is no a priori reason to accept this presumption. Keil (1994) suggested an alternative architecture. Intentional attributions may represent what Keil called a *mode of construal*. It may be that attributions of intentions to inanimate objects, say, are derived, but it is not necessarily the case that they derive from person-based folk psychology. Clearly an intentional mode of construal is expressed through individuals. Persons, however, are not the only kind of intentional agents. In fact, the particular kind of individual seems to be contingent on context. This is essentially the position that Keil (1994) and Sperber (1996) took when they suggested that several special-purpose modes of reasoning are not domain-specific (e.g., intentional, teleological, and essentialist modes). On this proposal, special-purpose modes of reasoning are independent of any particular domain and become associated with (implemented in thinking about) a particular domain because the domain meets the input conditions of the mode of construal.

Susan Gelman and I (1999; Hirschfeld, 1994) argued that this is the case for essentialist reasoning. We have suggested, for example, that the input condition for invoking an essentialist mode of construal is met when other modes of construal fail to account for highly salient everyday phenomena. The otherwise curious transformation of caterpillars turning into butterflies takes place because it is in the essential nature of caterpillars to become butterflies. As science this may not be satisfying. As folk belief it works quite well.

Gelman and I argued that essentialist reasoning is a particularly promiscuous modality of thought—one that can be deployed in a number of diverse domains (e.g., nonhuman living kinds, racial thinking) and can be applied to an almost haphazard set of phenomena (e.g., ranging from religious fetishes to Jackie O's faux pearls). We reviewed a number of these seemingly distinct domains and phenomena and concluded that the distribution of essentialist reasoning could not result from conceptual inheritance by analogy from folk biology. The idea that essentialism is a special-purpose mode of essentialist reasoning deployed in domains and to phenomena for which there are specific gaps in folk causality is a better fit with existing data.

Supporting evidence comes from studies exploring the developmental course and input conditions of essentialist reasoning about social entities (Hirschfeld, 1996). Contrary to the notion that races are conceptually modeled after nonhuman living kinds, biological and social kinds are in fact "triggered" by distinct kinds of input, visual information for folk-biological kinds, and verbal information for social kinds. This is not to deny that there are striking parallels between the way nonhuman living kinds and social groups like race are conceptually represented. Both sorts of kinds, for instance, are what has come to be called *highly naturalized*. A category is highly naturalized if membership in it is thought to be a function of the intrinsic nature of the organisms that constitute the category. Intrinsic nature in this characterization has three valences. First, an organism's intrinsic nature is something that cannot be (or cannot be easily) modified; it is part of the way an organism simply is. (Exceptions are informative. For instance, a tiger is a striped quadruped by nature. But an albino three-legged tiger is also a striped quadruped by nature. What has made it three-legged and nonstriped is a disruption of the expression of that intrinsic nature.) Second, an organism's intrinsic nature is thought to be a function of (and to reflect) the organization of the world's natural discontinuities. Third, the reproduction of an organism's intrinsic nature is grounded in mechanisms of natural reproduction. Organisms reproduce themselves using only their own resources.

Consider, for example, differences in the way social and nonhuman living kinds transmit properties to their offspring. Developmental studies reveal a pattern of both similarities and differences in the sorts of beliefs that can be inferred from knowledge of category membership, depending on whether the kind in question is social or nonhuman living. Convergence includes domain-specific principles of causality (like growth and inheritance) that apply in both folk biology and folk sociology. In both the social and biological domains, young children anticipate that category identity is largely immutable over one's lifetime, that family members resemble each other in nontrivial ways, and that relevant category properties are fixed at birth (for social categories, see Hirschfeld, 1996; Springer, Meier, & Berry, 1996; for biological kinds, see Wellman & Gelman, 1988).

There are two exceptions to this developmental pattern of convergence. By middle childhood, children begin to believe that the pattern of family resemblance of socially relevant properties is not the same as the pattern of family resemblance of nonsocially relevant properties. Children this age expect that couples who differ in a nonsocially relevant property will have offspring that are blends. Thus, a dark-haired father and blond mother will have a child whose hair color is intermediate. This pattern of reasoning, however, does not obtain when the property is socially relevant. Preadolescents predict that children of mixed-race couples will resemble their minority parent in qualities diagnostic of social category membership (e.g., skin color), although they will resemble both parents equally for qualities not diagnostic of social category membership (e.g., hair color; Hirschfeld, 1995b). In this case, differences in reasoning about biological and social properties reflect preadolescents' endorsement of a particular cultural ideology. That ideology is not one of biology—reasoning about other animals does not display this pattern—but it is nonetheless natural in that it reflects the children's beliefs about the intrinsic nature of race.

A second way in which folk biology and folk sociology diverge involves younger children. Although controversy remains about details of interpretation, young children possess an adult and theory-like understanding of body function, including the processes involved in disease, inheritance, and growth (Inagaki & Hatano, 2002; Kalish, 1996; Rosengren, Gelman, Kalish, & McCormick, 1991; Springer & Ruckel, 1992). Three-year-olds expect relevant folk-biological and folk-sociological kinds will remain unchanged over the life span, will be inherited, and will be fixed at birth. In these expectations, young children and adults converge. Interestingly, however, 3-year-olds also expect properties that American adults do not believe are biologically transmitted are in fact immutable, inheritable, and fixed a birth. North American 4-year-olds naturalize occupation, expecting that a parent and its offspring are as likely to have the same occupation as to be the same race, whereas 5-year-olds do not (Hirschfeld, 1995a).

This finding can be interpreted in several ways. It might simply reflect a progression in young children's thinking, in which they increasingly converge on a more adult-like belief system. They "shed" their naturalization of occupation as their understanding of biological transmission grows. The finding could also be interpreted as a convergent progression toward a particular cultural belief system. In this case, the shift would reflect a process by which a more abstract or broader array of hypotheses is narrowed by cultural experience. American 4-year-olds would not so much be wrong about occupation as initially open to cultural possibilities that are not supported by the cultural environment in which they live. If the child were to live in a different cultural environment, the shift might not take place. This appears to be the case. Mahalingam (1999) found that in South Asia, where occupation *is* naturalized, children believe that occupation is immutable, inherited, and fixed at birth. When Indian children naturalize caste, they are not getting biology wrong, they are getting the culturally appropriate version of biology right. Accordingly, when we conclude that even quite young children's beliefs are strikingly adult-like, we need to bear in mind that *adult-like* means "adult-like in some cultural environment."

Another way that reasoning about social and nonhuman living kinds differs is in young children's expectations about the way inherited properties are transmitted from adult to child. Many studies demonstrate that both adults and children reason as if nonobvious essences guide development of and fix the category identity of both biological and social categories. The mechanisms by which essences are fixed and how they transfer from one individual to another is typically only vaguely sketched in folk theory. Indeed, Medin and Ortony (1989) argued that psychological essences are precisely a "place-holder" for otherwise poorly understood processes. Some details, however, seem to be well understood. Springer (1996) found that young children believe that property resemblance among nonhuman living kinds involves the transfer of material particulates during pregnancy from mother to offspring. Adults everywhere believe that it is through intercourse that the crucial material particulate transfer takes place.

However, procreation is not the only way that children come to inherit physical and other intrinsic properties. For instance, in 17th-century France, it was speculated that physical properties could be inherited via the transfer of natural fluids that occurs during wet nursing:

> The nursing relationship was seen as the more profoundly influential on the developing nature of the child than the pre-natal experience. The threshold of birth was not the decisive one. Intrauterine gestation and extrauterine parasitism were regarded as one continuous process in the formation of the child's *naturel*. (Marvick, 1974, p. 224)

> It is an accepted thing that milk [. . .] has the power to make children resemble their nurses in mind and body, just as the seed makes them resemble their mother and father. (Fairchilds, 1984, p. 195)

Stoler (1995) described similar fears among 19th-century Dutch colonials about the use of indigenous wet nurses and nannies.

Preschoolers' beliefs about occupation demonstrate an openness to ideas about the naturalization of social kinds that are not shared by the adults with whom they live. It is not that they mistakenly naturalize categories that are not naturalizable. Instead, they remain open to a range of possibilities, only some of which are supported by cultural environment, and hence only some of which become stabilized in the child's social repertoire. Susan Gelman, Oren Kosansky, and I wondered if North American children might similarly be open to ideas about the reproduction of social properties that are also not culturally supported. If French physicians of the 17th century and Dutch planters of the 19th century believed that some social qualities could pass from wet nurse to child via breast milk, we wondered whether contemporary North American children might similarly be open, if only briefly, to the same possibility.

To test this, in an unpublished study, Gelman, Kosansky, and I adapted a switched-at-birth task I has used in previous studies (Hirschfeld, 1995a). The task poses a nature–nurture conflict. We told 4- and 5-year-old children about two families whose infants are switched at birth. As in standard switched-at-birth studies, children were then asked whether the switched infant would grow up having the properties ascribed to the birth parents or those ascribed to the adoptive parents. The modified version involved an experimental manipulation in which half the children were told that the switched infant was bottle fed by the adoptive mother, and the other half were told that the switched infant was nursed by the adoptive mother. In other words, half of the children were presented with a scenario in which a postpartum transfer of natural fluids occurred, whereas the other half presented with a scenario in which no natural transfer took place.

If children reasoned as they have in other switched-at-birth studies, then both the 4- and 5-year-olds should be nativist about physical properties (Gelman & Wellman, 1991; Hirschfeld, 1995a; Springer, Meier, & Berry, 1996). If children endorsed the model of inheritance reported for 17th-century France, then the children who heard about the infant who was nursed should be more nativist than children who heard about the infant who was bottle fed. There was no difference in the responses of 5-year-olds, consistent with a cultural model of contemporary North America in which physical properties are fixed at birth and contingent processes of sexual reproduction. However, 4-year-olds in the bottle-fed condition showed the expected birth parent or nativist bias, whereas 4-year-olds in the nursing condition were significantly more likely to predict that the infant would grow up to have physical properties of the adoptive parents. In short, 4- but not 5-year-olds were open to a theory of natural transmission supported by 17th-century French culture, but not 21st-century North American culture.

THE "NATURAL" OBJECTS OF INTENTIONS

Anyone who has worked with a personal computer has treated it as a sort of conversational partner at one time or another. Who hasn't cursed their computer, probably more than occasionally? Surely this is a case of conceptual inheritance by analogy. All seeming evidence aside, computers are not out to get us. We have great confidence in the intuition that computers are not sentient beings. Nor do we anticipate that they are moved by our words or sensitive to our moods. Computers are not people. We simply have a limited repertoire of expressing deeply felt exasperation, and yelling at computers reflects this: nothing deeply cognitive about this.

Nass and Moon, however, have conducted a number of studies suggesting otherwise. Humans, they have demonstrated, treat computers as much more *real* intentional agents than we might otherwise imagine. As a consequence, human–computer interactions are strikingly and profoundly like human–human interactions. In one study, Moon and Nass (1996) found that, consistent with similarity-attraction theory in social psychology, subjects were more attracted to computers with "personalities" like their own than with machines whose "personalities" did not match theirs. More relevant to the present discussion, Nass and Moon (2000) found that computer users used common gender and ethnic stereotypes when interacting with computers that were contrived to display gender or ethnic characteristics.

Perhaps more compelling support for the notion that nonhuman individuals are genuine intentional agents comes from work on the conceptual representations of social groupings. The idea that social groups can have agency, can share a common fate, can be constituted of individuals who are tokens of a type, and can engage in intense face-to-face contact (to use Campbell's, 1958, criteria for social groups to be moral individuals) is familiar. The English lexicon contains a rich repertoire of words that refer to social groups as moral individuals. Consider the following list, complied from an unsystematic search of the *Oxford English Dictionary*:

> *brood*, the young of certain animals, especially a group of young birds or fowl hatched at one time and cared for by the same mother; *nest*, a number of insects, birds, or other animals occupying such a place: "a nest of hornets"; *bevy*, a company of roe deer, larks, or quail; *cast*, the number of hawks or falcons cast off at one time, usually a pair; *cete*, a company of badgers; *covert*, a flock of coots; *covey*, a family of grouse, partridges, or other game birds; *drift*, a drove or herd, especially of hogs; *drove*, a flock or herd being driven in a body; *exaltation*, a flight of larks; *fall*, a family of woodcock in

flight; *farrow*, litter of pigs; *flight*, a flock of birds in flight; *fry*, a. small fish, especially young, recently hatched fish. b. the young of certain other animals; *gaggle*, a flock of geese; *gam*, a school of whales, or a social congregation of whalers, especially at sea; *hive*, a colony of bees; *kindle*, a brood or litter, especially of kittens; *litter*, the total number of offspring produced at a single birth by a multiparous mammal; *murder*, a flock of crows; *muster*, a flock of peacocks; *nide*, a brood of pheasants; *pack*, a group of animals, such as dogs or wolves, that run and hunt together; *pod*, a small herd of seals or whales; *pride*, a company of lions; *rout*, a company of wolves in movement; *school*, a congregation of fish, or aquatic mammals such as dolphins or porpoises; *shoal*, a large school of fish or other marine animals; *shrewdness*, a company of apes; *skein*, a flight of wildfowl, especially geese; *skulk*, a congregation of vermin, especially foxes; *sloth*, a company of bears; *sord*, a flight of mallards; *sounder*, a herd of wild boar; *stable*, a number of horses housed in one place or under the same ownership; *swarm*, a colony of insects, such as ants, bees, or wasps, especially on the move; *troop*, a number of animals, birds, or people, especially when on the move; *warren*, the inhabitants, such as rabbits, of a warren; *watch*, a flock of nightingales; *wisp*, a flock of birds, especially of snipe

Eskimo may not have 40 words for snow, but English speakers have at least that many for social aggregates. Some of the richness of this lexicon derives from utilitarian factors. I contend, however, that it also reflects a specialized curiosity about social entities that is distinct from curiosity about individual organisms. Three lines of research are relevant. The first concerns the case study of an autistic adult; the second work that Elizabeth Bartmess, Eva Loth, and I have done with autistic children; and the third work that Michael Baran, Paul Bloom, Susan Gelman, and I have done on children's attribution of intentionality to groups.

Sacks' (1995) case study of Temple Grandin, an autistic agricultural scientist, is a rich portrait of a person with impaired ToM. It is also a portrait of a person with an enhanced, or at least strikingly patent, theory of social groups. Given her autism, it is not surprising that Grandin finds human emotional interaction "completely baffling." Sacks devoted considerable time exploring heuristics that she employed to "normalize" social interaction. Still mental acts like pretense and emotions like embarrassment remain a puzzle to Grandin. The same is not true of nonhuman collective behavior. She possesses considerable ability to interpret the group dynamics of herd animals under stress. Grandin is an authority on the management of animals in commercial contexts and renowned, in Sacks' words, for her "understanding of the psychology and behavior of herd animals" (p. 281).[3] This insight into animals in groups has allowed her to design abat-

---

[3]Her writings are extensive. A sample topic, covered in her contribution to a volume on livestock handling that she edited, is "Behavioral principles of handling cattle and other grazing animals under extensive conditions" (Grandin, 1993). This gives a sense not only of her rich understanding of animals, but particularly animals in groups.

toir that are both humane and effective. Grandin attributes her sensitivity to animals to parallels in the sensory experience of cattle and of people with autism. Whatever its source, Grandin's extraordinary ability comes from her capacity to "see" the nature of animal social experience without anthropomorphizing it. This does not mean that she is insensitive to emotion. Indeed Sacks' portrait closed on an outburst of impassioned self-reflection by Grandin, and despite her extremely limited abilities to compute human feelings and intentions, Sacks noted that it is not the case

> that she was devoid of feeling or had a fundamental lack of sympathy. On the contrary, her sense of animals' moods and feelings was so strong that these almost took possession of her [. . .]. She feels that she can have sympathy for what is physical or physiological—for an animal's pain or terror—but lacks empathy for people's states of mind. . . . (p. 269)

Good animal husbandry, it seems, requires neither anthropomorphisms nor attributions of person-based ToM. It requires understanding how individuals coalesce into groups with unique behavioral and structural characteristics. We seem to have a fairly limited vocabulary for describing the motivations behind group-based behaviors, despite the rich lexicon that we have for referring the groups. That intentional *language* dominates descriptions of group behavior does not mean that intentional *attributions* do. Rather it means that, as with interactions with complex artifacts, intentional and dispositional language adheres to a domain of the world, perhaps in virtue of no more than a lexical lacunae.[4]

DOES THE AUTISTIC CHILD HAVE A THEORY OF SOCIETY?

The question of whether intentional agents are fundamentally the domain of persons is part of a broader concern: How fundamental are interpretations of behavior based on the mental states of individual persons? I began by suggesting that person- and mental state-based interpretations are important, but not fundamental. Humans regularly and readily interpret behavior as a function of the kinds of people who exist and the relationship between individuals and the social groups to which they belong. How can we test whether these latter modes of interpretation do not, in fact, derive

---

[4]Such lacunae are not uncommon. Considerable work in generative grammar explores the linguistic grounding of crucial aspects of the world—time, smell, emotion—in the rich vocabulary of space, taste, and mechanics. Suggestions aside by linguistic relativists from Whorf (1956) to Lakoff (1987) to Lucy (1992), this does not necessarily mean that conceptual repertoire follows vocabulary.

from person- and mental state-based interpretations? One strategy would be to explore whether people who struggle to construct person- and mental state-based interpretations have a parallel difficulty with group-based interpretations.

The extensive literature on autistic children's impairment with ToM points to a "natural" comparison with which to test this possibility. Autistic children, as observed earlier, are greatly impaired in their social lives, in part, because of significant impairment in their ability to use attribution of mental states to interpret the behavior of others. Are they similarly constrained in their capacity to interpret behavior in terms of the groups to which people belong? Perhaps the most common, and certainly the most precocious, group-based interpretations of behavior are stereotypes. By definition, a *stereotype* is a generalization that applies to an individual simply by virtue of the social group to which he or she belongs. A stereotype is a nondemonstrative inference that can be used to understand the behavior of another person. By definition, it ignores individuating information, such as the mental state of the person.

At first blush, ToM-impaired autistic children would not seem the ideal population in which to explore social stereotypes. These children have many cognitive difficulties and virtually all have social decrements. Presuming that children acquire common social stereotypes through everyday experience, it is plausible that autistic children, whose everyday experience is singular and constrained, would likely have difficulty developing them. In an unpublished study, Elizabeth Bartmess, Eva Loth, and I examined whether autistic children could use common social stereotypes and, if so, whether they use them as readily as normally developing children.

We tested 11 ToM-impaired Scottish autistic children, with a mean verbal age of 5.0. Children were presented a series of picture pairs, each pair contrasting either in the targets' gender or race. For gender items, children were asked which of the targets is the child who would behave in a stereotype-consistent way (e.g., likes to play with dolls). Race items were essentially parallel. Children were asked which target would behave in a racial stereotype-consistent way (e.g., would return a lost wallet). Children's responses were scored for whether they chose the stereotype-consistent target or not. Strikingly, the autistic children reasoned overwhelmingly in accord with common stereotypes: 80% of the time on gender items and 60% of the time on race items. Even more striking, their judgments were indistinguishable from that which other researchers have found with normally developing preschoolers (Aboud, 1988).

In short, children with significant impairment in their ability to interpret the behavior of others with respect to mental states were virtually unimpaired in their ability to interpret the behavior of others in terms of the groups of which they were members. The capacity for group-based reasoning about behavior thus appears to be independent of the capacity for person-based reasoning about behavior. Lacking a ToM, as I observed earlier, represents a serious disability. It is not, however, a disability in understanding behavior *tout court*. Insult to ToM does not affect the ability to use very common strategies for understanding others. ToM is not a social reasoning deficit, but a (admittedly significant) problem with one particular kind of interpersonal reasoning. Social reasoning in the sense of reasoning about group dynamics is intact in autistic children, just as reasoning about the group dynamics of herd animals is intact (perhaps enhanced) in Temple Grandin.

THE ROBUSTNESS OF GROUP IDENTITY

We have reviewed work indicating that ToM, person-based reasoning does not exhaust the strategies folk use to interpret the behavior of others. Indeed, the evidence suggests that ToM, person-based reasoning, and social group-based reasoning are largely autonomous modes of interpretation. Moreover, such reasoning is early emerging and essentially a spontaneous development. Other research suggests that strategies that have generally been thought as person-based, such as attributions of intentional agent, are in fact not so. This last line of evidence comes from studies of adult cognition. The final question that I want to explore is whether the willingness to attribute intentions to nonpersons, specifically aggregates, is precocious?

In a classic study, Heider and Simmel (1944) found that subjects who were shown films of geometric figures moving in an apparently purposeful manner readily used intentional language to describe the film's events. Subsequent research found that this willingness to perceive geometric objects as intentional agents is developmentally robust. Berry, Springer, and their collaborators (Berry & Springer, 1993; Springer et al., 1996) found that 5-year-olds were as likely as adults to attribute intentionality to the geometric objects in Heider and Simmel's films. This willingness gradually emerges between 3 and 4 years of age, and parallels the emergence and elaboration of both ToM abilities and theory-like reasoning about social kinds.

A similar willingness to attribute intentions was found when the targets were collections of objects rather than individual objects. Bloom and Veres (1999) asked subjects to describe the events of a series of films depicting the same individual geometric figures engaged in the same patterned movement as in Heider and Simmel's film. They also asked subjects to describe the series of events in otherwise identical films in which individual objects were replaced with collections of disconnected objects that in their ensemble mapped onto the same geometric space as the individual objects. They found virtually the same degree of intentional attributions in subjects' descriptions of the event depicted in the object films and those depicted in the group films. In contrast, in two control conditions—one in which the groups did not move and the other in which the three groups moved repeatedly up and down in a straight line at a constant rate—subjects attributed either no (stationary condition) or very low (repeated condition) degrees of intentionality. In both conditions, intentional attributions were lower than in the object or group conditions in which the objects and groups of objects moved in apparently purposeful ways.

In an unpublished study, Michael Baran, Paul Bloom, Susan Gelman, and I examined whether children would similarly treat groups of objects as intentional agents. Of particular interest is whether they would treat groups as corporate or moral individuals, not simply as collections. To test these questions, we slightly modified Bloom and Veres' (1999) task. In their study, subjects viewed six films, four in which the object and group films were played both forward and reverse and two in the control conditions described earlier. In our study, 24 four-year-olds and 24 adults viewed three films: the object forward, the group forward, and the repeated movement control film. After each viewing, subjects were asked to describe the events of the film.

We replicated Bloom and Veres' findings: Children were as likely as adults to use intentional language when describing events in the object and group conditions, whereas both children and adults used significantly less intentional language to describe events in the repeated condition. Children's willingness to attribute intentionality is not restricted to animate creatures. Consistent with Premack (1991) and Gergely, Nadasdy, Csibra, and Biro (1995), certain patterns of movement trigger intentional interpretation. It is, however, possible that subjects in both our study and Bloom and Veres' perceived the groups as intentional entities because they interpreted the stimuli as individual objects not groups. To rule this out, Bloom and Veres asked subjects to describe the stimuli. They found that almost

all of the subjects described the characters either as groups (e.g. "a group made of blue things"), or with a plural count noun (e.g. "blue circles"). This was consistent with their descriptions of the events, which almost always contained at least some instances of plural references. (p. B6)

We used a different strategy for ruling out the possibility that groups were seen as intentional by virtue of the intentions of their constituents. We were interested in determining how often plural and singular referring terms were used and under what conditions each was employed. We also wanted to know whether the use of singular versus plural references varied systematically with the degree to which intentional language was used. There are two advantages to this analysis. First, it allowed us to evaluate whether plural or singular references were consistent throughout a given subject's description. That is, if the subject used a singular reference in describing a particular event, did she use a singular reference to describe all of the events in a particular film? Second, this analysis allowed us to assess whether descriptions were a function of the objects themselves or of the movement the objects were engaged in. The logic here is that if subjects perceived a group as an individual object, then they should do so consistently throughout the description of any given film. In that there was no occlusion of the stimuli during the film, there was nothing leading the subjects to infer that a group might have, for instance, become or been replaced with a similar looking single object while out of view. Second, it allows us to determine whether the use of singular references means that the subject is interpreting the stimulus as an object or as a corporate individual. The logic here follows the suggestion in the literature on entitativity that highly entitative groups are perceived as acting as an entity despite the fact that they are constituted of independent members, whereas simple collections are less likely to be perceived as entities.

Subjects differed in the consistency with which they used singular and plural referring expressions. Analyses of individual performances found that three quarters of the children used *both* singular and plural references in the group condition (reliably above from chance), whereas slightly under half (46%) did so in the repeated condition (not significantly different from chance). For adults, 91% and 79%, respectively, used both singular and plural references (both reliably better than chance). Thus, assuming that subjects did not believe that a group was replaced by or transformed in the course of a film, the use of both singular and plural referring terms is consistent with each subject imagining that at various times, the aggregates were both collections of individuals and individuals themselves. We found that subjects' use of singular versus plural referring terms varied systematically with how the event was interpreted. In the group condition, more singulars were used when high degrees of intentionality were attributed than when low degrees of intentionality, and the inverse pattern was found in the repeated movement condition (viz., more singulars were used when low intentionality was perceived than when high intentionality was perceived; of course lower levels of intentionality were attributed in the repeated movement condition). A three-way (age × condition × level of intentionality) ANOVA revealed a nonsignificant trend, with the pattern of reasoning being more pronounced among adults than among children.

To repeat, this pattern is informative because it supports the claim that groups that are interpreted as acting in intentional ways are more likely to be seen as corporate individuals than groups that are interpreted as not acting in intentional ways. The data, of course, do not permit us to determine whether high intentionality drives perceptions of corporateness or whether perceptions of corporateness cause highly intentional interpretation. They are, however, more consistent with the former—that high intentionality causes attribution of corporateness—because the varying dimension here is attribution of intentionality, not the physical nature (or necessarily even the activity the stimulus is performing). After all, the stimuli were identical throughout the film. In short, intentional attributions adhere to the action, not the group.

The idea that a given aggregate might be viewed as a corporate individual at one moment and a mere collection at another on the face of it seems counterintuitive. Shouldn't a group's characteristic status remain constant? The degree to which an aggregate's activities are intentional is presumably fundamental to its nature and hence immutable. However, a little reflection suggests that this need not be the case. Consider a herd of cattle. When a number of cattle are quietly grazing together, there is little motivation to construe their behavior as corporate, so that intuitively the following is odd:

(1) The herd wasn't moving because it was hungry.

whereas the following is not:

(2) The herd wasn't moving because the cattle weren't hungry.

In contrast, if the same group of cattle is in the midst of a stampede, the use of a singular reference consistent with corporate individuality makes sense.

(3) A bolt of lightening startled the herd, causing it to stampede.

Contrast this with a person. Properties fundamental to the intentional states of a person are not something that should vary over time all that much. Indeed, a considerable literature in psychology details the psychological effort people must invest to convince themselves that an individual's personality remains constant over time (Mischel & Shoda, 2000; Ross & Nisbett, 1991).

THE INVISIBILITY OF GROUPS

Several studies using the Heider and Simmel task have shown that it is the specific pattern of motion that invites people to attribute intentions to the geometric figures (Berry & Springer, 1993; Springer et al., 1996), suggesting that perceptual features are crucial to intentional attributions. This makes sense with respect to nonhuman aggregates. Herds, flocks, troops, gaggles, and the manifold terms listed earlier that refer to social aggregates are readily perceived as unitary confederations. They literally jump out at the observer. Coordinated movement plus a degree of spatial contiguity would thus seem an important determinant in the perception of corporate individuality.

But this cannot be the whole story. With the exception of lynch mobs and troops in fairly arcane and decidedly ineffective strategies of military engagement, most human social aggregations do not afford the opportunity for perceptually driven, bottom–up appraisals. Indeed, it is almost *inevitably* the case that human groups high on entitativity are something we imagine more than something we experience as a perceptual "whole." Ironically, given his appeal to Gestalt principles in the article that set entitativity research going, Campbell (1958) noted that he could just as well have entitled his now-classic paper "Perceiving Invisible Entities Such as Social Groups." He continued:

> For an anthropologist in isolated areas, the specification of the social units of tribe and clan may pose little difficulty. That status of entity and system, the useful boundaries of aggregation, may be as apparent to him as to a vertebrate biologist. But for groups in the modern western world, the problems become difficult. (p. 16)

Although Campbell's confidence in the transparency of traditional social life is misplaced, his general point is well taken. Whatever else entitative groups are, they seldom present themselves as perceptually consolidated confederations.

It might be argued, however, that even if we do not encounter social groups in the form of perceptually consolidated confederations, the diagnostic features of many groups (e.g., skin color) are sufficiently blatant that groupness can be inferred (Taylor & Fiske, 1978). Visual experience is assumed to drive children's early representations (Aboud, 1988) and to be the most important factor in determining adult judgments of group cohesiveness (Campbell, 1958; Dasgupta et al., 1999). This claim, however, is assumed and seldom actually empirically examined. Indeed, historical and experimental research has revealed that visual differences in appearance do not map well onto racial categories. Nor do they figure importantly in the development of racial categories during early childhood (Hirschfeld, 1993) or over historical time (Domínguez, 1986; Fredrickson, 2002; Stoler, 1995). The same individual's race would be quite different depending on whether he or she were born in Brazil, the United States, or South Africa, or whether he or she were born in the United States in 2001 or 1901. Within a single system of classification, race is permeable. The historian Linda Gordon (1999) documented an intriguing account of the racial transformation of a group of children in the early 20th century who were not White when they left New York, but who were White when they arrived in Arizona 1 week later. Hahn, Mulinare, and Teutsch (1992) examined race identification of all infants who died before their first birthday in St. Louis between 1983 and 1985. Despite the fact that these were the same infants, they found that significantly more were Black when they were born than when they died. Hahn et al. attributed the inconsistency to differences in the way race is determined at birth and death: At birth race is identified by parents, at death by a physician. Self-identification is based on genealogy, whereas other identification is based on appearance.

Focusing on outward appearances is not only misleading, but draws attention away from the representation of groups and to the representation of their individual members. It also trivializes the achievement that representing groups actually is by reducing it to something achieved through low-order perceptual processes. Stereotypes, for example, typically have been viewed as properties of individuals, rather than properties of the groups of which the individuals are tokens of a type. For the most part, nature of the groups stereotyped are explicitly deemed unimportant to understanding the processes of stereotype formation (Hamilton & Trolier, 1986). Yet as Tajfel's (1981) minimalist experiments have shown, ingroup favoritism emerges *even in the absence of groups*.

CONCLUSION

How our minds effortlessly represent representations of other people's minds is a fascinating problem, and one that psychology has rightly devoted a great deal of attention. Much of what we take for granted about sociality and everyday social cognition rests on it. Although memory presumably limits how far we can cascade representations of representations, if there is a single cognitive capacity without which human culture would not be possible, metarepresentation, of which ToM is the prime example, would be it (Sperber, 1996).

This acknowledged, over the past 10 years, I have worked to develop a theory of lay theorizing I have identified as *naive sociology*. It is meant to capture the specificity, origins, and mechanisms involved in lay folks' reasoning about social entities, reasoning about aggregate kinds. It has been done in complement with and contrast to ToM, on the one hand, and folk biology, on the other hand. I have argued that thinking about groups the way lay folk think about groups forces a reconsideration of two foundational notions about social thinking: the primacy of ToM and the primacy of person as the prototypical individual. As fascinating as the problem of how people imagine other people's minds is, it is unfortunate that it has been taken as *the* problem of social cognition. *Person* is doubtless a cognitive primitive. Manipulations and computations over this primitive are crucial to making sense of the world. I contend, however, that social entity is also a cognitive primitive. Manipulations and computations over it are just as essential in making sense of the world. Indeed, making sense of the social world, at least making the particular kind of sense that we humans do, would not be possible without it. By folding social entity into person-hood—by assuming that one social primitive will do—we lose sight of how great an achievement parsing the social world is. I acknowledge that we need a ToM. It would be bizarre to doubt it. I also believe that we need a theory of society—one that is equally powerful, equally basic, and equally subject to deficit as ToM. The problem is, we will never know this if we do not look.

ACKNOWLEDGMENTS

I am grateful to Elizabeth Bartmess, Chris Judd, Paulo Sousa, Dan Sperber, and Ann Stoler for their helpful comments.

REFERENCES

Aboud, F. E. (1988). *Children and prejudice*. York: Basil Blackwell.

Atran, S. (1990). *Cognitive foundations of natural history: Towards an anthropology of science*. New York: Cambridge University Press.

Baldwin, D. A. (1991). Infants' contribution to the achievement of joint reference. *Child Development, 62*(5), 1875–1890.

Baldwin, D. A., & Baird, J. A. (2001). Discerning intentions in dynamic human action. *Trends in Cognitive Sciences: Special Issue, 5*(4), 171–178.

Baron-Cohen, S. (1996). *Mindblindness: An essay on autism and theory of mind*. Cambridge, MA: MIT Press.

Barrett, J. L., & Keil, F. C. (1996). Conceptualizing a non-natural entity: Anthropomorphism in God concepts. *Cognitive Psychology, 31*(3), 1219–1247.

Berry, D. S., & Springer, K. (1993). Structure, motion, and preschoolers' perceptions of social causality. *Ecological Psychology, 5*(4), 273–283.

Bloom, P., & Veres, C. (1999). The perceived intentionality of groups. *Cognition, 71*, B1–B9.

Boyer, P. (1990). *Tradition as truth and communication: A cognitive description of traditional discourse*. New York: Cambridge University Press.

Byrne, R. W., & Whiten, A. (1988). *Machiavellian intelligence: Social expertise and the evolution of intellect in monkeys, apes, and humans.* New York: Oxford University Press.

Campbell, D. (1958). Common fate, similarity, and other indices of the status of aggregates of persons as social entities. *Behavioral Science, 3,* 14–25.

Carey, S. (1985). *Conceptual change in childhood.* Cambridge, MA: MIT Press.

Chomsky, N. (1965). *Aspects of the theory of syntax.* Cambridge, MA: MIT Press.

Dasgupta, N., Banaji, M. R., & Abelson, R. P. (1999). Group entitativity and group perception: Associations between physical features and psychological judgment. *Journal of Personality & Social Psychology, 77*(5), 1991–2003.

Domínguez, V. R. (1986). *White by definition: Social classification in creole Louisiana.* New Brunswick, NJ: Rutgers University Press.

Durkheim, E. (1915). *The elementary forms of the religious life.* New York: Macmillan.

Fairchilds, C. C. (1984). *Domestic enemies: Servants and their masters in Old Regime France.* Baltimore: Johns Hopkins University Press.

Fodor, J. A. (1975). *The language of thought.* New York: Crowell.

Fredrickson, G. M. (2002). *Racism: A short history.* Princeton, NJ: Princeton University Press.

Gelman, S. A. (1988). Children's expectations concerning natural kind categories. *Human Development, 31*(1), 28–34.

Gelman, S. A. (1992). Children's conception of personality traits: Commentary. *Human Development, 35*(5), 280–285.

Gelman, S. A., & Hirschfeld, L. A. (1999). How biological is essentialism? In D. L. Medin & S. Atran (Eds.), *Folkbiology* (pp. 403–446). Cambridge, MA: MIT Press.

Gelman, S. A., & Wellman, H. M. (1991). Insides and essence: Early understandings of the non-obvious. *Cognition, 38*(3), 213–244.

Gergely, G., Nadasdy, Z., Csibra, G., & Biro, S. (1995). Taking the intentional stance at 12 months of age. *Cognition, 56*(2), 1165–1193.

Gergely, G. B., & Harold Kiraly, I. (2002). Rational imitation in preverbal infants. *Nature, 415*(6873), 755.

Gordon, L. (1999). *The great Arizona orphan abduction.* Cambridge, MA: Harvard University Press.

Grandin, T. (1993). *Livestock handling and transport.* Wallingford, UK: CAB International.

Hahn, R. A., Mulinare, J., & Teutsch, S. M. (1992). Inconsistencies in coding of race and ethnicity between birth and death in US infants: A new look at infant mortality, 1983 through 1985. *JAMA, 267,* 259–263.

Hamilton, D. L., & Sherman, S. J. (1996). Perceiving persons and groups. *Psychological Review, 103*(2), 1336–1355.

Hamilton, D. L., & Trolier, T. K. (1986). Stereotypes and stereotyping: An overview of the cognitive approach. In J. Dovridio & S. Gaertner (Eds.), *Prejudice, discrimination, and racism* (pp. 127–163). San Diego, CA: Academic Press.

Haslam, N., Rothschild, L., & Ernst, D. (2000). Essentialist beliefs about social categories. *British Journal of Social Psychology, 39*(1), 2113–2127.

Heider, F., & Simmel, M. (1944). An experimental study of apparent behavior. *American Journal of Psychology, 57,* 243–259.

Heyman, G. D., & Gelman, S. A. (2000a). Beliefs about the origins of human psychological traits. *Developmental Psychology, 36*(5), 2665–2678.

Heyman, G. D., & Gelman, S. A. (2000b). Preschool children's use of trait labels to make inductive inferences. *Journal of Experimental Child Psychology, 77*(1), 2001–2019.

Hilton, J. L., & von Hippel, W. (1996). Stereotypes. *Annual Review of Psychology, 47,* 237–271.

Hirschfeld, L. A. (1993). Discovering social difference: The role of appearance in the development of racial awareness. *Cognitive Psychology, 25,* 317–350.

Hirschfeld, L. A. (1994). Is the acquisition of social categories based on domain-specific competence or on knowledge transfer? In L. Hirschfeld & S. Gelman (Eds.), *Mapping the mind:*

Domain specificity in cognition and culture (pp. 201–233). New York: Cambridge University Press.

Hirschfeld, L. A. (1995a). Do children have a theory of race? *Cognition, 54*(2), 209–252.

Hirschfeld, L. A. (1995b). The inheritability of identity: Children's understanding of the cultural biology of race. *Child Development, 66,* 1418–1437.

Hirschfeld, L. A. (1996). *Race in the making: Cognition, culture, and the child's construction of human kinds.* Cambridge, MA: MIT Press.

Inagaki, K., & Hatano, G. (2002). *Young children's naive thinking about the biological world.* New York: Psychology Press.

Kalish, C. W. (1996). Preschoolers' understanding of germs as invisible mechanisms. *Cognitive Development, 11*(1), 83–106.

Katz, J. J. (1981). *Language and other abstract objects.* Totowa, NJ: Rowan & Littlefield.

Keil, F. (1979). *Semantic and conceptual development: An ontological perspective.* Cambridge, MA: Harvard University Press.

Keil, F. C. (1994). The birth and nurturance of concepts by domains: The origins of concepts of living things. In L. Hirschfeld & S. Gelman (Eds.), *Mapping the mind: Domain specificity in cognition and culture* (pp. 234–254). New York: Cambridge University Press.

Lakoff, G. (1987). *Women, fire, and dangerous things: What categories reveal about the mind.* Chicago: University of Chicago Press.

Leslie, A. M. (1987). Pretense and representation: The origins of theory of mind. *Psychological Review, 94*(4), 412–426.

Leslie, A. M. (1991). The theory of mind impairment in autism: Evidence for a modular mechanism of development? In W. Andrew (Ed.), *Natural theories of mind: Evolution, development and simulation of everyday mindreading* (pp. 63–78). Oxford: Basil Blackwell.

Lucy, J. A. (1992). *Grammatical categories and cognition: A case study of the linguistic relativity hypothesis.* New York: Cambridge University Press.

Mahalingam, R. (1999). *Essentialism, power and representation of caste: A developmental study.* Unpublished doctoral thesis, University of Pittsburgh.

Marvick, E. (1974). Nature versus nurture: Patterns and trends in seventeenth century French child-rearing. In L. de Mause (Ed.), *History of childhood* (pp. 259–301). New York: Psychohistory Press.

Medin, D. L. (1989). Concepts and conceptual structure. *American Psychologist, 44*(12), 1469–1481.

Medin, D. L., & Ortony, A. (1989). Psychological essentialism. In S. Vosniadou & A. Ortony (Eds.), *Similarity and analogical reasoning* (pp. 179–195). New York: Cambridge University Press.

Meltzoff, A. N., & Brooks, R. (2001). Like me as a building block for understanding other minds: Bodily acts, attention, and intention. In B. Malle, L. Moses, & D. Baldwin (Eds.), *Intentions and intentionality: Foundations of social cognition* (pp. 171–191). Cambridge, MA: MIT Press.

Miller, G., & Johnson-Laird, P. (1976). *Language and perception.* New York: Cambridge University Press.

Mischel, W., & Shoda, Y. (2000). A cognitive-affective system theory of personality: Reconceptualizing situations, dispositions, dynamics, and invariance in personality structure. In E. Higgins & A. Kruglanski (Eds.), *Motivational science: Social and personality perspectives* (pp. 150–176). Philadelphia: Psychology Press, Taylor & Francis.

Moon, Y., & Nass, C. (1996). How real are computer personalities? Psychological responses to personality types in human–computer interaction. *Communication Research, 23*(6), 1651–1674.

Nass, C., & Moon, Y. (2000). Machines and mindlessness: Social responses to computers. *Journal of Social Issues, 56*(1), 2081–2103.

Perner, J., Frith, U., Leslie, A. M., & Leekam, S. R. (1989). Exploration of the autistic child's theory of mind: Knowledge, belief, and communication. *Child Development, 60*(3), 689–700.

Premack, D. (1991). The infant's theory of self-propelled objects. In D. Frye & C. Moore (Eds.), *Children's theories of mind: Mental states and social understanding* (pp. 39–48). Hillsdale, NJ: Lawrence Erlbaum Associates.

Rosengren, K. S., Gelman, S. A., Kalish, C. W., & McCormick, M. (1991). As time goes by: Children's early understanding of growth in animals. *Child Development, 62*(6), 1302–1320.

Ross, L., & Nisbett, R. E. (1991). *The person and the situation: Perspectives of social psychology.* Philadelphia: Temple University Press.

Sacks, O. W. (1995). *An anthropologist on Mars: Seven paradoxical tales* (1st ed.). New York: Knopf.

Sperber, D. (1975). *Rethinking symbolism.* New York: Cambridge University Press.

Sperber, D. (1996). *Explaining culture: A naturalistic approach.* Cambridge, MA: Blackwell.

Springer, K. (1996). Young children's understanding of a biological basis for parent–offspring relations. *Child Development, 67*(6), 2841–2856.

Springer, K., Meier, J. A., & Berry, D. S. (1996). Nonverbal bases of social perception: Developmental change in sensitivity to patterns of motion that reveal interpersonal events. *Journal of Nonverbal Behavior, 20*(4), 1199–1211.

Springer, K., & Ruckel, J. (1992). Early beliefs about the cause of illness: Evidence against immanent justice. *Cognitive Development, 7*(4), 429–443.

Stoler, A. L. (1995). *Race and the education of desire: Foucault's "History of sexuality" and the colonial order of things.* Durham, NC: Duke University Press.

Tajfel, H. (1981). *Human groups and social categories.* New York: Cambridge University Press.

Taylor, S., & Fiske, S. (1978). Salience, attention, and attribution: Top of the head phenomena. In L. Berkowitz (Ed.), *Advances in experimental social psychology* (Vol. 11, pp. 249–288). New York: Academic Press.

Thibaut, J. W., & Kelley, H. H. (1959). *The social psychology of groups.* New York: Wiley.

Tomasello, M. (1999). *The cultural origins of human cognition.* Cambridge, MA: Harvard University Press.

Wellman, H. M. (1990). *The child's theory of mind.* Cambridge, MA: MIT Press.

Wellman, H. M., & Gelman, S. A. (1988). Children's understanding of the nonobvious. In *Advances in the psychology of human intelligence* (Vol. 4, pp. 99–135). Hillsdale, NJ: Lawrence Erlbaum Associates.

Whorf, B. L. (1956). *Language, thought, and reality; selected writings.* Cambridge, MA: Technology Press of Massachusetts Institute of Technology.

Woodward, A. L. (1998). Infants selectively encode the goal object of an actor's reach. *Cognition, 69*(1), 1–34.

Yuill, N. (1992). Children's conception of personality traits. *Human Development, 35*(5), 1265–1279.

Yzerbyt, V., Castano, E., Leyens, J.-P., & Paladino, M.-P. (2000). The primacy of the ingroup: The interplay of entitativity and identification. In W. Stroebe & M. Hewstone (Eds.), *European review of social psychology* (Vol. 11, pp. 257–295). Chichester, UK: Wiley.

Yzerbyt, V. Y., Rogier, A., & Fiske, S. T. (1998). Group entitativity and social attribution: On translating situational constraints into stereotypes. *Personality & Social Psychology Bulletin, 24*(10), 1089–1103.

Framing and the Theory-Simulation Controversy: Predicting People's Decisions

Josef Perner
Anton Kühberger
University of Salzburg

Human society is an interaction of minds. A central question is how minds understand each other. Two fundamental positions have been proposed. People have folk-psychological knowledge of what goes on in other people's minds and how that makes them act in particular situations. This kind of knowledge has been dubbed a "theory" (Churchland, 1981; Fodor, 1987) and the theoretical position the "Theory Theory" (TT). Alternatively, people imagine themselves being in another person's situation and thereby generate the same mental processes and action tendencies that the other person has in that situation, and then attribute the thus activated mental states and action tendencies to the other person. This process has been dubbed "replication" (Heal, 1986) and more commonly "simulation" (Gordon, 1986) and the theoretical position the "Simulation Theory" (ST).

THEORY THEORY VERSUS SIMULATION THEORY

This difference can be explained further on a simple example from Heal (2001) about how we might figure out what M is likely to conclude if she believes propositions p_1 to p_n and is interested in whether q is the case. An act of simulation would entail the following steps [capitalization ours]:

At t_1: I JUDGE that M believes that $p_1 - p_n$ and is interested in whether
 q.

At t_2: I ENTERTAIN reflectively the contents $p_1 - p_n$, and whether q.
At t_3: This reflection leads to my ENTERTAINING the content that q.
At t_4: I CONCLUDE that M believes that q.

With the capitalizations we try to highlight the mental processes (mental states) with which one entertains representations about the world and differentiate them from the description of what they represent. The inference from $p_1 - p_n$ to q is an act of *simulating* because I simply let my own reasoning process go from ENTERTAINING [that $p_1 - p_n$] to ENTERTAINING [that q]. In contrast, use of a *theory* would require entertaining a piece of knowledge about people making inferences (i.e., ENTERTAINING [that someone <u>believing</u> that $p_1 - p_n$ will also <u>believe</u> that q]).

The two approaches can, of course, also be applied to decision making. Assume a person is given the following options and problem:

(A) being paid € 18, or

(B) accepting a gamble and be paid € 36 with a winning probability of p = 1/2 (or else get nothing).

What will she choose? Using a theory or simulation to predict her choice, we would proceed as follows:

Theory:

I KNOW [when high amounts are involved, people tend to <u>be cautious</u>. € 18 is substantial. Therefore she will <u>opt for</u> (A)].

USE my knowledge to PREDICT: "She will take (A)."

Simulation:

I IMAGINE [being given this choice] and

DECIDE: [Hmmm! I take (A)].

Then I PREDICT [that she, too, will take (A)].

A BRIEF HISTORY OF THE THEORY-SIMULATION CONTROVERSY: TWO IMPORTANT POINTS

1. In the beginning, there was an all-or-none dispute between simulation theorists and theory theorists: How we predict and understand other people is purely a matter of using a theory or purely a matter of simulation. Apart from a worry that the distinction collapses conceptually (e.g., Davies & Stone, 2001), both sides (e.g., Heal, 1995; Stich & Nichols, 1995) have come to acknowledge that in most instances of predicting or understanding someone's mental state or action there is some theory and some simulation involved. Thus, methods are called for to decide when we use

theory and when we use simulation. Unfortunately, there is only one proposal on the table (Perner, Gschaider, Kühberger, & Schrofner, 1999) of how to assess which method is used in a given case. Next we briefly describe this method and use it to decide the case for two different predictions of people's choices in decision situations.

2. When it was thought that our predictions of others were exclusively based on either theory use or simulation, it seemed that simulation should be a fairly fail-safe process as long as we can assume a likeness in relevant aspects between predictor and predicted (Nichols, Stich, Leslie, & Klein, 1996). Because Nichols et al. (1996) purported that there is a rich body of findings to the contrary, they argued against the use of simulation. However, there are obvious reasons that simulation may yield wrong predictions: (a) People may fail to imagine the other person's situation correctly and, consequently, trigger in simulation different mental processes in the predictor than those operating in the predicted. (b) Moreover, some relevant features of real situations cannot be imagined in a way so that they trigger in imagination the same mental processes as they do in reality. Here we concentrate on a decision effect, the so-called "framing effect," to see what can and cannot be simulated.

THE FRAMING EFFECT

The original task is known as the *Asian Disease Problem* (Tversky & Kahneman, 1981). An Asian virus is expected to kill 600 people unless one of two treatments is being used:

- (positively framed)—Treatment *A* will save 200 lives for sure, Treatment *B* will save all 600, with a probability of 1/3; or
- (negatively framed)—With Treatment *C* 400 will die for sure, with Treatment *D* all 600 will die, with a probability of 1/3.

In the positively framed version of this problem, about three fourths of the respondents preferred saving 200 lives for sure, over the option that offered a one-third chance of saving 600 lives. In the negatively framed version, however, about three fourths of the respondents preferred the one-third chance of losing no lives over the sure loss of 200 lives. From a formal point of view, there should not be any systematic preference because the positively framed options as well as the negatively framed options yield either exactly 200 lives (sure options), or an expected value of 200 lives (risky options). But there is a *framing effect*—namely, the systematic tendency of risk aversion in the positively framed problem (preference for Treatment A) and of risk seeking in the negatively framed problem (preference for Treatment D).

Because people consider this finding puzzling, it shows that we do not have an explicit, consciously aware theory of the framing effect. So an interesting question is whether people can predict this effect. In pursuit of this question, we made a most obvious, yet for us still astounding, discovery—that the effect is actually not an effect of real decisions, but an effect of hypothetical decisions: "Which treatment would you take if you were in the situation of . . . ?" In other words, the famous framing effect is a finding about what people *think* how they (or others) would decide in particular situations. This is a very curious situation when one thinks of it. What would one say about a memory researcher who goes around asking people: "If I read 40 words to you and then asked you half an hour later what they were, how many would you be able to remember?" and then report people's estimates as findings on human memory? He would certainly not be taken seriously. Kühberger, Schulte-Mecklenbeck, and Perner (2002) pointed to the hypothetical nature of a core process in decision making that justifies, to some degree, why the practice of investigating behavior in hypothetical situations makes more sense in the case of decision making than for memory research. Moreover, the fact that the core component of real decisions consists of hypothesizing about the consequences of different actions, decision processes are particularly suited for simulation. By imagining how one would decide, one engages in the same process of considering possible consequences of action as when one makes actual decisions. Perhaps decision theorists have come to rely fairly uncritically on hypothetical experiments as evidence about real decisions because they are tacit simulation theorists.

However, there have been voices questioning the validity of such hypothetical investigation for real decision behavior (e.g., Grether & Plott, 1979; in the context of the *preference reversal phenomenon*, another anomaly in preferential choice). Actually, however, only a few empirical studies checked whether the framing effect exists when people gamble for real money (Levin, Chapman, & Johnson, 1988; Paese, 1995; Wiseman & Levin, 1996). Success was mixed. One problem with these studies was that they only used fairly trivial payoffs of a couple of dollars, whereas the classic effect was found with scenarios of life and death. Kühberger, Schulte-Mecklenbeck, and Perner (2002) systematically varied size of payoff: expected values of ATS 10 (approx. € 0.75) versus ATS 250 (approx. € 18), and whether the decision was real or merely hypothetical in four independent, randomly determined groups of university students. For example, in the *positive framing condition*, participants were offered, as part of their payment for participating in a tedious artificial grammar learning experiment, the following options:

Sure option (S+): Take your earned amount of € 18,

or

Risky option (R+): be given € 36 if bead of chosen color is drawn from an urn of black and white beads (p = 1/2), otherwise nothing.

In the negative framing condition, participants were given an advance of € 36 in the knowledge that they would have to repay part of this sum at the end. After the experiment, they were given the following options:

Sure option (S⁻): Pay back € 18 of the € 36,

or

Risky option (R⁻): pay back all of the € 36, if bead of other color than chosen color is drawn from an urn of black and white beads (p = 1/2), or else give back nothing.

The analysis of choices showed an interaction between payoff size and framing. For substantial payoffs (expected gain of € 18), there was indeed the expected framing effect (hitherto only reported for hypothetical decisions): 66% S+, but only 43% S⁻. In contrast, with small payoffs, there was no difference depending on how the option was framed. Both groups tended to risk their trivial payoffs and did not opt for the sure options: only 14% S+ and 20% S⁻.

Another four groups of students were paid for their participation directly and then asked hypothetically to predict their choice for these options: Their answers surprisingly closely matched the choices in the real decisions: 68% S+, but only 50% S⁻ for substantial payoffs, and only 16% S+ and 20% S⁻ for trivial payoffs, replicating the large literature of a hypothetical framing effect for large payoffs.

Together these data establish that a framing effect exists for substantial real payoffs (new), which can be predicted quite accurately in hypothetical decisions (previously established in the literature), and it establishes a large effect of payoff size especially for positively framed decisions (15% vs. 67% S+), which can also be accurately predicted (15% vs. 70% S+). We now can turn to our central question of whether these accurate predictions are based on theory (presumably implicit/unconscious knowledge) or simulation.

THE METHOD TO DECIDE

The basic idea behind the method developed by Perner, Gschaider, Kühberger, and Schrofner (1999) centers on the question of how people best deal with two different predictions. Will their predictions be more accurate if each person is *independently* given only one prediction task, or is it best to present both situations *juxtaposed* and let each person work on both predictions? These two prediction conditions are shown in Fig. 6.1 for the example of the framing effect.

The starting point is an imagined situation. This imagination then triggers mental processes and action tendencies in the person imagining these situations. The accuracy of the prediction depends on how well the imagined situation triggers the same processes in the imagining person as those that occur in the person who experiences these situations in real life. On face value, it seems plausible that imagining a single situation would serve this purpose optimally. When asked to simulate two different situations at a time, this might lead to interference or not. But in any case, it is hard to see how doing two predictions at a time (one after the other or really simultaneously) could lead to an improvement of the prediction. On the basis of these considerations, we can conclude (unless some additional assumptions are made):

> *If predictions for two juxtaposed situations are more accurate than predictions for each single situation presented independently, then* **simulation theory** *has no natural explanation at hand.*

In contrast, if we assume that predictions are based on theory, there is a ready explanation for why predictions for juxtaposed situations would be more accurate than predictions for each situation in isolation: The juxtaposition singles out the relevant factor that produces the target effect. Hence, the theory can be applied accurately without being distracted by other potentially relevant factors applicable to each situation in isolation. Hence, we can conclude:

> *If predictions for two juxtaposed situations are more accurate than predictions for each single situation presented independently, then* **theory theory** *has a natural explanation ready.*

Let us now consider the result that independent predictions for each single situation are more accurate than predictions for juxtaposed situations. Simulation theory has a ready answer: One can simulate only one situation at a time. The juxtaposition of the other situation interferes with the imaginatory process of the situation currently simulated. On this intuition, we can conclude:

> *If predictions for two independent situations are more accurate than predictions for two juxtaposed situations, then* **simulation theory** *has a natural explanation ready.*

SIMULATION OR THEORY

FIG. 6.1. Overview of target conditions and two different prediction conditions using the example of positively and negatively framed decision problems.

A problem for this method occurs at this point because theory theory—being somewhat more easily adjustable than simulation theory—can also account for this case. For instance, it can claim, with some plausibility, that juxtaposition makes people try to solve the two tasks simultaneously, leading to information overload with detrimental effects on prediction accuracy. Alternatively, juxtaposition by itself may trigger an additional theory—that would not come to mind in independent presentation—which interferes with the accurate independent predictions. How plausible such ad hoc explanations are depends, however, on the particular problem, and often one can find plausible arguments against them or use control conditions to empirically rule them out (see Perner et al., 1999, for how one such plausible ad hoc theory could be ruled out by appropriate controls). Under the assumption that for a given problem such additional assumptions can be ruled out, then theory theory finds it hard to account for this difference between prediction conditions and we can conclude (under the strong proviso that such amendments can be ruled out):

*If predictions for two independent situations are more accurate than predictions for two juxtaposed situations, then **theory theory** has no natural explanation at hand.*

In the following experiment, we contrasted independent with juxtaposed predictions for two effects: the framing effect for high payoffs, and the payoff-size effect for positively framed problems reported by Kühberger et al. (2002). Informal observations of how people react when being told about these effects indicate that people are surprised when they learn about the framing effect, but find the payoff-size effect quite understandable because with larger payoffs one tends to get more cautious. Hence, one would expect that for the conditions with different payoff sizes, predictions might show the pattern in favor of a theory, while in case of the framing effect independent predictions might be more accurate than juxtaposed predictions, indicating a use of simulation.

Experiment 1: Payoff Size—A Case of Theory

As a basis for this experiment, we use the finding by Kühberger et al. (2002) for positively framed problems that people choose the sure option (S+) 66% for large payoffs (EV = € 18), but only 14% of the time for trivial payoffs (EV = € 0.75). This provides the target effect that we use to measure the accuracy of our participants' hypothetical predictions of what people would choose in this situation under independent and juxtaposed prediction conditions.

Method

Participants. We distributed booklets among 217 volunteers from the University of Salzburg in a Research Methods Course (178 women, mean age of 22.1 years, and 39 males, mean age of 25.2 years).

Design and Procedure. The design was a 2 × 2 factorial design, with presentation condition (independent vs. juxtaposed) as a between-participants factor and payoff size (large payoff of € 18 vs. small payoff of € 0.75) as a factor that was varied between participants in the independent presentation condition and—per necessity—within participants in the juxtaposition condition. To present each participant in the juxtaposed condition with both payoffs defines the juxtaposition condition. To make this design tractable for statistical analysis, the group of participants in juxtaposed condition was split randomly in half; for one half only the prediction data for the large payoff condition was used, and for the other half only the prediction data for the small payoff condition was used. This somewhat conservative measure (because it ignores the information from half the data in this group; see Perner et al., 1999) makes the factor payoff size for the statistical analysis a purely between-participants manipulation. Participants were randomly assigned to one of three groups: independent prediction with large payoffs (n = 76), independent prediction with small payoffs (n = 65), and juxtaposed prediction with small and large payoffs (n = 76). They were then introduced to the task. They were asked to indicate how they would decide in their respective condition (of the experiment by Kühberger et al., described earlier). The description of the experiment included the fact that the choice was given as payment for participation in a 45-minute artificial grammar experiment.

Results and Discussion. Figure 6.2 shows the relevant data. The left panel shows the target effect for small and large payoffs reported by Kühberger et al. (2002). The other two panels show the data from this experiment. The third panel in Fig. 6.2 shows the mean percentage of sure option predictions under juxtaposed presentation. The means closely correspond to the original target effect that over 65% chose the sure option for large payoffs, but less than 25% chose it for the small payoff. The difference in predictions was also highly significant: McNemar $\chi^2(1, N = 76)$ = 28.19; $p < .001$. Also the independent predictions showed the payoff size effect [$\chi^2(1, N = 141) = 4.73; p < .05$], but the means are much closer together than in the original target effect. Moreover, the effect predicted in independent presentation is considerably smaller—hence the prediction

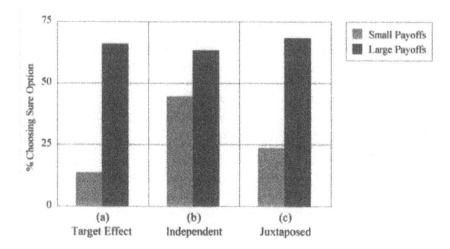

FIG. 6.2. Effect of payoff-size: (a) choice proportions as reported in Kühberger et al. (2002), (b) predicted choice proportions in independent presentation, and (c) predicted choice proportions in juxtaposed presentation.

is less accurate—than the effect predicted under juxtaposed presentation. To test this difference in accuracy, we used the mentioned method of reducing the juxtaposed prediction data to between-participant comparison by ignoring for half the participants the predictions for large payoffs and for the other half the small payoff predictions. The selected data (sure option choices) were analyzed by a 2 × 2 ANOVA with presentation (independent vs. juxtaposed) and size of payoff as two between-participants factors. Besides a significant effect for size of payoff [$F(1, 213) = 30.17, p < .001$], there was also a highly significant interaction between size of payoff and presentation [$F(1, 213) = 7.59, p < .01$], which confirms the impression from Fig. 6.2 that juxtaposed presentation led to a more accurate prediction of the original target effect than independent predictions. As a measure of caution, the same analysis was repeated with the other half (ignored set) of data from the juxtaposed condition. The same main effect of payoff size [$F(1, 213) = 23.38, p < .001$] and interaction [$F(1, 213) = 4.56, p < .05$] was significant.

The fact that juxtaposed predictions were significantly more accurate than independent predictions speaks for the use of theory in making these predictions. In some ways, this result was anticipated because people, when told of this effect, find it plausible and have an explanation ready: that people tend to be more cautious with larger than with smaller amounts of money.

Experiment 2: The Framing Effect—A Case of Simulation

Our second experiment investigated whether people can also predict the framing effect correctly and whether their predictions for this effect are similarly based on theory. As target effect, we use again the findings by Kühberger et al. (2002). This time, however, we use only large payoffs (approx. € 18) and compare positively framed (where 66% of the participants chose the sure option) with negatively framed choices (where only 43% of the participants chose the sure option).

Method

Participants. Three hundred and fifty-six psychology volunteers (173 women with a mean age of 21.6 years, and 183 men with a mean age of 23.6 years) from the University of Salzburg were recruited in seminars. They were tested in groups of up to 30 students.

Design and Procedure. The design was basically the same 2 × 2 factorial design as in Experiment 1; this time, however, we manipulated prediction condition (independent vs. juxtaposed) and framing (positive vs. negative) as between-participants factors. As we did in Experiment 1 with the factor payoff size, framing was turned into a between-participants factor by analyzing only half of the data in the juxtaposed condition. However, to preempt a plausible counterargument in case the findings will indicate use of simulation, a refinement needed to be added. If juxtaposed prediction were found to be inferior to independent prediction, it could plausibly be argued that by juxtaposing framing conditions participants were made aware that positively and negatively framed problems are actually equivalent. Additionally, this could trigger the theory that rational people should choose the same option in equivalent situations. Hence, the prediction accuracy would suffer under juxtaposed prediction, but not because of the use of simulation, but because juxtaposition triggers an additional theory. Note that the traditional presentation of options makes it particularly compelling that people recognize the equivalence of positively and negatively framed options: because juxtaposition makes it easy to see that (e.g., the payoff of the negatively framed sure option [S−; +36 − 18 = +18] is equivalent to the payoff of the positively framed sure option [S+; +18]). Hence, we aimed at obscuring this apparent equivalence by using different monetary values in the two framing conditions. Thus, we used two high payoff conditions: € 36/18, and € 26/13. Half of the participants in the framing juxtaposition groups were presented with identical payoffs, and half were

TABLE 6.1
The Refined Design of Experiment 2:
Individual Conditions With Sample Sizes

		% sure option choices		
Condition	n	S⁺	S⁻	Characterization
Independent predictions				
F⁺18/36	48	60.4		
F⁻18/36	41		31.7	
F⁺13/26	47	78.7		
F⁻13/26	40		47.5	
Juxtaposed predictions				
F⁺18/36 vs. F⁻18/36	48	62.5	60.4	Same payoffs
F⁺13/26 vs. F⁻13/26	45	53.3	37.8	Same payoffs
F⁺13/26 vs. F⁻18/36	45	53.7	70.7	Payoffs contra framing
F⁺18/36 vs. F⁻13/26	42	58.7	39.1	Payoffs reinforce framing

Note. F⁺, positively framed; 18/36, expected-value/maximum; F⁻, negatively framed.

presented with different payoffs. A stronger framing effect in the different payoff than in the pure payoff condition would indicate use of the alleged additional theory triggered by juxtaposition. To control for possible effects of the change in monetary value, several other counterbalancing conditions needed to be implemented (see Table 6.1).

Results and Discussion. We first analyzed the results for the independent prediction conditions with a 2 x 2 ANOVA with *framing* (positive, negative) and *payoff size* (€ 13, € 18) as two between-participants factors and the number of sure option choices as the dependent variable. There was a strong framing effect of 69.4% sure option choices for positive frames and 39.6% for negative frames [$F(1, 172) = 17.67, p < .001$]. Figure 6.3 shows the framing effect for independent predictions (center panel) in relation to the target effect (left panel) taken from Kühberger et al. (2002). The independent predictions match the target effect very closely.

For the juxtaposed conditions with equal payoffs a 2 × 2 ANOVA with *payoff size* as between factor and *framing* as within factor showed no framing effect [$F(1, 91) = 2.64, p > .10$]. The effect of payoff size was only marginally significant [$F(1, 91) = 3.33, p > .07$], and there was no interaction between the two factors [$F(1, 91) = 1.54, p > .22$].

For the juxtaposed conditions with different payoffs, we see in Table 6.1 (last two rows) that the framing effect (%S⁺ > %S⁻) depends on whether the size of payoff works in the same direction or whether it works against. However, when we cancel out the effects of the payoff by averaging the two last rows, we find no framing effect (S⁺ = 56%, S⁻ = 55%). Hence, there is no evidence that the framing effect diminishes because juxtaposed pre-

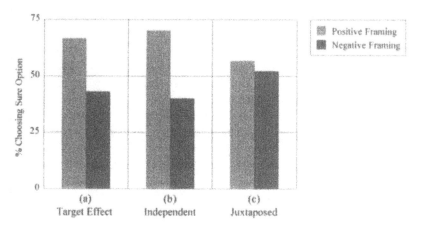

FIG. 6.3. Effect of framing: (a) choice proportions as reported in Kühberger et al. (2002), (b) predicted choice proportions in independent presentation, and (c) predicted choice proportions in juxtaposed presentation.

sentation makes participants realize the monetary equivalence of problems and triggers the wrong theory that people are rational and make the same choices in equivalent problems.

Figure 6.3 (right panel) shows the framing effect for juxtaposed predictions for equal and different payoffs combined. As one can see, the effect is much smaller than under independent prediction. To test the statistical reliability of this difference, the same technique of using only half the juxtaposition data as in Experiment 1 was used. The 2 × 2 ANOVA with framing (positive vs. negative) and presentation condition (independent vs. juxtaposed) as between factors showed a significant effect of framing [$F(1, 352) = 9.55, p < .01$] and a significant interaction between framing and presentation condition [$F(1, 352) = 7.15, p < .01$]. The same analysis computed with the complementary juxtaposition data that were ignored in the first analysis showed exactly the same significant effects [$F(1, 352) = 7.82, p < .01$, and $F(1, 352) = 5.50, p < .02$]. This significant interaction supports the idea that the accurate independent predictions are based on simulation rather than theory.

EVALUATION OF EXPERIMENTAL RESULTS

We are genuinely concerned to preempt any unwarranted overreliance and uncritical use of our empirical method for deciding between the use of simulation and theory. Although it is—to our knowledge—the only one available, we need to be aware of its limitations. From the informative prediction patterns, one can at best draw the following conclusions. The strongest case can be made when juxtaposed prediction outstrips independent prediction. Then simulation theorists have a difficult time explaining this difference in terms of simulation. Consequently there must be some element of theory responsible for the difference in prediction accuracy. Note that this does not mean that simulation might not play an important, even crucial part in the process as well. All that can be claimed is that there must be some piece of theory involved. To illustrate, prediction of the payoff size effect in Experiment 1, which showed a pattern that we interpret as a sign of theory use, may have been based on simulation (producing the independent prediction difference). However, the results of this simulation were instantly recognized as meaningful in the juxtaposed condition, giving rise to a corresponding theory, which then enhanced the difference even further, leading to the pattern of a larger difference under juxtaposed than under independent prediction. Although this pattern correctly indicates theory use, that theory was only triggered by simulation and accounts only for this additional enhancement.

The other informative pattern of independent prediction outstripping juxtaposed prediction occurred in the case of the framing effect in Experiment 2. Theory theorists would have a hard time explaining this difference without recourse to ad hoc explanations. Unfortunately, several fairly plausible ad hoc explanations come to mind. We have explicitly addressed one of them and successfully rejected it with appropriate control conditions. However, there are still other plausible explanations open to the theory theorist (e.g., that dealing with both decision problems at the same time overloads the system and leads to impaired accuracy). One can muster some argument against this by pointing out that it is unlikely that the complexity of these two tasks is any greater than the complexity of predicting the payoff size effect in Experiment 1. Because it did not lead to impaired accuracy there, why should it do so now?

To conclude, on the basis of a single finding, one cannot make a good case against the theory theorist. Only by comparing performance across different conditions can we firm up our case and make life difficult for the theory theorist. In the long run, our method only has value if we can use it to get consistent data in connection with a theory of when and what aspects of a problem we capture with theory and which by simulation. Here is a suggestion of how simulation can be developed to make empirical predictions that can then be tested by our method.

MAKING SIMULATION THEORY TESTABLE

Davies and Stone (1998) discussed whether one can accurately simulate the effect of alcohol or other drugs on our mind. Our suggestion is that one cannot: A principle of simulation is that only the effects of mental states, which one can reflectively entertain, on our mind can be successfully simulated. Now, let us contrast two real situations. In *Situation 1*, I drink *five really strong beers in the correct belief* that I am drinking five really strong beers. As an effect, my mind will become clouded and I will walk out of the room in a rather wobbly fashion. In *Situation 2*, I consume *five alcohol-free beers in the erroneous belief* that they are five really strong beers. Consequently, there will not be any particular effect on my mind and, barring any expectancy effects or consumption of any other substances with similar effects, I will walk out the room fairly straight. If I attempt to use simulation to predict my behavior, my simulation will yield the same result in each case because my mental states (i.e., how I perceive the situation to be, believe it to be, or want it to be) are the same in both situations. Only the invocation of these mental states through imagination will trigger the further mental states leading to my different gaits when leaving the room. Hence, simulation cannot arrive at different predictions for these situations.

One might suggest to simply imagine in *Situation 1* that the beers are real strong ones. This, however, will not help because the imagination of drinking real beers is not what causes the relevant further mental states. One can see this from the fact that my erroneous belief in *Situation 2* does not have that effect. It does not have that effect because alcohol affects the mind directly by being consumed and not via beliefs of being consumed.

So, from this principled prediction, which is based on the definition of how simulation works, it follows that if someone uses simulation to make predictions of how I will walk out of the room, this person will make the same prediction for both situations. If the predictions do differ, they must be based on theory. At this juncture, our method can be helpful. It can confirm that the correct predictions are based on theory and not on simulation. That is—cautiously formulated—it should never occur in this case that independent predictions are more accurate than juxtaposed predictions. With some luck, we might even get the stronger result that juxtaposed predictions are consistently better than independent predictions in every case of this kind, where simulation theory states that simulation cannot yield a difference.

In conclusion, we make a plea to simulation theorists for making an effort to spell out (for their respective versions of simulation theory) which differences can be made on the basis of simulation and which cannot. If we have those implications spelled out, we can make simulation theory empirically testable. Our method can thereby be usefully employed in checking whether accurate predictions are based on theory, when simulation theory states that it cannot be based on simulation, and that predictions are based on simulation, when simulation theory states that it can be and is based on simulation.

ACKNOWLEDGMENTS

Preparation of this chapter was financially supported by the Austrian Science Fund (FWF Project P11397-SOZ "Simulation and Decision Making" and FWF Project P16007-G05 "Theory and Simulation in Decisions"). This article was previously published in *Mind & Society*, 6(3), 2002, pp. 65–80.

REFERENCES

Churchland, P. M. (1981). Eliminative materialism and the propositional attitudes. *Journal of Philosophy, 78*, 67–90.

Davies, M., & Stone, T. (1998). Folk psychology and mental simulation. In A. O'Hear (Ed.), *Current issues in the philosophy of mind* (Suppl. 42, pp. 53–82). Cambridge: Cambridge University Press.

Davies, M., & Stone, T. (2001). Mental simulation, tacit theory, and the threat of collapse. *Philosophical Topics, 29*, 127–173.

Fodor, J. (1987). *Psychosemantics*. Cambridge, MA: MIT Press.

Gordon, R. M. (1986). Folk psychology as simulation. *Mind & Language, 1*, 158–171.

Grether, D., & Plott, C. (1979). Economic theory of choice and the preference reversal phenomenon. *American Economic Review, 69*, 623–638.

Heal, J. (1986). Replication and functionalism. In J. Butterfield (Ed.), *Language, mind, and logic* (pp. 135–150). Cambridge: Cambridge University Press.

Heal, J. (1995). How to think about thinking. In M. Davies & T. Stone (Eds.), *Mental simulation* (pp. 33–52). Oxford: Blackwell.

Heal, J. (2001). *Other minds, rationality and analogy*. Inaugural address, St. John's College, Cambridge University.

Kühberger, A., Schulte-Mecklenbeck, M., & Perner, J. (2002). Framing decisions: Real and hypothetical. *Organizational Behavior and Human Decision Processes, 89*, 1162–1175.

Levin, I. P., Chapman, D. P., & Johnson, R. D. (1988). Confidence in judgments based on incomplete information: An investigation using both hypothetical and real gambles. *Journal of Behavioral Decision Making, 1*, 29–41.

Nichols, S., Stich, S., Leslie, A., & Klein, D. (1996). Varieties of off-line simulation. In P. Carruthers & P. K. Smith (Eds.), *Theories of theories of mind* (pp. 39–74). Cambridge: Cambridge University Press.

Paese, P. W. (1995). Effect of framing on actual time allocation decisions. *Organizational Behavior and Human Decision Processes, 61*, 67–76.

Perner, J., Gschaider, A., Kühberger, A., & Schrofner, S. (1999). Predicting others through simulation or by theory? A method to decide. *Mind & Language, 14*, 57–79.

Stich, S., & Nichols, S. (1995). Folk psychology: Simulation or tacit theory? In M. Davis & T. Stone (Eds.), *Folk psychology* (pp. 123–158). Oxford: Blackwell.

Tversky, A., & Kahneman, D. (1981). The framing of decisions and the psychology of choice. *Science, 211*, 453–458.

Wiseman, D., & Levin, I. (1996). Comparing risky decision making under conditions of real and hypothetical consequences. *Organizational Behavior and Human Decision Processes, 66*, 241–250.

7

An Evolutionary Perspective on Testimony and Argumentation

Dan Sperber
Institut Jean Nicod

In the Preface of his seminal *Knowledge in a Social World*, Goldman (1999) wrote:

> Traditional epistemology has long preserved the Cartesian image of inquiry as an activity of isolated thinkers, each pursuing truth in a spirit of individualism and pure self-reliance. This image ignores the interpersonal and institutional contexts in which most knowledge endeavors are actually undertaken. Epistemology must come to grips with the social interactions that both brighten and threaten the prospect for knowledge. (p. vii)

In chapters 4 and 5, he discussed two generic social practices: testimony (i.e., the transmission of observed [or allegedly observed] information from one person to others), and argumentation (i.e., the defense of some conclusion by appeal to a set of premises that provide support for it). In discussing these practices, Goldman has many important things to say about the way they brighten the prospect for knowledge and very little about the way they threaten it. I would like to slightly redress the balance and put a touch of gray in Goldman's rosy picture by considering testimony and argumentation in the light of some evolutionary considerations.

My main claim will be that a significant proportion of socially acquired beliefs are likely to be false beliefs—and this not just as a result of the malfunctioning, but also of the proper functioning of social communication. I argue in particular that the cognitive manipulation of others is one of the effects that makes the practices of testimony and argumentation adaptive. This contributes to explaining why these practices have evolved and stabilized among humans. To highlight the claim, I start by contrasting social with individual mechanisms of belief production, arguing that individual mechanisms are, under normal conditions and in the absence of social interference, reliable sources of true beliefs. Humans, being permanently immersed in society and culture, are, even when on their own, the locus of ongoing cultural processes, and therefore never good examples of truly individual systems of belief production in the intended sense. The contrast I draw is not, therefore, between human individual and social cognition; it is between ideal types. Moreover, because I mention individual cognition just for the sake of this contrast, I do not spend time defending or hedging the evolutionary psychology approach I adopt on the topic.

Cognitive systems found in individual organisms are biological adaptations. Adaptations are traits that have evolved and stabilized because, by producing some characteristic effect, they have contributed to the fitness of the organisms endowed with them. Producing this fitness-enhancing effect can be described as the function of the adaptation, and I use *function* in this sense (for elaborations and variations of this notion of function, see Allen, Bekoff, & Lauder, 1998). Roughly, the function of a cognitive system is to provide the organism with information about itself and its environment, and thus guide its behavior. There may be cases and situations where it is adaptive for a cognitive system to introduce systematic biases—for instance, of excessive caution or, on the contrary, of overconfidence (see Stich, 1990). But such cases are, I believe, marginal. We should generally expect the beliefs produced by an evolved cognitive system to be true. In other terms, cognitive systems are basically producers of knowledge. Of course their function is not to produce knowledge per se, let alone scientific knowledge. It is to produce knowledge relevant to the organism's welfare. They do so reliably in the kind of environment in which they have evolved. Put in a different type of environment, whether by historical accident or experimental design, stimulated by phenomena the representation of which is irrelevant to the organism welfare, cognitive systems may well become quite unreliable. For instance, perceptual illusions, which are very rare in a natural and familiar environment, may be common in artificially devised settings.

A normative evaluation of evolved cognitive systems will find them to be, in the performance of their function, at least good enough to make them advantageous to the organisms endowed with them (or else they would have been selected out). Given the high risks involved in moving around (in contrast with the plant strategy of staying put and letting things happen), the cognitive systems on which self-mobile organisms rely must be quite good at producing genuine information rather than errors. However, the function of these systems can be performed by means of an articulation of task- and domain-specific subsystems (in fact it is not obvious that it could be performed in any other way; see Sperber, 1994; Tooby & Cosmides, 1994). Natural individual cognition is therefore likely to produce true beliefs of a limited variety and import, nothing to wax epistemological about. Beliefs and belief-producing systems worth a philosopher's evaluation come with communication, language, and culture.

Communication might be seen as a wonderful extension of individual cognition—a kind of "cognition by proxy." A communicating organism is not limited to information derived from its own perceptions and inferences. It can benefit from the perceptions and inferences of others. Of course it risks suffering from others' mistakes, but to the extent that individual cognition is reliable, so should communication be, or so the story goes. An early defender of such a view is Reid (1970)—approvingly quoted by Goldman (1999)—who maintained:

> The wise and beneficent Author of nature, who intended that we should be social creatures, and that we should receive the greatest and most important part of our knowledge by the information of others, hath, for these purposes implanted in our natures two principle that tally with each other. The first of these principles is a propensity to speak truth [. . . The second principle] is a disposition to confide in the veracity of others, and to believe what they tell us. (Reid, 1970, pp. 238–240)

In stark contrast to this view, Dawkins and Krebs (1978), in their famous article "Animal Signals: Information or Manipulation," argued that the prime function of communication is not information, but manipulation of others. They were focusing on the interests of the signaler as a driving force in the evolution of signals. These interests are generally different from the receiver's. Both Reid's view and Dawkins and Krebs' original view were too extreme. In a later article, "Animals' Signals: Mind-Reading and Manipulation," Krebs and Dawkins (1984) argued for taking into account both the signaler's and the receiver's perspective. This is obviously correct and should also apply for the study of human communication.

For communication to stabilize within a species, as it has among humans, both the production and reception of messages should be advantageous. If communication were on the whole beneficial to producers of messages (by contributing to their fitness) at the expense of receivers, or beneficial to receivers at the expense of producers, one of the two behaviors would be likely to have been selected out, and the other behavior would have collapsed by the same token (incidentally, there are exceptions, in particular in interspecies communication). In other words, for communication to evolve, it must be a positive-sum game where, in the long run at least, both communicators and receivers stand to gain. For this it is not necessary that the interests of the two parties coincide, it is enough that they overlap. The way these interests match and differ influences the manner in which communication evolves and works. Let us look, then, at testimony and argumentation as two communicative practices from the points of view of both communicators and receivers.

TESTIMONY

Unlike argumentation, which is specifically human, testimony (in the sense of "the transmission of observed information"; Goldman, 1999, p. 103) is also found in other species. A paradigmatic nonhuman example is the bee dance: One worker bee, having found a source of food, communicates to other worker bees the direction and distance at which it is to be found. At the end of the process, the receiver bees are, presumably, in the same cognitive state with respect to the source of food as they would have been had they found it themselves. This indeed can be described as cognition by proxy.

In the human case, testimony does not have quite the same effects as direct perception. When Mary tells John that there is beer in the refrigerator, John is not exactly in the same cognitive state regarding the whereabouts of the beer as he would be had he seen it there himself. To begin with, had John seen the beer, his knowledge of its location would be more detailed and more vivid than when he is just told. More important, understanding what one is told involves recognizing a speaker's meaning, which need not be automatically accepted as true (Millikan [1984] disagreed and defended the view that human communication is also cognition by proxy; for a discussion, see Origgi & Sperber, 2000).

From the point of view of receivers, communication, and testimony in particular, is beneficial only to the extent that it is a source of genuine (and of course relevant) information. Just as in the case of individual cognition, there may be cases where biases in communicated information are beneficial (e.g., think of exaggerated encouragement or warnings), but these cases are marginal and I ignore them.

From the point of view of producers of messages, what makes communication, and testimony in particular, beneficial is that it allows them to have desirable effects on the receivers' attitudes and behavior. By communicating, one can cause others to do what one wants them to do and to take specific attitudes to people, objects, and so on. To achieve these effects, the communicator must cause the audience to accept as true messages that in turn will cause the adoption of the intended behaviors or attitudes. Often these behaviors or attitudes are best brought about by messages that are indeed truthful. In other cases, however, they are best brought about by messages that are not. It is common and often practically (if not morally) appropriate for communicators to achieve the goals they pursue through communication by misleading or deceiving their audience to some small or large degree. Deception is found in nonhuman animals, but there, just like communication in general, it is quite limited in contents and highly stereotyped. Humans, thanks to their cognitive abilities and, in particular, their metarepresentational capacity to represent the mental states of others, are unique in their ability to engage in creative and elaborate distortion and deception, and also in their ability to question in a reasoned manner the honesty of communicators. Except in marginal cases, it is not in the audience's interest to be deceived or in the communicator's interest to be disbelieved. Dishonest communicators go against the interest of their audience, and distrusting addressees thwart the intentions of communicators.

Looking first at single communication events, we can sketch the possible payoffs of communicators and addressees in game-theoretical terms (see Fig. 7.1). Communicators can be truthful or untruthful. Addressees can be trusting or distrusting. From the point of view of the communicator, the payoff of communication depends not on her own truthfulness or untruthfulness, but solely on the addressee's trust or distrust. The communicator, whatever she chooses to communicate, is better off if the addressee is trusting and worse off (in that her effort is thwarted) if he is distrusting. From the point of view of the addressee, the payoff of communication depends both on his own trust and on the communicator's truthfulness. When he is trusting, the addressee is better off if the communicator is truthful and worse off if she is untruthful. When the addressee is distrusting, he neither gains nor loses from communication (apart from missing a possible gain if the communicator was in fact truthful).

	addressee	
	trusting	distrusting
truthful	*gain/gain*	*loss/no gain*
communicator		
untruthful	*gain/loss*	*loss/no gain*

FIG. 7.1. The communicator's truthfulness and the addressee's trust determine their possible payoffs.

Although a communication event where the communicator is truthful and the addressee is trusting is advantageous to both, there is no stable solution to the game. The optimal strategy varies with the circumstances for each party. Communicators do not gain just from having any message believed by the addressee. They gain from having the addressee believe a message that brings about effects beneficial to the communicator. Communicators, accordingly, do not choose between being truthful and being untruthful; they choose between expressing and withholding a message, whether truthful or not, that, if believed by the addressee, should have the desired effects. Addressees, on their side, know that it is not systematically in the interest of the communicator to speak truly, and therefore it is not in their interest to be systematically trusting.

How trusting should addressees be? If, in order never to be misled, addressees were to decide to be systematically distrusting, they would miss all the potential benefit of testimony. After all, it is not at all the case that the communicator's interests are always best served by misinforming the audience. Quite often, true testimony is the best or even the only way to have the intended effect on the addressee, who then stands to gain from accepting the testimony as truthful. However, if addressees were to decide to be systematically trusting, they would often be deceived (especially by communicators, who, having realized that they were systematically trusting, would not be hindered in the use of distortion and deception by the fear of detection). So, it is in the interest of addressees to calibrate their trust as closely as possible to match the trustworthiness of the communicator in the situation. However, there is no fail-safe way for addressees to reap all the benefits of communication without incurring the cost of being at times deceived. Still, if communication has stabilized among humans, it must be that there are ways to calibrate one's confidence in communicated information so that the expected benefits are greater than the expected costs. More about this later.

So far I have argued that part of the function of communication—the part having to do with the communicator's interest—is optimally fulfilled by the production of messages likely to have certain effects on the audience, irrespective of their truth. It is the causing of desirable effects on the audience that makes communication advantageous to the communicator; without these effects, communication would not have evolved and stabilized. In other words, it is naive to think, in the general case, and in particular in the human case, of the communicator as acting as proxy for the addressee's cognitive needs. The false beliefs spread by communication are not just due to communicators transmitting their own false beliefs or to their sometimes misusing communication to serve a purpose that goes against its function. Communication produces a certain amount of misinformation in the performance of its function, more specifically in the performance of those aspects of its function that are beneficial to the communicator.

There is, however, a possible Reidian objection. The game of communication is iterated again and again among the same parties, who moreover alternate in the roles of communicator and addressee. Just as the iteration of prisoner's dilemma games may cause the parties to converge on cooperation (see Axelrod, 1984; Kitcher, 1993), the iteration of acts of communication might stabilize a strategy of truthfulness on the part of communicators and of trust on the part of addressees. The evolution of communication is just, so the argument goes, a particular case of the evolution of cooperation, and reciprocal altruism is possible in that area just as it is in others.

The argument could be fleshed out as follows. In iterated communication, a communicator achieves on each occasion both short- and long-term effects. The short-term effects typically consist of modifying the addressee's beliefs and, indirectly, the addressee's attitude and behavior toward the things communication was about. The long-term effects achieved by an act of communication have to do with the opinion that the audience takes of the communicator's reliability as a source of information and, more generally, of her as a person who is helpful or unhelpful, modest or arrogant, considerate or inconsiderate, and so on. The authority, respect, and so on granted to a communicator affect the effectiveness of her future communications.

Whereas it is easy to see that, in many cases, one's short-term goals as a communicator may best be served by departing from the truth, it might seem that one's long-term goals of establishing or maintaining credibility—and therefore one's future short-term goals as a communicator—should always be best served by being truthful. Indeed, often one's overall interest is best served by forsaking the benefits that would come from misleading one's audience to maintain or increase one's ability to influence this audience in the future. Often yes, but not always. There are situations where communicators might better serve not just their short-term, but also their long-term goals, by being untruthful. Let me mention two considerations in passing. First, credibility is not always best served by truthfulness: Some lies are more credible than some truths. Second, credibility is not the only virtue addressees look for in communicators. For instance, it is often advantageous to flatter powerful people, who care as much about loyalty as credibility, even if it means misleading them. More to the point here is a third consideration—the fact that, in the communication game, long-term effects do not always trump short-term effects. To understand why, we must shift from the communicator's perspective to the audience's.

It is a matter of common observation that people are willing to believe, not everybody, but many other people—relatives, spouses, friends, colleagues, or politicians—even when they know these people have occasionally lied to them. Why shouldn't some version of the tit-for-tat strategy (Axelrod, 1984) prevail in the iterated game of communication (you lie to me, I cease believing you)? In games of the prisoner's dilemma type, it is always advantageous to defect, provided there is no sanction for defection. By the same token, in iterated prisoner's dilemma games, it is rational to sanction any defection of the other party by a refusal to cooperate for at least several turns. In the communication game, it is only sometimes advantageous to deceive; often it so happens that the communicator stands to benefit most by sharing true information. Therefore, the fact that a communicator has lied in specific circumstances is no evidence that he or she would in other circumstances.

The communication game is also different from the market situation, where the same goods can be obtained from many different sellers and where the buyer can and should turn away from dishonest sellers. Each communicator has information that no one else possesses, be it just information about him or herself. So, deciding to systematically ignore the messages of a particular communicator, especially a communicator with whom one stands in an ongoing relationship, can be very costly. The best choice for addressees is to adjust trust not just to each communicator, but to every combination of communicator, situation, and topic. Given this, it is not particularly advantageous for a communicator to adopt a (morally correct) policy of systematic truthfulness. It will generally not be sufficient to cause total trust in the audience, and occasional departures from truthfulness, even if discovered, are unlikely to cause radical distrust.

ARGUMENTATION

The effectiveness of nonhuman animal communication depends on receivers automatically accepting most signals. There may be forms of human unintentional communication where acceptance of a signal is also automatic, as in crowd panic. In the case of human intentional communication, acceptance of a testimony is dependent on trust in the communicator's truthfulness. Testimony, however, is not the only mode of communication of facts, and the effectiveness of human communication is not entirely dependent on the audience's trust. Given the cognitive capacities of humans, and in particular their metarepresentational abilities, human communicators are not limited to testifying to the truth of what they want their audience to accept. They can give reasons as to why the addressee should accept their assertion, and addressees can inspect these reasons and recognize their force even if they have no confidence at all in the communicator. To take an extreme example, a recognized liar whose testimony would never be accepted on anything could nevertheless convince his audience of a logical or mathematical truth by providing clear proof of it.

The capacity to reason is in evidence in both individual reflection and dialogical argumentation. However, it is typically viewed as, first and foremost, a property of the individual Cartesian thinker. Its function, besides practical reasoning, is seen as that of allowing the individual to go beyond perception-based beliefs and to discover facts with which it happens not to have had perceptual acquaintance and, more important, theoretical facts with which there is no way to be perceptually acquainted. On this view, reasoning is a higher level form of individual cognition, a superior tool for the pursuit of knowledge.

From an evolutionary psychology perspective, there is something implausible in this view of reasoning. The expectation is that there should be domain- and task-specific inferential mechanisms corresponding to problems and opportunities met in the environment in which a species has evolved. But, or so the argument goes, it is unclear that there would have been much pressure for the evolution of a general reasoning ability that would presumably be slow and costly and would perform less well than specialized mechanisms in their domains. At best such an ability would handle—and not too well—issues and data, the processing of which had not been preempted by more effective specialized devices. Some evolutionary psychologists have concluded that there is no general "logical" ability in the human psychological makeup. I have argued differently that there are evolutionary reasons to expect a kind of seemingly general reasoning mechanism in humans, but one that is, in fact, specialized for processing communicated or to-be-communicated information (Sperber, 2000). The function of this mechanism is linked to communication rather than individual cognition. It is to help audiences decide what messages to accept and to help communicators produce messages that will be accepted. It is an evaluation and persuasion mechanism, not, or at least not directly, a knowledge-production mechanism.

As I noted earlier, for communication to have stabilized among humans, audiences must have developed ways to calibrate their confidence in incoming information effectively enough for the benefits of communication to remain well above the costs. Actually, the potential benefits are so important, and the risks of deception so serious, that all available means of calibration of trust may well have evolved. Three such means come to mind. One is paying attention to behavioral signs of sincerity or insincerity (but these can be faked to some extent; see Ekman, 1985). A second, more important, means consists of trusting more or less as a function of the known degree of benevolence of the communicator (thus trusting relatives more than strangers, friends more than enemies, etc.; this may seem obvious, but note that it is very different from the Reidian idea—that Reid went on to qualify—of a "disposition to confide in the veracity of others, and to believe what they tell us"). There is a third means, which is to pay attention both to the internal coherence of the message and to its external coherence with what is already believed otherwise. It seems plausible that all three of these means have indeed evolved among humans. I want to focus on the third—coherence checking. (I use *coherence* and *incoherence* to refer to logical relationships and evidential relationships of support and undermining).

A problem well known to anybody who has ever tried to lie and stick to one's lie over time is that it is increasingly hard to keep it coherent with what is otherwise known to the audience without embellishing it, and it is increasingly difficult to embellish it without introducing internal inconsistencies. A sincere but false claim is also likely to encounter coherence problems. A useful method, then, to detect misinformation and, in particular, deception is to check for the internal and external coherence of messages.

Coherence checking should be useful for detecting all false beliefs, whether derived from communication or individual cognition. So why, if it exists at all, shouldn't it have evolved primarily as a tool of individual cognition? Here is the answer. Coherence checking involves a high processing cost, it cannot be done on a large scale because it would lead to a computational explosion, and it is fallible. Individual mechanisms of perception and inference, although not perfect, are probably reliable enough to make, on balance, checking the coherence of their outputs superfluous or even disadvantageous. We would be surprised to discover that coherence checking occurs in a nonhuman species (and if we did, we should look for peculiarity of the informational environment of the species that would make the procedure beneficial).

My first suggestion is this: Coherence checking—which involves metarepresentational attention to logical and evidential relationships between representations—evolved as a means of reaping the benefits of communication while limiting its costs. It originated as a defense against the risks of deception. This, however, was just the first step in an evolutionary arms race between communicators and audiences (who are of course the same people, but playing—and relying more or less on—two different roles).

The next move in the evaluation-persuasion arms race was from the communicator's side and consisted of displaying the coherence the audience might look for before accepting the message—a kind of "honest display" with many well-known analogs in animal interaction. Testimony can be given by a mere concatenation of descriptive sentences. Displaying coherence requires an argumentative form; the use of logical terms such as *if, and, or,* and *unless;* and use of words indicating inferential relationships such as *therefore, since, but,* and *nevertheless.* It is generally taken for granted that the logical and inferential vocabulary is—and presumably emerged as—tool for reflection and reasoning. From an evolutionary point of view, this is not particularly plausible. The hypothesis that such terms emerged as tools for persuasion may be easier to defend.

The next steps in the arms race are for the audience to develop skills at examining arguments of the communicator, and for communicators at improving their argumentative skills. Thus emerges an argumentation mechanism of rhetorical construction and epistemic evaluation of messages. This mechanism processes representations that have or are to be communicated. These are a very special kind of object in the world. Moreover, the mechanism pays attention only to some properties of these representations, their logical and evidential relationships. In other words, this metarepresentational device is highly domain- and task-specific. Yet the communicative representations it processes can be about anything. So, by causing these representations to be accepted, the argumentation mechanism contributes to the production of beliefs in all domains and possesses in this sense a kind of virtual domain-generality.

Regardless of whether you accept the evolutionary hypothesis I just suggested, the fact remains that argumentation has a different function for communicator and audience. To communicators, it is a means of persuasion; to audiences, it is a means to critically evaluate a message before accepting it. It might seem that, by displaying the coherence of their message, communicators handicap their ability to deceive their audience. This is true—honest argumentation is harder to fake than honest testimony—but only to a certain extent. As already noted, coherence checking cannot be thorough (especially when it is carried out at the speed of speech at the same time as the already effort-demanding comprehension process), and it is fallible. Real arguments are at best enthythematic and often just allude to the existence and structure of a complete demonstration. Effective argumentation, from the point of view of the persuader, is argumentation that can sustain the degree of checking that the audience is likely to submit it to. From the point of view of the audience, cost and benefit considerations are in play: The cost of risking being misled has to be weighed against both the cost of refusing some genuine and relevant information (as in the case of testimony) and the processing cost of checking the coherence of the argument. This latter cost can be modulated by checking more or less thoroughly, and clearly it would not be advantageous to check every argument quite thoroughly. This leaves room for a deceptive use of argumentation, as is well known since the Sophists.

From a logical and epistemological normative point of view, sophistry is a perversion of argumentation—a practice that goes against its very raison d'être. From the evolutionary perspective that I have just sketched, sophistry is a way to use the "honest display" strategy of argumentation in a dishonest way and thereby make it more advantageous for the communicator. In other words, sophistry contributes to making argumentation adaptive.

CONCLUSION

Wherever you have a function, you can normatively evaluate the degree to which the function is effectively fulfilled. In this limited sense, function entails norm. Because the function of communication presents itself differently for communicator and audience, one can evaluate to what extent a communicative practice allows communicators to achieve intended effects on the audience and to what extent it provides to the audience genuine and relevant information. One can work out a global evaluation of the extent to which a communicative practice provides to both parties sufficient overall benefits so as to cause them to perpetuate the practice.

It might seem then that to approach communicative practices from a veristic epistemological point of view, as does Goldman, is to espouse the point of view of the audience, to impose on it a norm that may be perfectly justifiable on ethical or pragmatic grounds, but that is not the norm that effectively governs the communicative process. However, the true situation is interestingly more complex. Communicators present themselves as honest, regardless of whether they are and whether it is their interest to be. Without presenting themselves as truthful, liars could not even begin to lie. Without presenting themselves as rational argumentators, sophists could not even begin to persuade. In other terms, the point of view of the audience determines a norm that is implicit in and intrinsic to all communication—a norm of truthfulness in testimony and of rationality in argumentation. These norms are not imposed from without, or from just one point of view in the communication process. They are overtly accepted by both parties to the process.

The point of this chapter could be rephrased by saying that the epistemic norms implicit in the process of communication (discussed in greater detail in Wilson & Sperber, 2002) are to a limited but interesting extent at odds with the very function of communication. Therefore, the prospect for knowledge discussed by Goldman is not just brightened—immensely so—it is also significantly threatened by well-functioning communicative practices.

ACKNOWLEDGMENTS

This article was previously published in *Philosophical Topics*, 29, 2001, pp. 401–413.

REFERENCES

Allen, C., Bekoff, M., & Lauder, G. (Eds.). (1998). *Nature's purposes: Analyses of function and design in biology*. Cambridge, MA: MIT Press.

Axelrod, R. (1984). *The evolution of cooperation*. New York: Basic Books.

Dawkins, R., & Krebs, J. R. (1978). Animal signals: Information or manipulation? In J. R. Krebs & N. B. Davies (Eds.), *Behavioural ecology* (pp. 282–309). Oxford: Basil Blackwell Scientific Publications.

Ekman, P. (1985). *Telling lies*. New York: Norton.

Goldman, A. (1999). *Knowledge in a social world*. Oxford: Clarendon.

Kitcher, P. (1993). The evolution of human altruism. *Journal of Philosophy, 90*, 497–516.

Krebs, J. R., & Dawkins, R. (1984). Animal signals: Mind-reading and manipulation. In J. R. Krebs & N. B. Davies (Eds.), *Behavioural ecology* (pp. 380–402). Sunderland, MA: Sinauer Associates.

Millikan, R. (1984). *Language, thought and other biological categories*. Cambridge, MA: MIT Press.

Millikan, R. (1993). *White Queen psychology and other essays for Alice*. Cambridge, MA: MIT Press.

Origgi, G., & Sperber, D. (2000). Evolution, communication, and the proper function of language. In P. Carruthers & A. Chamberlain (Eds.), *Evolution and the human mind: Language, modularity and social cognition* (pp. 140–169). Cambridge: Cambridge University Press.

Reid, T. (1970). *An inquiry into the human mind* (T. Duggan, Ed.). Chicago: University of Chicago Press.

Sperber, D. (1994). The modularity of thought and the epidemiology of representations. In L. A. Hirschfeld & S. A. Gelman (Eds.), *Mapping the mind: Domain specificity in cognition and culture* (pp. 39–67). New York: Cambridge University Press.

Sperber, D. (2000). Metarepresentations in an evolutionary perspective. In D. Sperber (Ed.), *Metarepresentations: A multidisciplinary perspective* (pp. 117–137). New York: Oxford University Press.

Stich, S. (1990). *The fragmentation of reason*. Cambridge, MA: MIT Press.

Tooby, J., & Cosmides, L. (1994). Origins of domain specificity: The evolution of functional organization. In L. A. Hirschfeld & S. A. Gelman (Eds.), *Mapping the mind: Domain specificity in cognition and culture* (pp. 85–116). New York: Cambridge University Press.

Wilson, D., & Sperber, D. (2002). Truthfulness and relevance. *Mind, 111*, 583–632.

Normativity and Epistemic Intuitions

Jonathan M. Weinberg
Indiana University

Shaun Nichols
University of Arizona

Stephen Stich
Rutgers University

In this chapter, we propose to argue for two claims. The first is that a sizeable group of epistemological projects—a group that includes much of what has been done in epistemology in the analytic tradition—would be seriously undermined if one or more of a cluster of empirical hypotheses about epistemic intuitions turns out to be true. The basis for this claim is set out in the next section. The second claim is that, while the jury is still out, there is now a substantial body of evidence suggesting that some of those empirical hypotheses *are* true. Much of this evidence derives from an ongoing series of experimental studies of epistemic intuitions that we have been conducting. A preliminary report on these studies is presented in turn. In light of these studies, we think it is incumbent on those who pursue the epistemological projects in question to either explain why the truth of the hypotheses does not undermine their projects, or to say why, in light of the evidence we present, they nonetheless assume that the hypotheses are false. In the fourth section, which is devoted to Objections and Replies, we consider some of the ways in which defenders of the projects we are criticizing might reply to our challenge. Our goal in all of this is not to offer a conclusive argument demonstrating that the epistemological projects we criticize are untenable. Rather, our aim is to shift the burden of argument. For far too long, epistemologists who rely heavily on epistemic intuitions have proceeded as though they could simply ignore the empirical hypotheses we set out. We will be well satisfied if we succeed in making a plausible case for the claim that this approach is no longer acceptable.

To start, it is useful to sketch a brief—and perhaps somewhat idiosyncratic—taxonomy of epistemological projects. With the aid of this taxonomy, we "locate in philosophical space" (as Wilfrid Sellars used to say) those epistemological projects that, we maintain, are threatened by the evidence we present. There are at least four distinct, although related, projects that have occupied the attention of epistemologists. Following Samuels (in preparation), we call them the Normative Project, the Descriptive Project, the Evaluative Project, and the Ameliorative Project.

The Normative Project, which we are inclined to think is the most philosophically central of the four, attempts to establish norms to guide our epistemic efforts. Some of these norms may be explicitly regulative, specifying which ways of going about the quest for knowledge should be pursued and which should not. This articulation of regulative norms is one of the more venerable of philosophical undertakings, going back at least to Descartes's *Regulae* and evident in the work of Mill, Popper, and many other important figures in the history of philosophy, and it continues in philosophy today. For example, when Goldman (1980) chastises internalism for being unable to provide us with "Doxastic Decision Principles", he challenges the ability of internalism to pull its weight in this aspect of the Normative Project. The Normative Project also aims to articulate what might be called *valuational* norms, which attempt to answer questions like: What is our epistemic good? How should we prefer to structure our doxastic lives? One may not be able to generate regulative principles from the answers provided; rather, the answers tell us at what target the regulative principles should aim.

The Descriptive Project can have a variety of targets, the two most common being epistemic concepts and epistemic language. When concepts are the target, the goal is to describe (or "analyze") the epistemic concepts that some group of people actually invoke. When pursued by epistemologists (rather than linguists or anthropologists), the group in question is typically characterized rather vaguely by using the first-person plural. They are "our" concepts, the ones that "we" use. Work in this tradition has led to a large literature attempting to analyze concepts like knowledge, justification, warrant, and rationality.[1] When language is the focus of the Descriptive Project, the goal is to describe the way some group of people use epistemic language or analyze the meaning of their epistemic terms. Here again the group is almost invariably "us".

Many epistemologists think there are important links between the Normative and Descriptive Projects. Indeed, we suspect that these (putative) links go a long way toward explaining why philosophers think the De-

---

[1]The literature on conceptual analysis in epistemology is vast. For an elite selection, see the essays assembled in Sosa (1994).

scriptive Project is so important. In epistemology, knowledge is "the good stuff," and to call a belief an instance of knowledge is to pay it one of the highest compliments an epistemologist can bestow.[2] Thus, terms like *knowledge, justification, warrant*, etc. and the concepts they express, are themselves plausibly regarded as implicitly normative. Moreover, many philosophers hold that sentences invoking epistemic terms have explicitly normative consequences. So, for example, "S's belief that p is an instance of knowledge" might plausibly be taken to entail "*Ceteris paribus*, S ought to believe that p" or perhaps "*Ceteris paribus*, it is a good thing for S to believe that p."[3] For reasons that will emerge, we are more than a bit skeptical about the alleged links between the Descriptive and Normative Projects. For the time being, however, we leave the claim that the two projects are connected unchallenged.

The Evaluative Project tries to assess how well or poorly people's actual belief-forming practices accord with the norms specified in the Normative Project. To do this, of course, another sort of descriptive effort is required. Before we can say how well or poorly people are doing at the business of belief formation and revision, we have to say in some detail how they actually go about the process of belief formation and revision.[4] The Ameliorative Project presupposes that we do not all come out with the highest possible score in the assessment produced by the Evaluative Project, and it asks how we can improve the way we go about the business of belief formation. In this chapter, our primary focus is on the Normative Project and on versions of the Descriptive Project which assume that the Descriptive and Normative Projects are linked in something like the way sketched earlier.

INTUITION-DRIVEN ROMANTICISM AND THE NORMATIVITY PROBLEM

Epistemic Romanticism and Intuition-Driven Romanticism

A central question that the Normative Project tries to answer is: *How ought we go about the business of belief formation and revision?* How are we to go

---

[2]This is a view with a venerable history. In Plato's (1892/1937) *Protagoras*, Socrates says that "knowledge is a noble and commanding thing," and Protagoras, not to be outdone, replies that "wisdom and knowledge are the highest of human things" (p. 352).

[3]Perhaps the most important advocate of extracting normative principles from analyses of our epistemic terms is Chisolm (1977). This approach is shared in projects as otherwise dissimilar as Bonjour (1985) and Pollock and Cruz (1999).

[4]For further discussion of the Evaluative Project, see Samuels, Stich, and Tremoulet (1999); Samuels, Stich, and Bishop (2002); and Samuels, Stich, and Faucher (2004). These papers are available on the Web site of the Rutgers University Research Group on Evolution & Higher Cognition: http://ruccs.rutgers.edu/ArchiveFolder/Research%20Group/research.html

about finding an answer to this question? Once an answer has been proposed, how are we to assess it? If two theorists offer different answers, how can we determine which one is better? Philosophers who have pursued the Normative Project have used a variety of methods or strategies. In this section, we want to begin by describing one influential family of strategies.

The family we have in mind belongs to a larger group of strategies that (just to be provocative) we propose to call *Epistemic Romanticism*. One central idea of 19th-century Romanticism was that our real self, the essence of our identity, is implanted within us, and that to discover who we really are we need but let that real identity emerge. Epistemic Romanticism assumes something rather similar about epistemic norms. According to Epistemic Romanticism, knowledge of the correct epistemic norms (or information that can lead to knowledge of the correct norms) is implanted within us in some way, and with the proper process of self-exploration we can discover them. As we read him, Plato was an early exponent of this kind of Romanticism about matters normative (and about much else besides). So *Epistemic Platonism* might be another (perhaps equally provocative) label for this group of strategies for discovering or testing epistemic norms.

There are various ways in which the basic idea of Epistemic Romanticism can be elaborated. The family of strategies that we want to focus on all accord a central role to what we call *epistemic intuitions*. Thus, we call this family of strategies *Intuition-Driven Romanticism* (IDR). As we use the notion, an epistemic intuition is simply a spontaneous judgment about the epistemic properties of some specific case—a judgment for which the person making the judgment may be able to offer no plausible justification. To count as an IDR strategy for discovering or testing epistemic norms, the following three conditions must be satisfied:

1. The strategy must take epistemic intuitions as data or input. (It can also exploit various other sorts of data.)

2. It must produce, as output, explicitly or implicitly normative claims or principles about matters epistemic. Explicitly normative claims include regulative claims about how we ought to go about the business of belief formation, claims about the relative merits of various strategies for belief formation, and evaluative claims about the merits of various epistemic situations. Implicitly normative claims include claims to the effect that one or another process of belief formation leads to justified beliefs or to real knowledge, or that a doxastic structure of a certain kind amounts to real knowledge.

3. The output of the strategy must depend, in part, on the epistemic intuitions it takes as input. If provided with significantly different intuitions, the strategy must yield significantly different output.[5]

Perhaps the most familiar examples of IDR are various versions of the reflective equilibrium strategy in which "a [normative] rule is amended if it yields an inference we are [intuitively] unwilling to accept [and] an inference is rejected if it violates a [normative] rule we are [intuitively] unwilling to amend" (Goodman, 1965, p. 66). In a much-discussed article called "Can Human Irrationality Be Experimentally Demonstrated," Cohen (1981) proposes a variation on Goodman's strategy as a way of determining what counts as rational or normatively appropriate reasoning.[6] It is of some importance to note that there are many ways in which the general idea of a reflective equilibrium process can be spelled out. Some philosophers, including Cohen, advocate a "narrow" reflective equilibrium strategy, whereas others advocate a "wide" reflective equilibrium strategy. Both of these alternatives can be elaborated in various ways.[7] Moreover, the details are often quite important because different versions of the reflective equilibrium strategy may yield different outputs, even when provided with exactly the same input.

Another example of the IDR strategy can be found in Goldman's (1986) important and influential book, *Epistemology and Cognition*. A central goal of epistemology, Goldman argues, is to develop a theory that specifies which of our beliefs are epistemically justified and which are not, and a fundamental step in constructing such a theory is to articulate a system of rules or principles evaluating the justificatory status of beliefs. These rules, which Goldman calls *J-rules*, specify permissible ways in which cognitive agents may go about the business of forming or updating their beliefs. They "permit or prohibit beliefs, directly or indirectly, as a function of some states, relations, or processes of the cognizer" (Goldman, 1986, p. 60). But, of course, different theorists may urge different and incompatible sets of J-rules. To decide whether a proposed system of J-rules is correct, we must appeal to a higher criterion—Goldman (1986) calls it "a criterion

---

[5]Note that as we have characterized them, epistemic intuitions are spontaneous judgments about *specific cases*. Some strategies for discovering or testing epistemic norms also take intuitions about general epistemic or inferential principles as input. These count as IDR strategies provided that the output is suitably sensitive to the intuitions about specific cases that are included in the input.

[6]For a useful discussion of the debate that Cohen's paper provoked, see Stein (1996), chapter 5.

[7]See, for example, Elgin (1996), chapter IV; Stein (1996), chapters 5 and 7.

of rightness"—which specifies a "set of conditions that are necessary and sufficient for a set of J-rules to be right" (p. 64). But now the theoretical disputes emerge at a higher level, for different theorists have suggested different criteria of rightness. Indeed, as Goldman notes, an illuminating taxonomy of epistemological theories can be generated by classifying them on the basis of the sort of criterion of rightness they endorse. So how are we to go about deciding among these various criteria of rightness? The answer, Goldman maintains, is that the correct criterion of rightness is the one that comports with the conception of justification that is "embraced by everyday thought and language" (p. 58). To test a criterion, we consider the judgments it would entail about specific cases, and we test these judgments against our "pretheoretic intuition". "A criterion is supported to the extent that implied judgments accord with such intuitions and weakened to the extent that they do not" (Goldman, 1986, p. 66).[8]

The examples mentioned so far are hardly the only examples of IDR. Indeed, we think a plausible case can be made that a fair amount of what goes on in normative epistemology can be classified as IDR. Moreover, to the extent that it is assumed to have normative implications, much of what has been written in descriptive epistemology in recent decades also counts as IDR. For example, just about all of the vast literature that arose

---

[8]In an insightful commentary on this chapter, presented at the Conference in Honor of Alvin Goldman, Joel Pust noted that in his recent work, Goldman (1992, 1999; Goldman & Pust, 1998) offered a rather different account of how epistemic intuitions are to be used:

> Very roughly, Goldman's more recent view treats the targets of philosophical analysis as concepts in the psychological sense of "concept," concrete mental representations causally implicated in the production of philosophical intuitions. On this new view, intuitions serve primarily as reliable evidence concerning the intuitor's internal psychological mechanisms [. . .]. Especially interesting in the context of this chapter is the fact that Goldman *explicitly disavows* the common assumption of "great uniformity in epistemic subjects" judgments about cases, noting that this assumption may result from the fact that philosophers come from a "fairly homogeneous subculture." (Goldman, 1992, p. 160)

This new psychologistic account makes it easier to explain why intuitions are reliable evidence of some sort. However, this reliability is gained by deflating the evidential pretensions of intuitions so that they are no longer treated as relevant to the *nonlinguistic* or *nonpsychological* question, which is the central concern of the Normative Project: "What makes a belief epistemically justified?" Although Goldman's approach solves *a* problem about the reliability of intuitions by telling us that *the fact that people have* certain intuitions is a reliable indicator of their psychological constitution, it does not resolve the problem that motivated Stich's argument because *that* problem was whether we are justified in treating *the content of* our epistemic intuitions as a reliable guide to the nature of justified belief. So, although Goldman's use of intuitions in his new project seems to me largely immune to [the criticisms in this chapter], this is because that project has aspirations quite different from those of traditional analytic epistemology.

in response to Gettier's classic (1963) article uses intuitions about specific cases to test proposed analyses of the concept of knowledge.[9]

For many purposes, the details of an IDR strategy—the specific ways in which it draws inferences from intuitions and other data—are of enormous importance. But since our goal is to raise a problem for all IDR strategies, the exact details of how they work play no role in our argument. Thus, for our purposes, an IDR strategy can be viewed as a "black box," which takes intuitions (and perhaps other data) as input and produces implicitly or explicitly normative claims as output. The challenge we are about to raise is, we claim, a problem for IDR accounts no matter what goes on within the black box.

The Normativity Problem

Reflective equilibrium and other IDR strategies all yield as outputs claims that putatively have normative force. These outputs tell us how people ought to go about forming and revising their beliefs, which belief-forming strategies yield genuinely justified beliefs, which beliefs are warranted, which count as real knowledge rather than mere opinion, etc. But there is a problem lurking here—we call it the *Normativity Problem*. What reason is there to think that the output of one or another of these IDR strategies has real (as opposed to putative) normative force? Why should we care about the normative pronouncements produced by these strategies? Why should we try to do what these outputs claim we should do in matters epistemic? Why, in short, should we take any of this stuff seriously?

We do not think there is any good solution to the Normativity Problem for IDR or indeed for any other version of Romanticism in epistemology. And because there is no solution to the Normativity Problem, we think the entire tradition of Epistemic Romanticism has been a very bad idea. These, obviously, are very big claims, and this is not the place to mount a detailed argument for all of them. We do, however, want to rehearse one consideration first raised in Stich's (1990) book, *The Fragmentation of Reason*. We think it lends some plausibility to the claim that satisfying solutions to the Normativity Problem for IDR are going to be hard to find. It also helps to motivate the empirical studies we recount in the section to follow.

What Stich notes is that the following situation seems perfectly possible. There might be a group of people who reason and form beliefs in ways that are significantly different from the way we do. Moreover, these

---

[9]For a review of literature during the first two decades after Gettier's paper appeared, see Shope (1983). For more recent work in this tradition, see Plantinga (1993a, 1993b) as well as the follow-up collection of papers in Kvanvig (1996).

people might also have epistemic intuitions that are significantly different from ours. More specifically, they might have epistemic intuitions that, when plugged into your favorite IDR black box yield the conclusion that *their* strategies of reasoning and belief formation lead to epistemic states that are rational (or justified, or of the sort that yield genuine knowledge—pick your favorite normative epistemic notion here). If this is right, then it looks like the IDR strategy for answering normative epistemic questions might sanction any of a wide variety of regulative and valuational norms. That sounds like bad news for an advocate of the IDR strategy because it does not tell us what we really want to know. It does not tell us how we should go about the business of forming and revising our beliefs. One might, of course, insist that the normative principles that should be followed are the ones that are generated when we put *our* intuitions into the IDR black box. But it is less than obvious (to put it mildly) how this move could be defended. Why should we privilege our intuitions rather than the intuitions of some other group?

One objection that was occasionally raised in response to this challenge focused on the fact that the groups conjured in Stich's argument are just philosophical fictions (cf. Pollock & Cruz, 1999). Although it may well be logically possible that there are groups of people whose reasoning patterns and epistemic intuitions differ systematically from our own, there is no reason to suppose that it is nomologically or psychologically possible. Without some reason to think that such people are psychologically possible, the objection continued, the thought experiment does not pose a problem that the defender of the IDR strategy needs to take seriously. We are far from convinced by this objection, although we are prepared to concede that the use of nomologically or psychologically impossible cases in normative epistemology raises some deep and difficult issues. Thus, for argument's sake, we are prepared to concede that a plausible case might be made for privileging normative claims based on actual intuitions over normative claims based on intuitions that are merely logically possible. But what if the people imagined in the thought experiment are not just logically possible, but psychologically possible? Indeed, what if they are not merely psychologically possible, but real—and to all appearances normal and flourishing? Under those circumstances, we maintain, it is hard to see how advocates of an IDR strategy can maintain that their intuitions have any special standing or that the normative principles these intuitions generate when plugged into their favorite IDR black box should be privileged over the normative principles that would be generated if we plugged the other people's intuitions into the same IDR black box. In the section to follow, we argue that these what-ifs are not *just* what-ifs. There really are people—normal, flourishing people—whose epistemic intuition are systematically different from "ours".

CULTURAL VARIATION IN EPISTEMIC INTUITIONS

Nisbett and Haidt: Some Suggestive Evidence

Our suspicion that people like those imagined in Stich's thought experiment might actually exist was first provoked by the results of two recent research programs in psychology. In one of these, Richard Nisbett and his collaborators (2001) showed that there are large and systematic differences between East Asians and Westerners[10] on a long list of basic cognitive processes including perception, attention, and memory. These groups also differ in the way they go about describing, predicting, and explaining events; in the way they categorize objects; and in the way they revise beliefs in the face of new arguments and evidence. This work makes it plausible that the first part of Stich's thought experiment is more than just a logical possibility. There really are people whose reasoning and belief-forming strategies are different from ours. Indeed, there are over a billion of them!

Although space does not permit us to offer a detailed account of the differences that Nisbett and his colleagues found, a few brief notes are useful in motivating the studies we describe later in this section. According to Nisbett and his colleagues (2001), the differences "can be loosely grouped together under the heading of holistic vs. analytic thought" (p. 293). Holistic thought, which predominates among East Asians, is characterized as "involving an orientation to the context or field as a whole, including attention to relationships between a focal object and the field, and a preference for explaining and predicting events on the basis of such relationships" (p. 293). Analytic thought, the prevailing pattern among Westerners, is characterized as "involving detachment of the object from its context, a tendency to focus on attributes of the object in order to assign it to categories, and a preference for using rules about the categories to explain and predict the object's behavior" (Nisbett, Peng, Choi, & Norenzayan, 2001, p. 293). One concomitant of East Asian holistic thought is the tendency to focus on chronological, rather than causal patterns in describing and recalling events. Westerners, by contrast, focus on causal patterns in these tasks.[11] Westerners also have a stronger sense of agency and independence, whereas East Asians have a much stronger commitment to social harmony. In East Asian society, the individual feels "very much a part of a

---

[10]The East Asian subjects were Chinese, Japanese, and Korean. Some of the experiments were conducted in Asia, and others used East Asian students studying in the United States or first- and second-generation East Asian immigrants to the United States. The Western subjects were Americans of European ancestry.

[11]Nisbett (personal communication). Watanabe (1999), Abstract. See also Watanabe (1998).

large, complex and generally benign social organism in which prescriptive role relations were a guide to ethical conduct. Individual rights were construed as one's 'share' of the rights of the community as a whole" (Nisbett et al., 2001, p. 292).

The second research program that led us to suspect that there might actually be people like those in Stich's thought experiment was the work by Haidt, Koller, and Dias (1993).[12] These investigators were interested in exploring the extent to which moral intuitions about events in which no one is harmed track judgments about disgust in people from different cultural and socioeconomic groups. For their study, they constructed a set of brief stories about victimless activities that were intended to trigger the emotion of disgust. They presented these stories to subjects using a structured interview technique designed to determine whether the subjects found the activities described to be disgusting and also to elicit the subjects' moral intuitions about the activities. As an illustration, here is a story describing actions that people in all the groups studied found (not surprisingly) to be quite disgusting:

> A man goes to the supermarket once a week and buys a dead chicken. But before cooking the chicken, he has sexual intercourse with it. Then he cooks it and eats it.

The interviews were administered to both high and low socioeconomic status (SES) subjects in Philadelphia (U.S.) and in two cities in Brazil. Perhaps the most surprising finding in this study was that there are large differences in moral intuitions between social classes. Indeed, in most cases, the difference between social classes was significantly greater than the difference between Brazilian and American subjects of the same SES. Of course we have not yet told you what the differences in moral intuitions were, although you should be able to predict them by noting your own moral intuitions. (Hint: If you are reading this chapter, you count as high SES.) Not to keep you in suspense, low SES subjects tend to think that the man who has sex with the chicken is doing something that is seriously morally wrong, whereas high SES subjects do not. Much the same pattern was found with the other scenarios used in the study.

Four Hypotheses

For our purposes, Haidt's work, like Nisbett's, is only suggestive. Nisbett gives us reason to think that people in different cultural groups exploit very different belief-forming strategies. Haidt's work demonstrates that

---

[12]We are grateful to Christopher Knapp for bringing Haidt's work to our attention.

people in different SES groups have systematically different moral intu-itions. Neither investigator explored the possibility that there might be differences in *epistemic* intuitions in different groups. However, the results they reported were enough to convince us that the following pair of hy-potheses *might* be true and that it was worth the effort to find out:

Hypothesis 1: Epistemic intuitions vary from culture to culture.

Hypothesis 2: Epistemic intuitions vary from one socioeconomic group to another.

To these two experimentally inspired hypotheses, we added two more that were suggested by anecdotal rather than experimental evidence. It has often seemed to us that students' epistemic intuitions change as they take more philosophy courses, and we have often suspected that we and our colleagues were, in effect, teaching neophyte philosophers to have in-tuitions that are in line with those of more senior members of the profes-sion. Perhaps we are not modifying intuitions at all, but simply weeding out students whose intuitions are not mainstream. If either of these is the case, then the intuitions that "we" use in our philosophical work are not those of the man and woman in the street, but those of a highly trained and self-selecting community. These speculations led to:

Hypothesis 3: Epistemic intuitions vary as a function of how many phi-losophy courses a person has had.

It also sometimes seems that the order in which cases are presented to people can have substantial effects on people's epistemic intuitions. This hunch is reinforced by some intriguing work on neural networks suggest-ing that a variety of learning strategies may be "path dependent" (see Clark, 1997, pp. 204–207). If this hunch is correct, the pattern of intuitions that people offer on a series of cases might well differ systematically as a function of the order in which the cases are presented. This suggested our fourth hypothesis:

Hypothesis 4: Epistemic intuitions depend, in part, on the order in which cases are presented.

Moreover, it might well be the case that some of the results of order effects are very hard to modify.[13]

---

[13]Nisbett and Ross's work on "belief perseverance" shows that, sometimes at least, once a belief is formed, it can be surprisingly impervious to change. See, for example, Nisbett and Ross (1980), chapter 8.

If any one of these four hypotheses turns out to be true, then, we maintain, it poses a serious problem for the advocate of IDR. If all of them are true, then it is hard to believe that any plausible case can be made for the claim that the normative pronouncements of IDR have real normative force—that they are norms that we (or anyone else) should take seriously.

Some Experiments Exploring Cultural Variation in Epistemic Intuitions

Are any of these hypotheses true? To find out, we have been conducting a series of experiments designed to test Hypotheses 1 and 2. Although the results we have so far are preliminary, they are sufficient, we think, to at least shift the burden of argument well over in the direction of the defender of IDR strategies. What our results show, we believe, is that the advocates of IDR can no longer simply ignore these hypotheses or dismiss them as implausible because there is a growing body of evidence which suggests that they might well be true.

In designing our experiments, we were guided by three rather different considerations. First, we wanted our intuition probes—the cases that we would ask subjects to judge—to be similar to cases that have actually been used in the recent literature in epistemology. Second, because the findings reported by Nisbett and his colleagues all focused on differences between East Asians (EAs) and Euro-Americans (Ws for Westerners), we decided that would be the obvious place to look first for differences in epistemic intuitions. Third, because Nisbett and his colleagues argue that Ws are significantly more individualistic than EAs, who tend to be much more interdependent and "collectivist" and thus much more concerned about community harmony and consensus, we tried to construct some intuition probes that would tap into this difference. Would individualistic Ws, perhaps, be more inclined to attribute knowledge to people whose beliefs are reliably formed by processes that no one else in their community shares? The answer, it seems, is yes.

Truetemp Cases. An issue of great moment in recent analytic epistemology is the internalism–externalism debate. Internalism, with respect to some epistemically evaluative property, is the view that *only* factors within an agent's introspective grasp can be relevant to whether the agent's beliefs have that property. Components of an agent's doxastic situation available to introspection are internalistically kosher; other factors beyond the scope of introspection, such as the reliability of the psychological mechanisms that actually produced the belief, are epistemically external to the agent. Inspired by Lehrer (1990), we included in our surveys a number of cases designed to explore externalist–internalist dimensions of

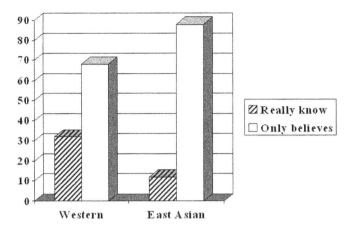

FIG. 8.1.   Individualistic Truetemp case.

our subjects' intuitions. Here is one of the questions we presented to our subjects, all of whom were undergraduates at Rutgers University.[14]

> One day Charles is suddenly knocked out by a falling rock, and his brain becomes re-wired so that he is always absolutely right whenever he estimates the temperature where he is. Charles is completely unaware that his brain has been altered in this way. A few weeks later, this brain re-wiring leads him to believe that it is 71 degrees in his room. Apart from his estimation, he has no other reasons to think that it is 71 degrees. In fact, it is at that time 71 degrees in his room. Does Charles really know that it was 71 degrees in the room, or does he only believe it?

> REALLY KNOWS   ONLY BELIEVES

Although Charles' belief is produced by a reliable mechanism, it is stipulated that he is completely unaware of this reliability. So his reliability is epistemically external. Therefore, to the extent that a subject population is unwilling to attribute knowledge in this case, we have evidence that the group's *folk epistemology* may be internalist. We found that although both groups were more likely to deny knowledge, EA subjects were much more likely to deny knowledge than were their W classmates. The results are shown in Fig. 8.1.[15]

---

[14]In classifying subjects as East Asian or Western, we relied on the same ethnic identification questionnaire that Nisbett and his colleagues had used. We are grateful to Professor Nisbett for providing us with a copy of the questionnaire and for much helpful advice on its use.

[15]The numerical data for all the experiments reported in this chapter are assembled in the appendix. The y-axis represents the percentage of each group giving the red-rated response.

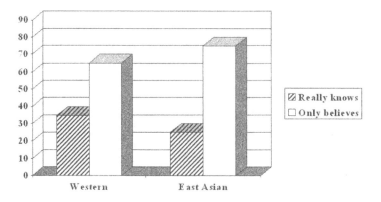

FIG. 8.2.   Truetemp: The elders version.

After finding this highly significant difference, we began tinkering with the text to see whether we could construct other "Truetemp" cases in which the difference between the two groups would disappear. Our first thought was to replace the rock with some socially sanctioned intervention. The text we used was as follows:

> One day John is suddenly knocked out by a team of well-meaning scientists sent by the elders of his community, and his brain is re-wired so that he is always absolutely right whenever he estimates the temperature where he is. John is completely unaware that his brain has been altered in this way. A few weeks later, this brain re-wiring leads him to believe that it is 71 degrees in his room. Apart from his estimation, he has no other reasons to think that it is 71 degrees. In fact, it is at that time 71 degrees in his room. Does John really know that it was 71 degrees in the room, or does he only believe it?
>
> REALLY KNOWS   ONLY BELIEVES

As we had predicted, the highly significant difference between the two groups disappeared. The results are shown in Fig. 8.2.

Encouraged by this finding, we constructed yet another version of the "Truetemp" case, in which the mechanism that reliably leads to a true belief is not unique to a single individual, but rather is shared by everyone else in the community. The intuition probe read as follows:

> The Faluki are a large but tight knit community living on a remote island. One day, a radioactive meteor strikes the island and has one significant effect on the Faluki—it changes the chemical make-up of their brains so that they are always absolutely right whenever they estimate the temperature. The Faluki are completely unaware that their brains have been altered in this way. Kal is a member of the Faluki community. A few weeks after the

meteor strike, while Kal is walking along the beach, the changes in his brain lead him to believe that it is 71 degrees where he is. Apart from his estimation, he has no other reasons to think that it is 71 degrees. In fact, it is at that time exactly 71 degrees where Kal is. Does Kal really know that it is 71 degrees, or does he only believe it?

REALLY KNOWS   ONLY BELIEVES

As predicted, on this case too there was no significant difference between Ws and EAs (see Fig. 8.3).

Intriguingly, although the difference is not statistically significant, the percentage of EAs who answered "Really Knows" in this case was *greater* than the percentage of Ws who gave that answer, reversing the pattern in the individualistic "hit by a rock" case. Figure 8.4, which is a comparison of the three Truetemp cases, illustrates the way in which the large difference between Ws and EAs in the Individualistic version disappears in the Elders version and looks to be reversing direction in the Faluki version.

Gettier Cases.   A category of examples that has loomed large in the recent epistemology literature are "Gettier cases", in which a person has good (although, as it happens, false, only accidentally true, or in some other way warrant-deprived) evidence for a belief that is true. These cases are, of course, by their very construction in many ways quite similar to unproblematic cases in which a person has good and true evidence for a true belief. As Norenzayan and Nisbett have shown, EAs are more inclined than Ws to make categorical judgments on the basis of similarity. Ws, in contrast, are more disposed to focus on causation in describing the world and classifying things (Norenzayan, Nisbett, Smith, & Kim, 1999).

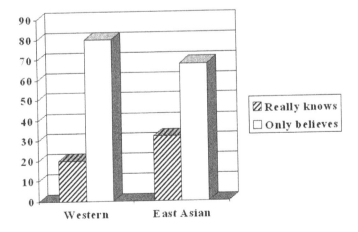

FIG. 8.3.   Community-wide Truetemp case ("Faluki").

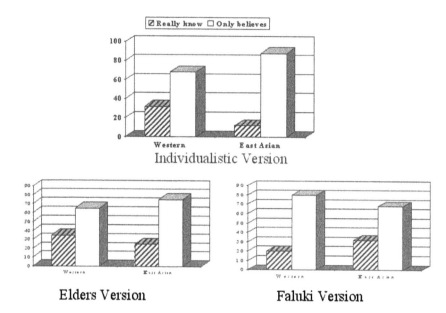

FIG. 8.4.   Comparison of Truetemp cases.

In a large class of Gettier cases, the evidence that *causes* the target to form a belief turns out to be false. This suggests that EAs might be much less inclined than Ws to withhold the attribution of knowledge in Gettier cases. Indeed, they are.

The intuition probe we used to explore cultural differences on Gettier cases was the following:

> Bob has a friend, Jill, who has driven a Buick for many years. Bob therefore thinks that Jill drives an American car. He is not aware, however, that her Buick has recently been stolen, and he is also not aware that Jill has replaced it with a Pontiac, which is a different kind of American car. Does Bob really know that Jill drives an American car, or does he only believe it?
>
> REALLY KNOWS   ONLY BELIEVES

The striking finding in this case is that a large majority of Ws give the standard answer in the philosophical literature—viz. "Only Believes". But among EAs, this pattern is actually *reversed*! A majority of EAs say that Bob really knows. The results are shown in Fig. 8.5.

Evidence From Another Ethnic Group.   The experiments we have reported thus far were done in lower division classes and large lectures at Rutgers. Because Rutgers is the State University of New Jersey and New

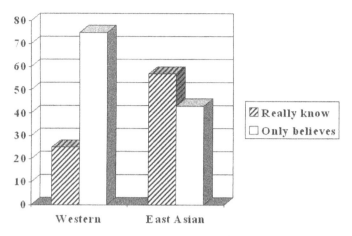

FIG. 8.5.   Gettier case Western and East Asian.

Jersey is home to many people of Indian, Pakistani, and Bangladeshi descent, in the course of the experiments we collected lots of data about these people's intuitions. Initially we simply set these data aside because we had no theoretical basis for expecting that the epistemic intuitions of people from the Indian subcontinent (SCs) would be systematically different from the epistemic intuitions of Ws. But after finding the extraordinary differences between Ws and EAs on the Gettier case, we thought it might be interesting to analyze the SC data as well. We were right. It turns out that the epistemic intuitions of SCs are even more different from the intuitions of Ws than the intuitions of EAs are. The SC results on the Gettier case are shown in Fig. 8.6. If these results are robust, it seems that what counts as knowledge on the banks of the Ganges does not count as knowledge on the banks of the Mississippi!

There were two additional intuition probes used in our initial experiments that did not yield statistically significant differences between Ws and EAs. But when we analyzed the SC data, it turned out there were significant differences between Ws and SCs. The text for one of these probes, the *Cancer Conspiracy* case, was as follows:

It's clear that smoking cigarettes increases the likelihood of getting cancer. However, there is now a great deal of evidence that just using nicotine by itself without smoking (for instance, by taking a nicotine pill) does not increase the likelihood of getting cancer. Jim knows about this evidence and as a result, he believes that using nicotine does not increase the likelihood of getting cancer. It is possible that the tobacco companies dishonestly made up and publicized this evidence that using nicotine does not increase the likelihood of cancer, and that the evidence is really false and misleading. Now, the tobacco companies did not actually make up this evidence, but Jim

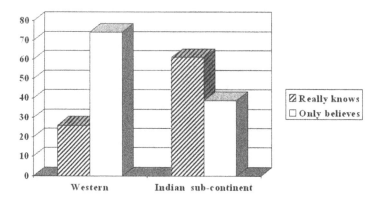

FIG. 8.6.   Gettier case Western and Indian.

is not aware of this fact. Does Jim really know that using nicotine doesn't increase the likelihood of getting cancer, or does he only believe it?

REALLY KNOWS   ONLY BELIEVES

The results are shown in Fig. 8.7.

The other probe that produced significant differences is a version of
Dretske's (1970) *Zebra-in-Zoo* case:

> Mike is a young man visiting the zoo with his son, and when they come to
> the zebra cage, Mike points to the animal and says, "that's a zebra." Mike is
> right—it is a zebra. However, as the older people in his community know,
> there are lots of ways that people can be tricked into believing things that
> aren't true. Indeed, the older people in the community know that it's possi-
> ble that zoo authorities could cleverly disguise mules to look just like zebras,
> and people viewing the animals would not be able to tell the difference. If
> the animal that Mike called a zebra had really been such a cleverly painted
> mule, Mike still would have thought that it was a zebra. Does Mike really
> know that the animal is a zebra, or does he only believe that it is?

REALLY KNOWS   ONLY BELIEVES

The results are shown in Fig. 8.8.

What is going on in these last two cases? Why do SCs and Ws have
different epistemic intuitions about them. The answer, to be quite frank,
is that we are not sure how to explain these results. But, of course, for our
polemical purposes, an explanatory hypothesis is not really essential.
The mere fact that Ws, EAs, and SCs have different epistemic intuitions
is enough to make it plausible that IDR strategies, which take these intuitions as inputs, would yield significantly different normative pro-

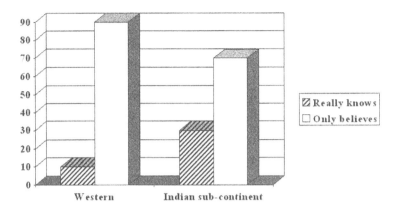

FIG. 8.7.   Cancer conspiracy case (W vs. SC).

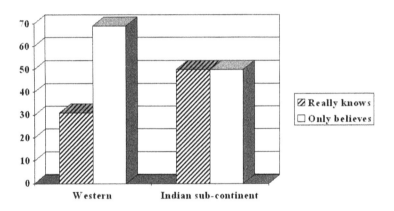

FIG. 8.8.   Zebra case (W vs. SC).

nouncements as output. This, we think, puts the ball squarely in the court of the defenders of IDR strategies. They must either argue that intuitive differences of the sort we have found would not lead to diverging normative claims, or they must argue that the outputs of an IDR strategy are genuinely normative despite the fact that they are different for different cultures. Nor is this the end of the bad news for those who advocate IDR strategies.

Epistemic Intuitions and Socioeconomic Status.   Encouraged by our findings in these cross-cultural studies, we have begun to explore the possibility that epistemic intuitions might also be sensitive to the SES of the people offering the intuitions. Although our findings here are also quite preliminary, the apparent answer is that SES does indeed have a major impact on subjects' epistemic intuitions.

Following Haidt (and other research in social psychology), we used years of education to distinguish low and high SES groups. In the studies we recount in this section, subjects were classified as low SES if they reported that they had never attended college. Subjects who reported that they had 1 or more years of college were coded as high SES. All the subjects were adults; they were approached near various commercial venues in downtown New Brunswick, New Jersey, and (because folks approached on the street tend to be rather less compliant than university undergraduates in classrooms) they were offered McDonald's gift certificates worth a few dollars if they agreed to participate in our study.

Interestingly, the two intuition probes for which we found significant SES differences both required the subjects to assess the importance of possible states of affairs that do not actually obtain. Here is the first probe, which is similar to the Dretske-type case discussed earlier:

> Pat is at the zoo with his son, and when they come to the zebra cage, Pat points to the animal and says, "that's a zebra". Pat is right—it is a zebra. However, given the distance the spectators are from the cage, Pat would not be able to tell the difference between a real zebra and a mule that is cleverly disguised to look like a zebra. And if the animal had really been a cleverly disguised mule, Pat still would have thought that it was a zebra. Does Pat really know that the animal is a zebra, or does he only believe that it is?
>
> REALLY KNOWS   ONLY BELIEVES

The results are shown in Fig. 8.9.

The second probe that produced significant (indeed enormous) differences between our two SES groups was the Cancer Conspiracy case that also generated differences between Western subjects and subjects from the Indian subcontinent. The results are shown in Fig. 8.10.

Why are the intuitions in these two SES groups so different? Here again we do not have a well-worked-out theoretical framework of the sort that Nisbett and his colleagues provided for the W versus EA differences. So any answer we offer is only a speculation. One hypothesis is that one of the many factors that subjects are sensitive to in forming epistemic intuitions of this sort is the extent to which possible but nonactual states of affairs are relevant. Another possibility is that high SES subjects accept much weaker knowledge defeaters than low SES subjects because low SES subjects have lower minimum standards for knowledge. More research is

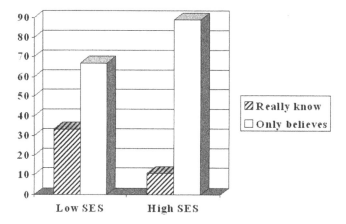

FIG. 8.9.   Zebra case (SES).

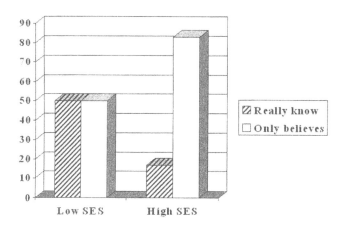

FIG. 8.10.   Cancer conspiracy case (SES).

needed to determine whether either of these conjectures is correct. But whatever the explanation turns out to be, the data we have reported look to be yet another serious embarrassment for the advocates of IDR. As in the case of cultural difference, they must either argue that these intuitive differences, when plugged into an IDR black box, would not lead to different normative conclusions, or they must bite the bullet and argue that diverging normative claims are genuinely normative, and thus that the sorts of doxastic states that should be pursued by relatively rich and well-educated people are significantly different from the sorts of doxastic states that poor and less-well-educated folks should seek. We do not pretend to have an argument showing that neither of these options is defensible, but we certainly do not envy the predicament of the IDR advocate who has to opt for one or the other.

OBJECTIONS AND REPLIES

In this section, we propose to assemble some objections to the case against IDR that we set out in the preceding sections along with our replies.

What Is So Bad About Epistemic Relativism?

Objection. Suppose we are right. Suppose that epistemic intuitions *do* differ in different ethnic and SES groups, and that because of this IDR strategies will generate different normative conclusions depending on which group uses them. Why, the critic asks, should this be considered a problem for IDR advocates? At most it shows that different epistemic norms apply to different groups, and thus that epistemic relativism is true. But why, exactly, is that a problem? What is so bad about epistemic relativism? "Indeed," we imagine the critic ending with an *ad hominem* flourish, "one of the authors of this chapter has published a book that *defends* epistemic relativism" (Stich, 1990; see especially chap. 6).

Reply. We certainly have no argument that could show that *all* forms of epistemic relativism are unacceptable, and the one avowed relativist among us is still prepared to defend some forms of relativism. But if we are right about epistemic intuitions, then the version of relativism to which IDR strategies lead would entail that the epistemic norms appropriate for the rich are quite different from the epistemic norms appropriate for the poor, and that the epistemic norms appropriate for white people are different from the norms appropriate for people of color.[16] We take this to be quite a preposterous result. The fact that IDR strategies lead to this result is, we think, a strong reason to think that there is something wrong with those strategies. Of course, a defender of an IDR strategy might simply bite the bullet and insist that the strategy he or she advocates is the right one for uncovering genuine epistemic norms, despite the fact that it leads to a relativistic consequence that many find implausible. But the IDR advocate who responds to our data in this way surely must offer some *argument* for the claim that the preferred IDR strategy produces genuine epistemic norms. And we know of no arguments along these lines that are even remotely plausible.

---

[16]Although there is little evidence on this point, we do not think the differences we found are innate. Rather, we suspect they are the product of deep differences in culture.

There Are Several Senses of Knowledge

Objection. The next objection begins with the observation that episte-mologists have long been aware that the word *knows* has more than one meaning in ordinary discourse. Sometimes when people say that they "know" that something is the case, what they mean is that they have a strong sense of subjective certainty. So, for example, someone at a horse race might give voice to a strong hunch by saying: "I just know that Ivory Armchair is going to win." Even after Lab Bench comes in first, this collo-quial sense of *know* still permits them to say, "Drat! I just knew that Ivory Armchair was going to win." At other times, however, when people use *know* and *knowledge*, the sense they have in mind is the one that is of inter-est to epistemologists. The problem with our results, this objection main-tains, is that we did nothing to ensure that when subjects answered "Really Know" rather than "Only Believe," the sense of *know* that they had in mind was the one of philosophical interest, rather than the subjective certainty sense. "So," the critic concludes, "for all you know, your subjects might have been offering you philosophically uninteresting judgments about people's sense of subjective certainty."

Reply. It is certainly possible that some of our subjects were interpret-ing the "Really Know" option as a question about subjective certainty. But there is reason to think that this did not have a major impact on our find-ings. For all of our subject groups (W, EA, and SC in the ethnic studies and high and low SES in the SES study), we included a question designed to uncover any systematic differences in our subjects' inclination to treat mere subjective certainty as knowledge. The question we used was the following:

> Dave likes to play a game with flipping a coin. He sometimes gets a "special feeling" that the next flip will come out heads. When he gets this "special feeling", he is right about half the time, and wrong about half the time. Just before the next flip, Dave gets that "special feeling", and the feeling leads him to believe that the coin will land heads. He flips the coin, and it does land heads. Did Dave really know that the coin was going to land heads, or did he only believe it?
>
> REALLY KNOWS   ONLY BELIEVES

As shown in Fig. 8.11, there was no difference at all between the high and low SES groups on this question; in both groups, almost none of our

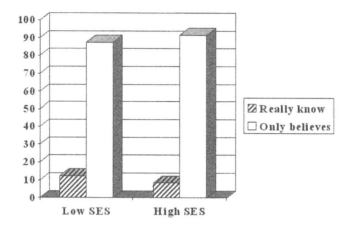

FIG. 8.11.   "Special feeling" case.

subjects judged that this was a case of knowledge. The results in the ethnic studies were basically the same.[17]

This might be a good place to elaborate a bit on what we are and are not claiming about epistemic intuitions and the psychological mechanisms or "knowledge structures" that may subserve them. For polemical purposes, we have been emphasizing the diversity of epistemic intuitions in differ-ent ethnic and SES groups because these quite different intuitions, when plugged into an IDR black box, generate different normative claims. But we certainly do not mean to suggest that epistemic intuitions are com-pletely malleable or that there are no constraints on the sorts of epistemic intuitions that might be found in different social groups. Indeed, the fact that subjects from all the groups we studied agreed on not classifying be-liefs based on "special feelings" as knowledge suggests that there may well be a universal core to "folk epistemology". Whether this conjecture is true and, if it is, how this common core is best characterized are questions

---

[17]Another possible interpretation of "Really Know" in our intuition probes would invoke what Sosa (1991) termed merely *animal* or *servo-mechanical* knowledge. We sometimes say that a dog knows that it is about to be fed or that the thermostat knows the temperature in the room. But we philosophers are hunting different game—fully normative game, which, the critic maintains, these surveys might not capture. However, if our subjects had this no-tion in mind, one would predict that they would overwhelmingly attribute such knowledge in the Truetemp cases because the protagonists in each of the stories clearly has a reliable, thermostat-like information-registering capacity. Yet they did not do so—in none of the Truetemp cases did a majority of subjects opt for "Really Knows." So this rival gloss on "knows" will not help the IDR theorist to explain our data away.

that require a great deal more research. Obviously, these are not issues that can be settled from the philosopher's armchair.

The Effect Size We Found Is Small and Philosophically Uninteresting

Objection.   If it were the case that virtually all Ws judged various cases in one way and virtually all EAs or SCs judged the same cases in a different way, that might be genuine cause for concern among epistemologists. But that is not at all what you have found. Rather, what you have shown is merely that in various cases there is a 20% or 30% difference in the judgments offered by subjects in various groups. So, for example, a majority in all of your groups withhold knowledge attributions in all the Truetemp cases that were designed to test the degree to which subjects' intuitions reflected epistemic internalism. Because the majority in all groups agree, we can conclude that the correct account of epistemic norms is internalist. So it is far from clear why epistemologists should find the sort of cultural diversity you have found to be at all troubling, or even interesting.

Reply.   Here we have two replies. First, the sizes of the statistically significant group differences that we reported are quite comparable with the size of the differences that Nisbett, Haidt, and other social psychologists take to show important differences between groups. The second reply is more important. Although in some cases what we reported are just the brute facts that intuitions in different groups differ, in other cases what we found is considerably more interesting. The differences between Ws and EAs look to be both systematic and explainable. EAs and Ws appear to be sensitive to different features of the situation—different *epistemic vectors* as we call them. EAs are much more sensitive to communitarian factors, whereas Ws respond to more individualistic ones. Moreover, Nisbett and his colleagues have given us good reason to think that these kinds of differences can be traced to deep and important differences in EA and W cognition. We have no reason to think that equally important differences could not be found for SCs. Our data also suggest that both high and low SES Westerners stress the individualistic and noncommunitarian vector because there was no difference between high and low SES groups on questions designed to emphasize this vector. What separates high and low SES subjects is a quite different vector—sensitivity to mere possibilities, perhaps. What our studies point to, then, is more than just divergent epistemic intuitions across groups; the studies point to divergent epistemic *concerns*—concerns that appear to differ along a variety of dimensions. It is plausible to suppose that these differences would significantly affect the output of just about any IDR process.

We Are Looking at the Wrong Sort of Intuitions; The Right Sort Are Accompanied by a Clear Sense of Necessity

Objection. The central idea of this objection is that our experiments are simply not designed to evoke the right sort of intuitions—the sort that the IDR process really requires. What we are collecting in our experiments are unfiltered, spontaneous judgments about a variety of cases. But what is really needed, this objection maintains, are data about quite a different kind of intuition. The right sort of intuitions are those that have modal import and are accompanied by a clear sense of necessity. They are the kind of intuitions that we have when confronted with principles like: If p, then not-not-p. Unless you show cultural or SES diversity in these sorts of intuitions, this objection continues, you have not shown anything that an IDR advocate needs to be concerned about because you have not shown that the right sort of intuitions are not universal.[18]

Reply. It is true that the sorts of intuitions that our experiments collect are not the sorts that some IDR theorists would exploit. However, our findings do raise serious questions about the suggestion that intuitions which come with a clear sense of necessity and modal import—*strong intuitions*, as we propose to call them—are anything close to universal. Many epistemologists would no doubt insist that their own intuitions about many cases are strong. Simple Gettier case intuitions are a good example. Indeed, if these intuitions, which led a generation of epistemologists to seek something better than the traditional justified true belief analysis of knowledge, are not strong intuitions, then it is hard to believe that there are enough strong intuitions around to generate epistemic norms of any interest. But if philosophers' intuitions on simple Gettier cases *are* strong intuitions, then our data indicate that strong intuitions are far from universal. Although our experiments cannot distinguish strong from weak intuitions, they do indicate that almost 30% of W subjects do not have either strong or weak intuitions that agree with those of most philosophers because almost 30% of these subjects claim that, in our standard Gettier scenario, Bob really knows that Jill drives an American car. Among EA subjects, over 50% of subjects have the intuition (weak or

---

[18]See, for example, Bealer (1999), who insisted that "the work of cognitive psychologists such as Wason, Johnson-Laird, Nisbett, Kahneman and Tversky tells us little about intuitions in our [philosophical] sense" (p. 31).

strong) that Bob really knows, and among SC subjects the number is over 60! It may well be that upper middle-class Westerners who have had a few years of graduate training in analytic philosophy do indeed all have strong, modality-linked intuitions about Gettier cases. However, because most of the world's population apparently does not share these intuitions, it is hard to see why we should think that these intuitions tell us anything at all about the modal structure of reality, about epistemic norms, or indeed about anything else of philosophical interest.

We Are Looking at the Wrong Sort of Intuitions; The Right Sort Require at Least a Modicum of Reflection

Objection.   We have also heard a rather different objection about the type of intuitions examined in our study.[19] The proper input intuitions for the IDR strategy, the critics maintain, are not "first-off" intuitions, which may be really little better than mere guesses. Rather, IDR requires what might be called *minimally reflective intuitions*—intuitions resulting from some modicum of attention, consideration, and, above all, reflection on the particulars of the case at hand as well as one's other theoretical commitments. We have, this objection continues, done nothing to show that such minimally reflective intuitions would exhibit the sort of diversity we have been reporting; until we show something along those lines, the IDR theorist need not worry.

Reply.   This objection is right as far as it goes because we have not (yet) examined intuitions produced under conditions of explicit reflection. But the objection really does not go very far and certainly not far enough to allow IDR theorists to rest easy. First of all, many of our subjects clearly reflected at least minimally before answering, as evidenced in the many survey forms on which the subjects wrote brief explanatory comments after their answers. Moreover, as we stressed in an earlier Reply, it is not just that we found group differences in epistemic intuition; much more interestingly, W and EA subjects' intuitions seem to respond to quite different epistemic vectors. It is extremely likely that such differences in sensitivities would be recapitulated—or even strengthened—in any reflective process. If EA subjects have an inclination to take into account factors involving community beliefs, practices, and traditions, and W subjects do not have such an inclination, then we see no reason to expect that such vectors will not be differentially present under conditions of explicit reflection. IDR theorists who want to make use of any purported difference between first-off and minimally reflective intuitions had better go get

---

[19]This objection was offered by Henry Jackman, Ram Neta, and Jonathan Schaffer.

some *data* showing that such differences would point in the direction they would want.

We Are Looking at the Wrong Sort of Intuitions;
The Right Sort Are Those That Emerge After
an Extended Period of Discussion and Reflection

Objection. The last objection we consider was proposed (although not, we suspect, endorsed) by Philip Kitcher. What IDR strategies need, this objection maintains, is neither first-off intuitions nor even minimally reflective intuitions, but rather the sorts of intuitions that people develop after a lengthy period of reflection and discussion—the sort of reflection and discussion that philosophy traditionally encourages. Kitcher suggested that they be called *Austinian intuitions.*

Your experiments, the objection insists, do nothing to show that Austinian intuitions would exhibit the sort of cultural diversity you have found in first-off intuitions or, indeed, that they would show any significant diversity at all. When sensible people reflect and reason together, there is every reason to suppose that they will ultimately reach a meeting of the minds.

Reply. We certainly concede that we have not shown that Austinian intuitions would not ultimately converge. However, to echo the theme of our previous reply, in the absence of any evidence, we do not think there is any reason to suppose that the sorts of marked cultural differences in sensitivity to epistemic vectors that our experiments have demonstrated would simply disappear after reflection and discussion. Moreover, even if these cultural differences do dissipate after extended reflection, it might well be the case that they would be replaced by the sorts of order effects suggested in our Hypothesis 4. If that hypothesis is correct, then the Austinian intuitions on which a group of reflective people would converge would depend, in part, on the order in which examples and arguments happened to be introduced. Different groups might well converge on quite different sets of Austinian intuitions, which then proved quite impervious to change. Experiments demonstrating the sort of path dependence that we suggest in Hypothesis 4 are much harder to design than experiments demonstrating cultural differences in initial intuitions. In the next stage of our ongoing empirical research on intuitions, we hope to run a series of experiments that will indicate the extent to which the evolution of people's intuitions is indeed a function of the order in which examples and counterexamples are encountered. Neither those experiments nor any of the evidence we cited in this chapter suffice to demonstrate that Austinian intuitions or IDR processes that propose to use them will fail to converge. But, to end with the theme with which we began, our goal has not been to establish that IDR strategies *will* lead to very different (putatively) normative conclusions, but simply to make it plausible that they *might*. The assumption that they will not is an empirical assumption; it is not an assumption that can be made without argument.

Our data indicate that when epistemologists advert to "our" intuitions when attempting to characterize epistemic concepts or draw normative conclusions, they are engaged in a culturally local endeavor—what we might think of as *ethno-epistemology*. Indeed, in our studies, some of the most influential thought experiments of 20th-century epistemology elicited different intuitions in different cultures. In light of this, IDR seems a rather bizarre way to determine the correct epistemic norms. For it is difficult to see why a process that relies heavily on epistemic intuitions that are local to one's own cultural and socioeconomic group would lead to genuinely normative conclusions. Pending a detailed response to this problem, we think that the best reaction to the high SES Western philosophy professor who tries to draw normative conclusions from the facts about "our" intuitions is to ask: What do you mean "we"?

ACKNOWLEDGMENTS

This chapter was previously published in *Philosophical Topics, 29*, 2001, pp. 429–460. We are grateful to Joe Cruz, Gilbert Harman, Philip Kitcher, and Joel Pust for helpful feedback on earlier versions of this chapter. Our deepest debt is to Richard Nisbett, who provided us with invaluable advice and assistance in designing and interpreting the studies reported herein.

REFERENCES

Bealer, G. (1999). A theory of the *a priori*. *Philosophical Perspectives, 13*, 29–55. (Reprinted in *Pacific Philosophical Quarterly*, vol. 81, *Special Issue on A Priori Knowledge*, 2000.)

Bonjour, L. (1985). *The structure of empirical knowledge*. Cambridge, MA: Harvard University Press.

Chisolm, R. (1977). *Theory of knowledge*. Englewood Cliffs, NJ: Prentice-Hall.

Clark, A. (1997). *Being there: Putting brain, body and world together again*. Cambridge, MA: MIT Press.

Cohen, L. (1981). Can human irrationality be experimentally demonstrated? *Behavioral and Brain Sciences, 4*, 317–370.

Dretske, F. (1970). Epistemic operators. *Journal of Philosophy, 67*(24), 1007–1023. (Reprinted in F. Dretske [2000]. *Perception, knowledge, and belief*. Cambridge: Cambridge University Press.)

Elgin, C. (1996). *Considered judgment*. Princeton, NJ: Princeton University Press.

Gettier, E. (1963). Is justified true belief knowledge? *Analysis, 23*, 121–123.

Goldman, A. (1980). The internalist conception of justification. In P. French, T. Uehling, & H. Wettstein (Eds.), *Midwest studies in philosophy: Vol. 9. Causation and causal theories* (pp. 27–51). Minneapolis: University of Minnesota Press.

Goldman, A. (1986). *Epistemology and cognition*. Cambridge, MA: Harvard University Press.

Goldman, A. (1992). Epistemic folkways and scientific epistemology. In *Liaisons*. Cambridge, MA: MIT Press.

Goldman, A. (1999). A priori warrant and naturalistic epistemology. In J. E. Tomberlin (Ed.), *Philosophical perspectives* (Vol. 13, pp. 1–28). Cambridge, MA: Blackwell.

Goldman, A., & Pust, J. (1998). Philosophical theory and intuitional evidence. In M. DePaul & W. Ramsey (Eds.), *Rethinking intuition: The psychology of intuition and its role in philosophical inquiry* (pp. 179–197). Lanham, MD: Rowman & Littlefield.

Goodman, N. (1965). *Fact, fiction and forecast*. Indianapolis: Bobbs-Merrill.

Haidt, J., Koller, S., & Dias, M. (1993). Affect, culture and morality. *Journal of Personality & Social Psychology, 65*(4), 613–628.

Kvanvig, J. (Ed.). (1996). *Warrant in contemporary epistemology: Essays in honor of Plantinga's theory of knowledge*. Lanham, MD: Rowman & Littlefield.

Lehrer, K. (1990). *Theory of knowledge*. Boulder, London: Westview, Routledge.

Nisbett, R., Peng, K., Choi, I., & Norenzayan, A. (2001). Culture and systems of thought: Holistic vs. analytic cognition. *Psychological Review, 108*(2), 291–310.

Nisbett, R., & Ross, L. (1980). *Human inference: Strategies and shortcomings of social judgment*. Englewood Cliffs, NJ: Prentice-Hall.

Norenzayan, A., Nisbett, R. E., Smith, E. E., & Kim, B. J. (1999). *Rules vs. similarity as a basis for reasoning and judgment in East and West*. Ann Arbor: University of Michigan.

Plantinga, A. (1993a). *Warrant: The current debate*. Oxford: Oxford University Press.

Plantinga, A. (1993b). *Warrant and proper function*. Oxford: Oxford University Press.

Plato. (1892/1937). *The dialogues of Plato* (B. Jowett, Trans.). New York: Random House.

Pollock, J., & Cruz, J. (1999). *Contemporary theories of knowledge*. Lanham, MA: Rowman & Littlefield.

Samuels, R. (in preparation). Naturalism and normativity.

Samuels, R., Stich, S., & Bishop, M. (2002). Ending the rationality wars: How to make disputes about human rationality disappear. In R. Elio (Ed.), *Common sense, reasoning and rationality. Vancouver studies in cognitive science* (Vol. 11, pp. 236–268). Oxford: Oxford University Press.

Samuels, R., Stich, S., & Faucher, L. (2004). Reason and rationality. In I. Niiniluoto, M. Sintonen, & J. Wolenski (Eds.), *Handbook of epistemology* (pp. 1–50). Dordrecht: Kluwer.

Samuels, R., Stich, S., & Tremoulet, P. (1999). Rethinking rationality: From bleak implications to Darwinian modules. In E. LePore & Z. Pylyshyn (Eds.), *What is cognitive science?* (pp. 74–120). Oxford: Blackwell.

Shope, R. (1983). *The analysis of knowing*. Princeton, NJ: Princeton University Press.

Sosa, E. (1991). *Knowledge in perspective*. Cambridge: Cambridge University Press.

Sosa, E. (Ed.). (1994). *Knowledge and justification*. Brookfield, VT: International Research Library of Philosophy, Dartmouth Publishing Company Limited.

Stein, E. (1996). *Without good reason: The rationality debate in philosophy and cognitive science*. Oxford: Clarendon.

Stich, S. (1990). *The fragmentation of reason*. Cambridge, MA: MIT Press.

Watanabe, M. (1998, August). *Styles of reasoning in Japan and the United States: Logic of education in two cultures*. Paper presented at the American Sociological Association Annual Meeting, San Francisco.

Watanabe, M. (1999). *Styles of reasoning in Japan and the United States: Logic of education in two cultures*. Unpublished doctoral dissertation, Columbia University.

APPENDIX

The Fisher Exact test was used to calculate statistical significance between groups.

Individualistic Truetemp Case (Fig. 8.1)

	Really Knows	*Only Believes*
Western	61	128
East Asian	3	22

The p-exact = 0.020114.

Elders Truetemp Case (Fig. 8.2)

	Really Knows	*Only Believes*
Western	77	140
East Asian	5	15

The p-exact = 0.131784.

Community-Wide Truetemp Case (Fig. 8.3)

	Really Knows	*Only Believes*
Western	2	8
East Asian	10	21

The p-exact = 0.252681.

Gettier Case: Western and East Asian (Fig. 8.5)

	Really Knows	*Only Believes*
Western	17	49
East Asian	13	10

The p-exact = 0.006414.

Gettier Case: Western and Indian (Fig. 8.6)

	Really Knows	*Only Believes*
Western	17	49
Indian subcontinental	14	9

The p-exact = 0.002407.

Cancer Conspiracy Case: Western and Indian (Fig. 8.7)

	Really Knows	Only Believes
Western	7	59
Indian subcontinental	7	16

The p-exact = 0.025014.

Zebra-in-Zoo Case: Western and Indian (Fig. 8.8)

	Really Knows	Only Believes
Western	19	43
Indian subcontinental	12	12

The p-exact = 0.049898.

Zebra-in-Zoo Case: Low and High SES (Fig. 8.9)

	Really Knows	Only Believes
Low SES	8	16
High SES	4	30

The p-exact = 0.038246.

Cancer Conspiracy Case: Low and High SES (Fig. 8.10)

	Really Knows	Only Believes
Low SES	12	12
High SES	6	29

The p-exact = 0.006778.

Special Feeling Case: Low and High SES (Fig. 8.11)

	Really Knows	Only Believes
Low SES	3	32
High SES	3	21

The p-exact = 0.294004.

Special Feeling Case: Western and East Asian (no figure)

	Really Knows	Only Believes
Western	2	59
East Asian	0	8

The p-exact = 0.780051.

9

Probabilistic Reasoning and Natural Language

Laura Macchi
Maria Bagassi
Università degli Studi di Milano–Bicocca

The debate on the structure of "natural" probability—in cultural terms, a relatively recent concept in the history of thought (it can be dated to approximately the middle of the 16th century; Hacking, 1975)—has been animated by various and contrasting currents of thought, ranging from the diverse theories of probability (Carnap, 1962; De Finetti, 1968) to studies of so-called *intuitive statistics*. Here we are referring to the psychological study of probabilistic judgment, the main object of which is to describe and explain reasoning processes under uncertainty.

The first studies on probabilistic judgment were carried out by Edwards (1968), while the concept of heuristics was subsequently developed by Tversky and Kahneman (1974) and Kahneman, Slovic, and Tversky (1982) and characterized as a series of automatic and simplifying modalities that, given the limitations of our mental system, reduce problem complexity, but in most cases result in errors (biases).

Natural heuristics, then, can be defined as "strategies of simplification that reduce the complexity of judgment tasks, to make them tractable for the kind of mind that people happen to have" (Kahneman, Slovic, & Tversky, 1982, p. xii). The *availability* is an example of a natural heuristic based on limits of memory; the assessment of the frequency of a class or the probability of an event increased by the ease with which instances or occurrences can be brought to mind. In this perspective, the cultural aspect is represented by the normative human judgment models; in the case

223

of the study of subjective probability, this is the Bayesian paradigm, which is an articulated model of optimal performance under uncertainty, with which human judgment has been compared.

The representational errors resulting from the application of such mechanisms are likened to perceptual illusions (Tversky & Kahneman, 1974, 1981). This implies that there exists one, and only one, correct representation for each problem, just as there exists only one veridical representation of the physical world. Inconsistent preferences are understood to be the result of deficient perception and interpretation of the decisional problem (Jungermann, 1986).

In our opinion, inferring mental limitations from the presence of biases represents an indebitous inferential gap that assumes only this objective cause for the observed phenomena. Anyway, also in the critical approach to this theory emerges the dichotomy between the natural and cultural sides of human inference. In fact, the frequentist approach (Cosmides & Tooby, 1996; Gigerenzer, 1991, 1994) considers probabilistic reasoning as being based—on an evolutionary level—on observed frequencies, sequences of events, and limited samples. Gigerenzer and Hoffrage (1995) defined natural sampling as: "The sequential acquisition of information by updating event frequencies" (p. 686). Probabilities expressed in percentages, in both single-case probabilities and relative frequencies, are considered to be a highly processed cultural product, and are therefore considered inappropriate for the study of intuitive statistics. The numerous and recurring errors individuated by the first approach (the so-called *heuristics and biases* research program), which did in fact make use of percentages, should not be considered as being an expression of the limits of our rationality, but rather of the inadequacy of the system we use to study this rationality. In fact, this approach considers percentages as a thoroughly unnatural form of probabilistic expression.

It could be said that the natural dimension for the heuristics and biases approach is concerned with mental limitations, whereas the cultural dimension is represented by the theory of probability. With regards to the frequentist approach, however, the natural dimension can be defined as the earlier methods of categorizing events (by sequence of events) as opposed to more recent elaborations (by the use of forms of generalization such as percentages). Recently, the mental models theory (MMT) has been extended to the probabilistic field (Johnson-Laird et al., 1999). This theory emphasizes the sources of difficulties encountered in problems, including the number of models, the degree to which the models are fleshed out, and the need to grasp that a problem calls for conditional probability. Again, the concept of mental limitations emerges, justified by the poor performance of the subjects in the task of estimating the ratio between favorable and possible cases.

The different theoretical perspectives have been subjected to numerous experimental verifications, and the results obtained are extremely interesting. Generally speaking, if the *natural dimension* of probabilistic reasoning is linked to the limitations of our cognitive system, there should be no possibility of intervening to eliminate the biases. However, several research studies (see the pragmatic approach considered later) have demonstrated that it is, in fact, possible to eliminate most of the judgmental biases by modifying certain textual elements of the problems quite independently of the alleged cognitive limitations (whose proofs are, for instance, the natural heuristics). The fact that even statistical experts perform poorly in some experimental tasks (an excellent example of this can be found in the conjunction fallacy; Tversky & Kahneman, 1983) also renders the dichotomy between natural and cultural dimensions difficult to sustain.

In our view, the natural versus cultural distinction loses significance as everything we learn is originally cultural and destined to become natural once it has been consolidated by use. An example of this is the lexicalization of linguistic metaphors, even if we are not anymore aware of it (it seems that in a minute we produce three or four metaphors without realizing it).

A pragmatic approach (Grice, 1975; Mosconi, 1990; Sperber & Wilson, 1986) to the study of reasoning, however, opens the way to new interpretations of the factors that are responsible for the generation of a judgmental bias. What the prior approaches, compared to the pragmatic approach, ignore is the importance of the context activated by the formulation of a problem.

The *pragmatic* approach gave many contributions to the study of probabilistic reasoning (for the conjunction fallacy, see Adler, 1984; Dulany & Hilton, 1991; Macdonald & Gilhooly, 1990; Mosconi & Macchi, 2001; Politzer & Noveck, 1991; Schwarz, 1996; for the disjunction effect, see Bagassi & Macchi, 2006; for the base-rate fallacy, see Ginossar & Trope, 1987; Macchi, 1995, 2000; Margolis, 1987; Morier & Borgida, 1984; Politzer & Macchi, 2005; for general reviews, see Hilton, 1995; Levinson, 1995). By pragmatic approach, we refer to, on one side at a microstructure level, an analysis of the perceptual[1] or linguistic stimula that constitutes the problem to make sure that they convey the meaning intended by the experimenter (particularized implicatures evoked in a specific context or generalized implicatures as may occur when dealing with connectives or quantifiers; Grice, 1975). At a macrostructure level, which is strictly inter-

---

[1]The information submitted to a pragmatic analysis are not necessarily a linguistic one, but can be also visual stimula (see, for instance, the studies by Mosconi, 1990, on the virtual square of Mayer).

connected with the previous one, the analysis consists of identifying the representation of the task, the intention and state of knowledge of the experimenter, and the required skills that participants are likely to build. This latter analysis takes a serious view on the special relationship between experimenter and participant. But what is of interest to the experimenter (often the logical correctness and not the informativeness, in Gricean sense) is not always clear to the participant; it results from a process of attribution whose outcome may be different from the experimenter's expectations. In case this occurs without being detected by the experimenter, the interpretation of the task by the participant will cause misinterpretation of the results by the experimenter (Politzer & Macchi, 2005).

Let consider now two exemplary cases of probabilistic reasoning: The first concerns the process of updating probabilities and the second the process of estimating the ratio between favorable and possible cases.

We try to show that in both cases the neglect of the pragmatical structure of the text of problems (by researchers) is responsible for the apparent biases of probabilistic reasoning. By consequence, those biases are independent of, respectively, in the first problem, the statistical format adopted (frequentist vs. probabilistic) and, in the second one, the numerosity of mental models.

THE USE AND UNDERSTANDING
OF CONDITIONAL PROBABILITY

The study of conditional probability has been one of the main topics in the last decades, crucial for the comprehension of the natural way of updating evidence. One exemplar experimental task consists of two types of information: the base rate (in the following example, the incidence of the illness) and likelihoods (hit rate and false alarms, based on the proportion of sick and healthy people with a positive mammography). A classical example of this kind of task (Eddy, 1982; Gigerenzer & Hoffrage, 1995) is the diagnosis problem:

> *The probability of breast cancer is 1% for women at age forty who participate in routine screening.*
>
> *If a woman has breast cancer, the probability is 80% that she will get a positive mammography. If a woman does not have breast cancer, the probability is 9.6% that she will also get a positive mammography.*
>
> *A woman in this age group had a positive mammography in a routine screening. What is the probability that she actually has breast cancer? ____%*

To assess the requested probability, it is first necessary to consider 80% (the probability that someone who has breast cancer will get a positive mammography) of 1% (the probability of having the breast cancer) (= 0.8%). It is then possible to determine the probability of getting a positive mammography in the case of ill (= 0.8%) or healthy people (9.6% of 99% = 9.5%) and consider the proportion of cases of illness and positive mammography (0.8%) among all of the cases of positive mammography (0.8% + 9.5% = 10.3%, then 0.8/10.3 = 0.07). According to the Bayes Theorem:

$$P(M/T+) = \frac{P(T+/M) \times P(M)}{P(T+/M) \times P(M) + P(T+/S) \times P(S)}$$

$$= \frac{.80 \times .01}{.80 \times .01 + .10 \times .90} = \frac{.008}{.107} = .07$$

In reasoning with problems of this type, people typically ignore the incidence of the disease and focus their attention on the likelihood of cancer given a positive test result, giving rise to the well-known phenomenon of base-rate neglect.

According to the heuristics and biases model, in this kind of task, the implicated heuristic principle is said to be specificity (i.e., more importance is given to specific information) and/or the schemas of causality (i.e., the base rate has no causal relevance; Bar-Hillel, 1990; Casscells, Schoenberger, & Graboys, 1978; Eddy, 1982; Kahneman & Tversky, 1996; Koehler, 1996; Tversky & Kahneman, 1982).

As said earlier, the traditional research program supporting the heuristic thesis has been opposed by two main perspectives: the *frequentist* approach and the *pragmatic* approach. According to the first critical perspective, difficulties with base-rate problems are said to be caused by the probabilistic formulation of the single-case-oriented information (Cosmides & Tooby, 1996; Gigerenzer & Hoffrage, 1995). By giving classical problems a frequentist format, the authors obtained a reduction in the number of classical errors (for similar studies involving the conjunction fallacy, see Fiedler, 1988; Hertwig & Gigerenzer, 1997; Jones, Jones Taylor, & Frisch, 1995; Reeves & Lockhart, 1993).

On the other critical side, for what concerns the kind of problems we proposed previously, a pragmatic analysis of the text has brought to the identification of a particular formulation of the likelihood, as the explicative factor of the fallacy, more than to an intrinsic difficulty to reason in Bayesian terms (Koehler & Macchi, 2004; Macchi, 1995, 2000; Macchi & Mosconi, 1998; Mosconi, 1990). Our own interpretation, which is also intended as a critical review of the heuristic approach (see Macchi, 1995), suggests a different explanation for the better results achieved using frequentist versions of base-rate fallacy tasks.

A PRAGMATICS PERSPECTIVE:
THE PARTITIVE HYPOTHESIS

We propose that neither heuristic nor frequentist factors underlie the occurrence or elimination of the base-rate fallacy. What is crucial, given that all of the other elements of difficulty are the same (Macchi & Mosconi, 1998), is the presence or absence of a particular formulation of the likelihood information. This formulation, called *partitive* (Macchi, 2000), consists of defining the set of which the datum (expressed in percentage or frequency terms) represents a part and then relativizing its numerical content. Thus:

> "80% of the people affected by the disease . . . have a positive mammography"

defines the proportion (or subset) of the population with the disease (i.e., the base-rate probability) and has particular properties (having a positive mammography). Specifically, this wording clearly indicates the relationships between the probabilities relating to the subsets, which is a basic condition for Bayesian reasoning. This kind of formulation seems to express the intrinsic nature of a conditional probability, which conditions an event (A) to the occurrence of another one (B). Then it represents the cases in which, given the occurrence of B, also A happens or, said in other words, the subset that is the conjunction of two sets of events (A & B), indicating what is A and what is B without ambiguities.

When such a formulation is used, be it in terms of percentages as relative frequencies or ratio (Macchi, 1995, 2000) or natural sampling frequencies (Gigerenzer & Hoffrage, 1995), it communicates the independence of the hit rate from the base rate. This is a crucial assumption for proper Bayesian analysis (Birnbaum, 1983) because the posterior probability (i.e., the probability of the hypothesis given the datum, $P[H/D]$) is calculated on the basis of the base rate and therefore dependent on it. If the hit rate depended on the base rate, it would already include it and, if this were the case, we would already have the a posteriori probability ($P[H/D]$) and the consequent uselessness of considering the base rate. This is what often underlies the base-rate fallacy, which consists of a failure to consider the base rate as a result of the privileging of hit-rate information. In our view, the confusion sometimes generated between the two types of conditional probability (the hit rate and a posteriori probability) is due to an ambiguous formulation of conditional probability or, in other words, to the absence of a partitive formulation.

If this is true, the partitive formulation has the triple effect of identifying the data reference set, eliminating confusion (by showing the independence of the data), and making it possible to perceive and make use of the relationships between the data. In this light, the published results showing the use of Bayesian reasoning by naive subjects (Tversky & Kahneman, 1980, using the heuristic of causality; Gigerenzer & Hoffrage, 1995, using frequentist formulations) do not depend on the principles proposed by the authors (the presence of certain heuristics or probabilistic formats), but on the partitive expression of the hit rate.

Consistent with this perspective, we found that: (a) partitive formulations prevent the confusion of probabilities (Macchi, 1995, 2000); (b) there is no difference in performance between texts formulated in frequentist or percentage (and also ratio terms) provided that these are partitive; (c) both frequencies (if partitive) and percentages (relative frequencies) lead to performances that are different and better than those obtained using versions relating to single events (Tversky & Kahneman, 1980) insofar as these are not partitive;[2] and (d) even when probabilities are expressed in terms of frequency, the elimination of the partitive formulation leads to the reemergence of the error.

In a series of studies, these results were obtained (for the notorious cab problem and suicide ones, see Macchi, 1995; for the medical diagnosis and diploma problems, see Macchi, 2000; for the disease problem, see Macchi, 2003). Consider, for instance, the following problem:

Diploma Problem

About 360 out of every 1,000 students who sit for their high school diploma fail.

If a student is not awarded a diploma, there is a 75% probability that he/she failed the written Italian paper.

However, even if a student is awarded a diploma, there is a 20% probability that he/she failed the written Italian paper.

One student failed the written Italian paper. What is the probability that he/she was not awarded a diploma?

Two groups of partitive and nonpartitive versions of the same problem were created. The *partitive* versions we consider here consisted of:

- a control frequency format text (Partitive Frequency [PF]) following the formulaic layout of the texts of Gigerenzer and Hoffrage (1995),

---

[2]In this last case, an idea is given of the extent of an effect or the impact of a property, but not of the relationship between them. This would explain the difficulties encountered in using Bayesian reasoning in the classical experiments based on this type of formula.

which, on the basis of our analysis, has a partitive structure: ". . . 270 out of every 360 students who are not awarded a Diploma fail the written Italian paper . . ."; and

- a partitive probabilistic version (Partitive Probability [PP]) involving relative frequency: ". . . 75% of the students who are not awarded a diploma fail the written Italian paper. . . ."

The *nonpartitive* versions consisted of:

- a nonpartitive frequency format (Nonpartitive Frequency [NPF]) that was identical to text PF except for its nonpartitive formulation: ". . . 750 out of every 1,000 students who are not awarded a diploma fail the written Italian paper . . ."; and
- a nonpartitive probabilistic (single-case) version (NPP): ". . . If a student is not awarded a diploma, there is a 75% probability that he/she failed the written Italian paper. . . ."

As shown in Table 9.1, there was a significant difference [χ^2 (1) = 47,06, p < 0.001] between the results obtained using the partitive and nonpartitive texts, although they should invoke the same heuristics regardless of whether they had a frequentist formulation. Our results do not support the approach that attributes the base-rate fallacy to certain heuristics (specificity, causality, etc.), but show that the use or otherwise of Bayesian reasoning to solve problems based on the same heuristics depends exclusively on the indicated partitive element. Furthermore, the fact that problems with a frequentist formulation in partitive format produced a high percentage of Bayesian responses, but also, in nonpartitive format, a high percentage of *non*-Bayesian responses, implies that a frequentist formulation is not the crucial element for eliciting correct reasoning (we do not consider here the debate about normalized frequency and natural sampling; see Macchi, 2003).

TABLE 9.1
Solutions Produced to Nonpartitive Versus Partitive Versions

	Partitive		Nonpartitive	
	PF (n = 30)	PP (n = 30)	NPF (n = 30)	NPP (n = 30)
Bayesian and pseudo-Bayesian answers	22	21	4	9
Base rate				3
Hit (frequency or rates)	2	2	4	5
Other	6	7	17	11
No answer			5	2

THE PROCESS OF ESTIMATING THE RATIO
BETWEEN FAVORABLE AND POSSIBLE CASES

Let now consider a problem of evaluating/estimating the ratio between possible cases and favorable ones recently studied by MMT. According to one of the main theories of thinking, the MMT (Johnson-Laird, 1983; Johnson-Laird & Byrne, 1991), people reason by building initial models of the content of a premise or, more generally, models of a situation. The MMT suggests that the main factors responsible for difficulties encountered in reasoning are the amount of mental models and the failure to represent false cases. The use of such explanatory factors has been recently extended to the study of probabilistic reasoning (Johnson-Laird et al., 1999). However, it has also been found that the responses to probabilistic problems may be significantly influenced by pragmatic factors even in the presence of the same number of models with the same degree of explicitness (Macchi, 2000).

The following problem (Johnson-Laird et al., 1999) was considered:

Marbles Problem

There is a box in which there is at least a red marble, or else there is a green marble and there is a blue marble, but not all three marbles.

Given the preceding assertion, what is the probability of the following situation?

In the box there is a red marble and a blue marble.

On the basis of MMT, subjects should consider:

Red	¬Green	¬Blue
¬Red	Green	Blue
Red	*¬Green*	*Blue*
Red	Green	¬Blue

The correct response would therefore be $p = 1/4$. However, the authors found that almost all of the subjects (18 out of 20) participating in the test replied that the box could not contain a red marble and a blue marble.

This erroneous evaluation was attributed to the explanatory factors mentioned before (the amount of mental models and the failure to represent false cases). In this case, it was claimed that there was a failure to represent the cases in which the conjunction "green and blue" is false[3]:

---

[3]In reality, in addition to being a real case of disjunction, it cannot be excluded that the case "Red, ¬Green ¬Blue" is also a false case of conjunction.

¬Green	¬Blue
¬Green	Blue
Green	¬Blue

PRAGMATIC ANALYSIS OF THE PROBLEM

From a pragmatic perspective, the source of the difficulty of the present problem could be attributed less to an inability to represent false cases (because of memory limitations or other reasons) than to the construction itself of the "discourse of the problem," to which the following three factors synergistically concur.

First of all, the syntactic action of the exclusive *or* presupposes that the two counterposed elements (*"red marble, or else there is a green marble and there is a blue marble"*) are of equal weight, thus transforming the *and* from a simple connective element to a cohesive one that indissolubly unites the green and blue marbles as the second element of the disjunction. This cohesion is inevitable given the semantic identity of the involved elements. The two marbles that constitute the conjunction (green and blue) are necessarily represented as being both present or both absent, almost as if the alternative to the red marble in the box were a "green-blue" marble (then it is impossible to have a green marble without a blue marble). Consequently, only one of the three cases in which the conjunction is false is represented (i.e., that in which the negation concerns both the conjuncts, ¬green and blue).

Furthermore, the quantitative adverb *at least* has two possible senses: in its maximal acception as: "at least this and possibly more" (e.g., *"he will make at least a million [and perhaps more]"*), or in its minimal acception as: "at least this and nothing else" (e.g., *"if he were at least sorry [if he cannot put things right]"*).

Johnson-Laird et al. (1999) used it in its maximal acception, which is one of the two possible senses of the term, but not the one that is relevant for the context: *"a red marble alone or together with one of the other two."* However, an examination of the protocols of the control version shows that the subjects making the mistake (by replying that "the box cannot contain both the red and the blue marble at the same time") interpreted *at least* as meaning *"a red marble alone."* On the basis of a pragmatic analysis of the text, this interpretation of *at least* may depend on the context activated by the use of *there is* in:

> *"there is at least* a red marble, or else *there is* a green marble and *there is* a blue marble, but not all three marbles."

The "discourse of the problem," in the intention of the experimenter, would transmit the following information: (a) the box contains one or two marbles; (b) when there is only one marble, its color can only be red; and (c) vice versa—when there are two marbles, there is no fixed color–number association. It is this last information that is the critical point of the message, which is intended by the subjects as the opposite: the color limitation, which is right when there is one marble alone, is extended to the case of two marbles, the colors of which are thus wrongly presumed to be also predetermined (*green and blue*).

In such a context, *there is* limits the content of the box to the two alternatives: one marble (red) or two marbles (one green and one blue). This could impede the interpretation of *at least* in its maximal sense, which could potentially increase the number of marbles from one ("red") to two ("one red and one green" or, alternatively, "one red and one blue"). The function of the adverb *at least* excludes the possibility that the box may be empty.

An analogous phenomenon happens with the scalar implicatures of undefined quantitative terms such as *some*, which depends on the knowledge the interlocutor attributes to the speaker (Gazdar, 1979; Levinson, 1985; Politzer & Macchi, 2000). In the absence of other signals, the interlocutor considers such a state of knowledge to be complete. Consequently, the word *some* (which only potentially expresses an undefined quantity) takes on a meaning that places it at the minimum level of the quantitative scale ("some and not all"). If the speaker had wanted to use *some* in its maximal acception in the sense of *all*, he would have said *all* or canceled the conversational implicature *only some, not all* by adding a further premise: "*some, perhaps all.*" In the same way, in the problem investigated in the present chapter, if the speaker has wanted us to understand *at least* in its maximal acception, we would be surprised at the use of *there is* instead of the more pragmatically appropriate *there may be*. "*There may be at least one red marble*" conveys the implicature that, as far as the speaker knows, it is possible that the box contains "one red marble alone or together with another marble."

In a first experiment, to verify this hypothesis, we formulated two different versions in which we respectively acted on the identified pragmatic factors of *at least* and *there is*. In the first version, we made the literal significance of *at least* explicit by replacing it with "*alone or together with one of the other two*" (Version 1). In the second, we replaced *there is* with *there may be* to impede the extension of the color/number association to the second element of the conjunction and to allow *at least* to be interpreted in its maximal sense, thus conveying the conversational implication that the box may also contain "one red and one blue marble" (Version 2).

Version 1—Marbles

In a box, there is a green marble and there is a blue marble, or there is a red marble *alone or together with one of the other two*, but not all three marbles together. What is the probability that the box contains one red marble and one blue marble?

Version 2—Marbles

In a box, *there may be* at least one red marble, or *there may be* one green marble and one blue marble, but not all three marbles together. What is the probability that the box contains one red marble and one blue marble?

The experimental subjects ($n = 31$ for Version 1, $n = 17$ for Version 2, and $n = 21$ for the control version), who were all university students attending arts faculties, each received only one problem to solve in written form, with a request to indicate the reason for the answer and the reasoning followed. We used the original problem of Legrenzi (2000) as the control version.

None of the subjects who participated in Version 1 considered the simultaneous presence of "one red marble and one blue marble" impossible, and approximately 80% (24 out of 31) gave the correct answer "1/4."

The results were significantly different from those obtained with the control version [χ^2 (2) = 30.34, $p < .01$).

In the case of Version 2, only two subjects said "0," four said "1/4," and nine gave different answers that in any case revealed the representation of false cases of the conjunction (green and blue; see Table 9.2).

To evaluate the generality of the syntactically exclusive action of *or* described earlier when the disjuncts are semantically identical, we formulated two further versions of the problem in which the second disjunct consisted of the conjunction of two elements with different semantic characteristics (*necklace* vs. *flowers*). Our hypothesis was that the conjunction can be split only if the requirements of the disjunction are satisfied (i.e., that the two elements contiguous to the exclusive *or* have a pragmatically equal weight—Version 3: Flowers).

TABLE 9.2
Solutions Produced to Versions 1, 2, and 5 in the Marble Problem

	J–L (n = 20)	*Control Version* (n = 21)	*Version 1* (n = 31)	*Version 2* (n = 17)	*Version 5* (n = 30)
Correct answers	0	1 (5%)	24 (77%)	4 (24%)	16 (53%)
"0"	18 (90%)	9 (43%)	0	2 (12%)	2 (7%)
Other false cases*	2 (10%)		7 (23%)	9 (64%)	12 (40%)
¬ False cases**		11 (52%)		2 (12%)	

*Answers in which the subjects represented all of the false cases of the conjunction.
**Vice versa.

When this is not the case (Version 4: Flowers), the contiguous element that does not have an equal weight (bouquet of flowers) is seen as forming part of a whole with the second element of the conjunction (necklace).

Version 3—Flowers

On their retirement, the well-known Roman jeweler Bulgari usually gives its employees *at least a bracelet or a necklace and a bouquet of flowers*, but not all three. What is the probability of the gift being a bracelet and a bouquet of flowers?

Of the 38 subjects to whom the version was submitted (see Table 9.3), 25 answered "50%," thus splitting the conjunction "*a necklace and a bouquet of flowers*" and revealing that the disjuncts were seen as *a bracelet* and *a necklace* and *a bouquet of flowers* as an accessory simply connected to the necklace, but not indissolubly so.

Version 4—Flowers

On their retirement, the well-known Roman jeweler Bulgari usually gives its employees *at least a bracelet or a bouquet of flowers and a necklace*, but not all three. What is the probability of the gift being a bracelet and a bouquet of flowers?

On the contrary, of the 23 subjects to whom this version was submitted (see Table 9.3), only 4 answered "50%," thus confirming what intuitively already appears obvious: that "a bouquet of flowers" does not have the same weight as "a bracelet"; consequently, the two real disjuncts in this version become "a bracelet" versus "a necklace [and a bouquet of flowers]."

Finally, with the aim of investigating the MMT hypothesis that attributes the error to the excessive *number of mental models* that would be involved if the false cases were represented, a third experiment was conducted in which the same problem was modified in such a way as to *increase the number of mental models* necessary for its solution. If this were to

TABLE 9.3
Solutions Produced to Versions 3 and 4 in the Flowers Problem

	Version 3—Flowers (n = 38)	Version 4—Flowers (n = 23)
Correct answers ("1/4")	0	0
"0"	6	15
"50%"	25	4
Other	7	4

lead to more correct answers than the original version, this would refute the explanatory connection between the failure to represent false cases and the number of mental models.

Using the same procedure as adopted in the previous experiment, the following version was submitted to another group of subjects ($n = 30$).

Version 5—Marbles

There is a box in which there is at least one red marble, or one green marble or one blue marble, but not all three marbles together. What is the probability that the box contains one red and one blue marble?

The solution implies the representation of six mental models:

Red	¬Green	¬Blue
Red	*¬Green*	*Blue*
Red	Green	¬Blue
¬Red	Green	¬Blue
¬Red	¬Green	Blue
¬Red	Green	Blue

In this version, the simultaneous presence of "one red and one blue marble" was considered impossible by only two subjects, while more than 50% correctly replied "1/6" (see Table 9.2). The results were significantly different from those obtained using the control version [$\chi^2 (2) = 16.67, p < .01$].

CONCLUSIONS

The results of the first study indicate that the source of difficulty in certain types of probabilistic reasoning is related more to the structure of the text than to heuristic factors or the statistical format in which the probabilities are expressed (independently of the use of the "cultural percentages" or "natural frequencies": whether the text contains a *partitive* description of likelihood, which consists of defining the set of which the datum [expressed in percentage or frequency terms] represents a part, and then defining the proportion [or subset] of the population with particular properties [the base-rate probability]). When such a formulation is used, be it in terms of percentages (relative frequencies), ratio, or (natural sample) frequencies, it transmits the independence of the hit rate from the base rate. The partitive formulation thus has the triple effect of identifying the data reference set, eliminating confusion, and making it possible to perceive and make use of the relationships between the data.

We suggest that it has not to be intended as a "cueing" or a facilitating way to express these data, but as a direct way to express them, intrinsically connected to the nature of this kind of probability. Actually, the comparison between partitive and nonpartitive formulations shows that the majority of the subjects answer the partitive versions of the problem correctly and the nonpartitive versions incorrectly.

In general, the idea that it is important to understand the relationship between items of information as parts of sets actually seems to be quite shared, although the explanations for it are very different (see Krauss, Martignon, & Hoffrage, 2000; Lewis & Keren, 1999; Mellers & McGraw, 1999).

The results of the second study show that the source of the difficulty of a probabilistic reasoning problem as the "Marbles" one does not lie in the failure to represent false cases of the conjunction nor in the number of mental models because these were exactly the same as those required by the original version of Johnson-Laird et al. (1999) in Versions 1 and 2 and even more in Version 5. In fact the difficulty depends on, again, the pragmatic dimension of the discourse of the problem.

In our opinion, therefore, theories on reasoning cannot ignore the pragmatic dimension of the discourse involved in solving the problem as not to acknowledge the connection between the organization of thought and the organization of the discourse.

REFERENCES

Adler, J. E. (1984). Abstraction is uncooperative. *Journal for the Theory of Social Behavior, 14*, 165–181.

Bagassi, M., & Macchi, L. (2006). Pragmatic approach to decision making under uncertainty: The case of the disjunction effect. *Thinking & Reasoning*.

Bar-Hillel, M. (1990). Back to base rates. In R. M. Hogarth (Ed.), *Insights in decision making: A tribute to Hillel J. Einhorn* (pp. 200–216). Chicago: University of Chicago Press.

Birnbaum, M. H. (1983). Base rates in Bayesian inference: Signal detection analysis of the cab problem. *American Journal of Psychology, 96*, 85–94.

Carnap, R. (1962). *Logical foundations of probability*. Chicago: University of Chicago Press.

Casscells, W., Schoenberger, A., & Graboys, T. B. (1978). Interpretation by physicians of clinical laboratory results. *New England Journal of Medicine, 299*, 999–1001.

Cosmides, L., & Tooby, J. (1996). Are humans good intuitive statisticians after all? Rethinking some conclusions from the literature on judgment under uncertainty. *Cognition, 58*, 1–73.

De Finetti, B. (1968). Probability: Interpretation. In D. E. Sills (Ed.), *International encyclopedia of the social sciences* (Vol. 12, pp. 496–504). New York: Macmillan.

Dulany, D. E., & Hilton, D. J. (1991). Conversational implicature, conscious representation, and the conjunction fallacy. *Social Cognition, 9*(1), 85–110.

Eddy, D. M. (1982). Probabilistic reasoning in clinical medicine: Problems and opportunities. In D. Kahneman, P. Slovic, & A. Tversky (Eds.), *Judgement under uncertainty: Heuristics and biases* (pp. 249–267). Cambridge: Cambridge University Press.

Edwards, W. (1968). Conservatism in human information processing. In B. Kleinmuntz (Ed.), *Formal representation of human judgment* (pp. 17–52). New York: Wiley.

Fiedler, K. (1988). The dependence of the conjunction fallacy on subtle linguistic factors. *Psychological Research, 50,* 123–129.

Gastwirth, J. L. (2000). *Statistical science in the courtroom.* New York: Springer.

Gazdar, G. (1979). *Pragmatics, implicature, presupposition and logical form.* New York: Academic Press.

Gigerenzer, G. (1991). On cognitive illusion and rationality. In E. Eells & T. Maruszewski (Eds.), *Probability and rationality: Studies on L. Jonathan Cohen's philosophy of science* (Vol. 21, pp. 225–249). Poznan', Poland: Rodopi.

Gigerenzer, G. (1994). Why the distinction between single-event probabilities and frequencies is important for psychology (and vice versa). In G. Wright & P. Ayton (Eds.), *Subjective probability* (pp. 129–162). Chichester, England: Wiley.

Gigerenzer, G., & Hoffrage, U. (1995). How to improve Bayesian reasoning without instruction: Frequency formats. *Psychological Review, 102*(4), 684–704.

Ginossar, Z., & Trope, Y. (1987). Problem solving in judgment under uncertainty. *Journal of Personality and Social Psychology, 52,* 474–484.

Grice, H. P. (1975). Logic and conversation. In P. Cole & J. L. Morgan (Eds.), *Syntax and semantics: Vol. 3. Speech acts* (pp. 41–58). New York: Academic Press.

Hacking, I. (1975). *The emergence of probability.* Cambridge: Cambridge University Press.

Hertwig, R., & Gigerenzer, G. (1997). *The "conjunction fallacy" revisited: How intelligent inferences look like reasoning errors.* Unpublished manuscript.

Hilton, D. (1995). The social context of reasoning: Conversational inference and rational judgment. *Psychological Bulletin, 118,* 248–271.

Johnson-Laird, P. N. (1983). *Mental models.* Cambridge: Cambridge University Press.

Johnson-Laird, P. N., & Byrne, R. M. J. (1991). *Deduction.* Hillsdale, NJ: Lawrence Erlbaum Associates.

Johnson-Laird, P. N., Legrenzi, P., Girotto, V., Sonino Legrenzi, M., & Caverni, J.-P. (1999). Naive probability: A mental model theory of extensional reasoning. *Psychological Review, 106,* 62–88.

Jones, S. K., Jones Taylor, K., & Frisch, D. (1995). Biases of probability assessment: A comparison of frequency and single-case judgments. *Organizational Behavior and Human Decision Processes, 61,* 109–122.

Jungermann, H. (1986). The two camps on rationality. In H. R. Arkes & K. R. Hammond (Eds.), *Judgment and decision making. An interdisciplinary reader* (pp. 575–591). Cambridge: Cambridge University Press.

Kahneman, D., & Tversky, A. (1996). On the reality of cognitive illusions: A reply to Gigerenzer's critique. *Psychological Review, 103,* 582–591.

Kahneman, D., Slovic, P., & Tversky, A. (Eds.). (1982). *Judgment under uncertainty: Heuristics and biases.* Cambridge: Cambridge University Press.

Koehler, J. J. (1996). The base rate fallacy reconsidered: Descriptive, normative and methodological challenges. *Behavioral and Brain Sciences, 19*(1), 1–17.

Koehler, J. J., & Macchi, L. (2004). Thinking about low probability events: An exemplar cueing theory. *Psychological Science, 15*(8), 540–546.

Krauss, S., Martignon, L., & Hoffrage, U. (2000). Simplifying Bayesian inference: The general case. In L. Magnani, N. Nersessian, & P. Thagard (Eds.), *Model-based reasoning in scientific discovery* (pp. 165–179). New York: Plenum.

Legrenzi, P. (2000). *Modelli mentali e illusioni nel ragionamento: I giudizi di coerenza e probabilità.* Unpublished manuscript.

Levinson, S. C. (1983). *Pragmatics.* Cambridge: Cambridge University Press.

Levinson, S. C. (1995). Interactional biases in human thinking. In E. Goody (Ed.), *Social intelligence and interaction* (pp. 303–318). Cambridge: Cambridge University Press.

Lewis, C., & Keren, G. (1999). On the difficulties underlying Bayesian reasoning: A comment on Gigerenzer and Hoffrage. *Psychological Review, 106*, 411–416.

Macchi, L. (1995). Pragmatic aspects of the base rate fallacy. *The Quarterly Journal of Experimental Psychology, 48A*(1), 188–207.

Macchi, L. (2000). Partitive formulation of information in probabilistic problems: Beyond heuristics and frequency format explanations. *Organizational Behavior and Human Decision Processes, 82*(2), 217–236.

Macchi, L. (2003). The partitive conditional probability. In D. Hardman & L. Macchi (Eds.), *Thinking: Psychological perspectives on reasoning, judgment and decision making* (pp. 165–187). Chichester, England: Wiley.

Macchi, L., & Mosconi, G. (1998). Computational features vs. frequentist phrasing in the base-rate fallacy. *Swiss Journal of Psychology, 57*(2), 79–85.

Macdonald, R. R., & Gilhooly, K. J. (1990). More about Linda or conjunction in context. *European Journal of Cognitive Psychology, 2*, 57–70.

Margolis, H. (1987). *Patterns, thinking, and cognition.* Chicago: University of Chicago Press.

Mellers, B. A., & McGraw, A. P. (1999). How to improve Bayesian reasoning: Comment on Gigerenzer and Hoffrage. *Psychological Review, 106*, 417–424.

Morier, D. M., & Borgida, E. (1984). The conjunction fallacy: A task specific phenomenon? *Personality and Social Psychology Bulletin, 10*, 243–252.

Mosconi, G. (1990). *Discorso e pensiero.* Bologna: Il Mulino.

Mosconi, G., & Macchi, L. (2001). The role of pragmatic rules in the conjunction fallacy. *Mind & Society, 3*(2), 31–58.

Politzer, G., & Macchi, L. (2000). Reasoning and pragmatics. *Mind and Society, 1*, 73–94.

Politzer, G., & Macchi, L. (2005). The representation of the task: The case of the lawyer-engineer. In V. Girotto & P. N. Johnson-Laird (Eds.), *The shape of reason. Essays in honor of Paolo Legrenzi* (pp. 119–135). Hove: Psychology Press.

Politzer, G., & Noveck, I. A. (1991). Are conjunction rule violations the result of conversational rule violations? *Journal of Psycholinguistic Research, 15*, 47–92.

Reeves, T., & Lockhart, R. S. (1993). Distributional versus singular approaches to probability and errors in probabilistic reasoning. *Journal of Experimental Psychology: General, 122*, 207–226.

Schwarz, N. (1996). *Cognition and communication: Judgmental biases, research methods, and the logic of conversation.* Hillsdale, NJ: Lawrence Erlbaum Associates.

Sperber, D., & Wilson, D. (1986). *Relevance: Communication and cognition.* Oxford: Basil Blackwell.

Tversky, A., & Kahneman, D. (1974). Judgment under uncertainty: Heuristics and biases. *Science, 185*, 1124–1131.

Tversky, A., & Kahneman, D. (1980). Causal schemata in judgments under uncertainty. In M. Fishbein (Ed.), *Progress in social psychology* (Vol. 1, pp. 49–72). Hillsdale, NJ: Lawrence Erlbaum Associates.

Tversky, A., & Kahneman, D. (1981). The framing of decisions and the rationality of choice. *Science, 221*, 453–458.

Tversky, A., & Kahneman, D. (1982). Evidential impact of base rates. In D. Kahneman, P. Slovic, & A. Tversky (Eds.), *Judgment under uncertainty: Heuristics and biases* (pp. 153–160). Cambridge: Cambridge University Press.

Tversky, A., & Kahneman, D. (1983). Extensional versus intuitive reasoning: The conjunction fallacy in probability judgment. *Psychological Review, 90*, 293–315.

Author Index

Subject Index

A

Adversarial debate, 89
Affordances in the environment, 61, 68
Affordances to perception, 61
Anthropology, vii, viii
Argumentation, 20, 21, 177, 178, 180, 184, 187, 188
Attention, 55, 67, 68
    to the field, 55, 57, 67
    to the object, 66
    salience, 58
Autism, 147–150

B

Belief formation, 72
Bias, 7, 224, 225
    anthropocentric bias, 16, 97
    base-rate neglect, 227
    belief bias effect, 85, 86
    bias of perseverance, 8
    hindsight bias, 73, 90
Biological affinity, 104, 106

C

Cancer conspiracy case, 207
Categorization, 54, 66, 72, 120, 124
    categorical judgment, 24
    category, 4, 14, 142, 143
    context-free categorization, 107
    exemplar-based categorization, 13, 74, 76, 77, 90
    family resemblance, 54, 77, 79, 82, 143
    highly naturalized category, 142
    relationship, 54
    rule-based categorization, 54, 74, 76, 77, 79
    Similarity-Coverage Model (SCM), 115, 116
        coverage, 115, 116
        diversity (*see also* Diversity principle), 36, 37, 40, 41, 116, 118, 119, 121
        similarity, 40, 103, 104, 115, 119, 125
    taxonomy
        basic level, 110
        generic species, 99, 100, 102, 110, 114, 115, 123, 124
        subordinate category, 110
        superordinate category, 110
    typicality, 118, 119
Causal attribution, 1, 7, 13, 23, 52, 66, 89

www.ingramcontent.com/pod-product-compliance
Ingram Content Group UK Ltd.
Pitfield, Milton Keynes, MK11 3LW, UK
UKHW020432010325
455677UK00029B/1123